ASPIRE
SUCCEED
PROGRESS

exam success

in Cambridge International AS & A Level

Economics

Second Edition

Terry Cook

OXFORD
UNIVERSITY PRESS

Great Clarendon Street, Oxford, OX2 6DP, United Kingdom

Oxford University Press is a department of the University of Oxford.

It furthers the University's objective of excellence in research, scholarship, and education by publishing worldwide. Oxford is a registered trade mark of Oxford University Press in the UK and in certain other countries

British Library Cataloguing in Publication Data
Data available

978-1-38-202299-6

10 9 8 7 6 5 4

Paper used in the production of this book is a natural, recyclable product made from wood grown in sustainable forests.

The manufacturing process conforms to the environmental regulations of the country of origin.

Printed and bound by CPI Group (UK) Ltd, Croydon, CR0 4YY

Acknowledgements
The publisher would like to thank the following for permissions to use copyright material:

Cover: Nikada/Getty Images.

Artwork by Aptara and Q2A Media.

Every effort has been made to contact copyright holders of material reproduced in this book. Any omissions will be rectified in subsequent printings if notice is given to the publisher.

IGCSE® is the registered trademark of Cambridge Assessment International Education

This Exam Success Guide refers to the Cambridge International AS & A ... nomics (9708) Syllabus published by Cambridge Assessment ... onal Education.

Th... has been developed independently from and is not end... or otherwise connected with Cambridge Assessment Inter... Education.

Contents

Introduction

The *Exam Success* series has been designed to help you reach your highest potential and achieve the best possible grade. Each book fully covers the syllabus and is written in syllabus order to help you prepare effectively for the exam. In contrast to traditional revision guides, these new books contain advice and guidance on how to improve answers, giving you a clear insight into what examiners are expecting of candidates. Each of the *Exam Success* titles consists of two parts: the first part covers the content of the subject, with clear syllabus references, while the second part contains exam-style questions and advice on how to improve your performance in the exam. All of the titles are written by authors who have a great deal of experience in knowing what is required of candidates in exams.

Exam Success in Cambridge International AS and A Level Economics has been written specifically to meet the requirements of the AS Level and A Level Cambridge 9708 Economics syllabus. The first part of the guide consists of 11 units. The first six of these cover the content that is required for the AS exam, while the last five cover the additional content that is required for the A Level exam. Each unit closely follows the syllabus and includes diagrams to help you fully understand the content, with exam tips, key terms, worked examples and advice on what to remember throughout. There are also examples of exam-style questions at the end of each unit, covering both multiple choice questions (featured in Papers 1 and 3) and structured questions (featured in Papers 2 and 4). On the supporting website you can find Units 12 and 13 where there are further examples of exam-style questions and useful advice on how you can best prepare for the Economics exam. There is also an appendix on maths skills for Economics, which includes worked examples to show how mathematics can be used by economists, and a list of the more important formulae that you may need to use in the exam.

Each of the titles in the *Exam Success* series contains common features to help you do your best in the exam. These include the following:

Key terms

These give you easy-to-understand definitions of important terms and concepts of the subject.

★ Exam tip

These give you guidance and advice to help you understand exactly what the examiners are looking for from you in the exam.

♡ Remember

These include key information that you will need to remember in the exam if you are to achieve your highest possible grade.

Raise your grade

In these sections, you will be able to read answers by candidates who do not achieve maximum marks. This feature provides advice on how to improve the grade for these answers.

Worked Example

Each unit contains a Worked Example section. This provides an exam-style question and an example of an answer to this question to indicate what examiners are looking for from candidates in their answers.

Exam-style questions

Each unit contains examples of exam-style questions so you understand the sort of questions you can expect to see on each topic when you take your exam. There is also a complete unit of exam-style questions hosted on the supporting website, which are arranged by paper. These questions provide ample opportunities to practise the skills and techniques required of you in the exam.

 The answers to all of the exam-style questions included in the book can be found on the OUP support website.

The *Exam Success* series is clearly focused on giving you practical advice that will help you to do your best in the exam. The 'sample' candidate answers, in particular, are extremely useful as they include examiner commentary and feedback. The expectations of examiners are made very clear throughout the books, so you can fully understand what is expected of you in the exam. This will also help to boost your confidence as you approach the exam.

 Access your support website for additional content here:
http://www.oxfordsecondary.com/caie-al-econ2e-exam-success

Basic economic ideas and resource allocation

Key topics

- Scarcity, choice and opportunity cost
- Economic methodology
- Factors of production
- Resource allocation in different economic systems
- Production possibility curves
- The classification of goods and services

1.1 Scarcity, choice and opportunity cost

1.1.1 The fundamental economic problem of scarcity

The fundamental **economic problem** refers to a situation where there is a relative scarcity of resources in relation to the unlimited wants and needs of people.

> ★ **Exam tip**
>
> It may appear, in some countries, that certain resources are not scarce. For example, there may be a high level of unemployment, suggesting an abundant supply of labour, and yet there may be an insufficient supply of labour with the right skills and/or in the right places.

1.1.2 The need to make choices at all levels

Scarcity refers to a condition where there are insufficient resources to satisfy all the **needs** and **wants** of people. This makes **choice** inevitable, because there will be a requirement to make decisions about the possible alternative uses of scarce economic resources. Choice will involve all levels of economic decision making, that is, at the level of:

- individuals
- firms
- governments.

> **Key terms**
>
> **Scarcity:** a condition where there are insufficient resources to satisfy all the wants and needs of people.
>
> **Needs:** the demand for something that is essential, such as food or shelter.
>
> **Wants:** the demand for something (such as a new television) that is less important than the demand for a need and which is not necessarily achieved by a consumer.
>
> **Choice:** the need to make decisions about the possible alternative uses of scarce resources, given the existence of limited resources and unlimited wants and needs.

> **Key term**
>
> **Economic problem:** the situation of the relative scarcity of resources in relation to the unlimited wants and needs of people.

> ★ **Exam tip**
>
> Do not confuse the existence of the fundamental economic problem, which is a universal problem, with particular economic problems in specific countries, such as a high level of unemployment.

> 💡 **Remember**
>
> Resources are limited, whereas the needs and wants of people are unlimited.

> 💡 **Remember**
>
> You need to understand that the fundamental economic problem occurs in all economies, including both developed and developing economies.

> 💡 **Remember**
>
> Economic resources have alternative possible uses and so a choice will need to be made about the use of each particular resource.

> 💡 **Remember**
>
> You need to understand that the existence of scarcity makes choice inevitable.

> ★ **Exam tip**
>
> The inevitability of choice applies at all levels in an economy, that is, at the level of individuals, firms and governments.

1.1.3 The nature and definition of opportunity cost, arising from choices

It was pointed out in section 1.1.2 that the condition of scarcity makes **choice** inevitable. This is because there will be a requirement to make decisions about the possible alternative uses of scarce economic resources.

These decisions will be taken in terms of **opportunity cost**. This is the next best alternative that is foregone, as a result of taking a decision.

1.1.4 The basic questions of resource allocation

There are three basic questions that need to be asked in every economy:

- **What to produce?**: decisions will need to be taken about what is going to be produced with the economic resources and how much will be produced. For example, a decision will need to be made in terms of how many agricultural products will be produced in an economy and how many industrial products.

- **How to produce?**: production involves the combination of the four factors of production – land, labour, capital and enterprise – and decisions will need to be taken in terms of exactly how these factors will be combined to produce the required output.

- **For whom to produce?**: if it is not possible to satisfy the needs and wants of people in an economy, decisions will need to be taken as to which needs and wants will be satisfied, that is, how is the output to be distributed?

> 💡 **Remember**
>
> There are different ways of producing a given output – for example, to what extent production is capital-intensive, that is, where there is a relatively high proportion of capital used relative to labour, or labour-intensive, that is, where there is a relatively high proportion of labour used relative to capital.

> ★ **Exam tip**
>
> You need to recognise that a decision to produce more of one product, such as agricultural products, may lead to a lower production of another product, such as industrial products. This will be considered later in terms of the production possibility curve.
>
> Candidates often focus on production, but it is also necessary to consider how the output that has been produced is to be distributed to different people in an economy.

1.2 Economic methodology

1.2.1 Economics as a social science

Economics is social in the sense that it studies different aspects of human behaviour, especially the choices that humans make in different circumstances. It is a science in the sense that it uses theories and facts to make verifiable predictions of behaviour. Economics can therefore be regarded as a social science in that it uses scientific methods to establish theories and laws that can help explain the behaviour of individuals and groups in societies.

> **Key term**
>
> **Opportunity cost:** the cost of something in relation to a foregone opportunity, that is, it indicates the benefits that could have been obtained by choosing the next best alternative.

> ★ **Exam tip**
>
> The concept of opportunity cost does not only apply to production decisions; it can be applied to consumption decisions as well.

> ★ **Exam tip**
>
> Make sure you do not refer to opportunity cost in terms of any choice that is made. The foregone opportunity needs to be seen in terms of the next best alternative that is foregone, not just any possible alternative.

> ★ **Exam tip**
>
> These three basic questions will be asked in every economy, however developed it is.

> 💡 **Remember**
>
> You need to understand that answers to these three questions will provide a very good indication of the nature of different economies.

> **Key term**
>
> **Social science:** the branch of science devoted to the study of human societies and the relationships among individuals within those societies.

1.2.2 Positive and normative statements (the distinction between facts and value judgements)

Candidates need to be able to clearly distinguish between a **positive statement** and a **normative statement**. A positive statement is one that is based on factual evidence, that is, it will be objective rather than subjective. A normative statement is one that involves making a **value judgement** or expressing an opinion, that is, it will be subjective rather than objective.

1.2.3 The meaning of the term *ceteris paribus*

The term *ceteris paribus* literally means 'all other things being equal'. This is important in Economics because it emphasises that the other factors which could influence a relationship between two variables are assumed to remain constant.

It has already been pointed out in section 1.2.1 that Economics is regarded as one of the social sciences and yet it would be very difficult to regard it as a science in the same way that chemistry, biology or physics can be regarded as sciences given that it is concerned with human behaviour. The very nature of the subject matter of Economics can therefore cause difficulties. The use of *ceteris paribus* means that for the purposes of establishing a theory or a model in Economics, it can be assumed that other possible influences on behaviour, apart from what is the focus of the theory or model, are held constant.

1.2.4 The importance of the time period (short run, long run and very long run)

Economists distinguish between three different time periods:

- The **short run** refers to a time period in which only some variables may change, that is, some factors of production will be fixed and some will be variable. Technical progress is held to be constant.

- The **long run** refers to a time period in which all of the factors of production will be variable. Technical progress is held to be constant.

- The **very long run** refers to a time period in which it is possible for supply to change as a result of technical progress. This distinguishes the very long run from both the short run and the long run.

Key terms

Short run: a period of time in which at least one factor of production is fixed in supply and output can only be increased by using more of the variable factors.

Long run: a period of time when all factors of production are variable and output can be increased by using more of all factors.

Very long run: a time period when technical progress is taking place, affecting the ability of firms to supply products.

Key terms

Positive statement: a statement that is based on facts and factual evidence.

Normative statement: a statement that is based on beliefs rather than on factual evidence.

Value judgement: a judgement that is a reflection of particular values or beliefs.

⭐ **Exam tip**

Do not confuse positive and normative statements and objective and subjective statements. Make sure that you understand how they are different.

💡 **Remember**

A positive statement usually uses the word 'is', for example, 'value added tax is an example of an indirect tax'. However, a normative statement usually uses the words 'ought' or 'should', for example, 'the government should spend more money on defence than on transport'.

Key term

Ceteris paribus: literally 'all other things being equal', that is, the other factors which could influence a relationship between two variables are assumed to be constant.

⭐ **Exam tip**

Make sure that you fully understand what is meant by the term *ceteris paribus* and can explain its importance in relation to the claim of Economics to be a social science.

1.3 Factors of production

1.3.1 The nature and definition of factors of production

There are four factors of production:

* **land**
* **labour**
* **capital**
* **enterprise.**

> ★ **Exam tip**
>
> Make sure that you do not get confused by the term 'land'. It doesn't just mean land in the sense of a space that can be used for agricultural production, such as a farm, or industrial production such as a factory. It has a wider meaning in the sense of referring to the natural resources of an economy, including forests, lakes and rivers.
>
> The term 'labour' can also be confusing. It refers to all aspects of labour, including both physical and mental work. The term can also be used to apply to the skills, knowledge, experience and abilities of the labour force, which is why labour is also frequently referred to by economists as human or intellectual capital.
>
> Capital, in the sense of being an economic resource or factor of production, can also be a misleading term. In this sense, it refers to the human-made aids to production, such as tools, machinery and equipment. It can also refer to factories. It should not be confused with the word 'capital' when it is used to mean money.
>
> The term 'enterprise' can also cause difficulties. It refers to the role of the entrepreneur in combining, organising and coordinating the other three factors of production to enable production to take place, and this involves taking a risk.

1.3.2 The difference between human capital and physical capital

Human capital refers to the human element of the production process. This involves the talent, knowledge, abilities, training, education and skills of a country's labour force.

Physical capital refers to the non-human element of the production process. This involves the tools, plant, equipment, buildings and machinery used in the production of products.

> **Key terms**
>
> **Human capital:** the skills, knowledge and experience possessed by an individual or population in terms of their value or cost to a business organisation or country.
>
> **Physical capital:** the human-made objects that a firm uses to produce products, such as tools, machinery and equipment.

> ★ **Exam tip**
>
> Make sure that you can distinguish between labour, in the form of human capital, and capital, in the form of machinery or equipment.

> ★ **Exam tip**
>
> Do not be confused into thinking that the short run and the long run refer to a specific period of time; this is not the case. The period of time involved before the short run becomes the long run will vary from one industry to another. It could be a matter of weeks or months in one industry and a matter of years in another.

> **Key terms**
>
> **Land:** the factor of production that is concerned with the natural resources of an economy, such as farmland or mineral deposits.
>
> **Labour:** the factor of production that is concerned with the workforce of an economy in terms of both the physical and mental effort involved in production.
>
> **Capital:** the factor of production that relates to the human-made aids to production, such as tools and equipment.
>
> **Enterprise:** the factor of production that takes a risk in organising the other three factors of production. The individual who takes this risk is known as an entrepreneur.

1.3.3 The rewards to the factors of production

There are rewards that are paid to these factors of production:

- rent to land
- wages or salaries to labour
- interest to capital
- profit to enterprise.

1.3.4 Division of labour and specialisation

Specialisation refers to concentration on the provision of particular goods and services rather than other products. Specialisation allows for, and encourages, a concentration on what producers are best at doing and so enables production to increase. When there is specialisation of economic activity by product or process, this is known as the **division of labour**.

1.3.5 The role of the entrepreneur in contemporary economies: risk and organisation of the other factors of production

The factor enterprise has already been referred to and it is important to understand its role in contemporary economies, both in terms of organising the other factors of production and, in doing so, taking a risk.

In many countries, there has developed what can be called an 'enterprise culture' which encourages the emergence of entrepreneurs, although in some of these countries the encouragement has come from a variety of government initiatives

1.4 Resource allocation in different economic systems

1.4.1 and 1.4.2 Decision making and resource allocation in market, planned and mixed economies

There are three types of economic system:

- market economies
- planned economies
- mixed economies.

Market economies

A **market economy**, or **market system**, is one that is characterised by a relatively low level of state or government intervention in the economy, where decisions about the allocation of resources are taken in the private sector by producers and consumers. The **price mechanism** is the means through which these decisions are taken, bringing about changes in the allocation of resources in such an economy.

> ★ **Exam tip**
>
> A market economy can also be known as a free economy. However, this description can sometimes cause confusion. It does not mean that goods and services are 'free', but that they are provided through a 'free market', that is, one that relies on the private, rather than the public, sector.
>
> It is sometimes thought that there is no state or government intervention in a market economy, but there is no economy in the world with no state or government intervention. The term 'market economy' simply means that the role of the state or government is relatively small.
>
> A market economy, operating through the price mechanism and stressing the importance of profit maximisation, is often regarded as a better system than the alternatives. However, it also has to be understood that there are a number of disadvantages, as well as advantages, of such an economic system, giving rise to what is called 'market failure'.

Planned economies

A **planned economy**, or **command economy**, is one that is characterised by a relatively high level of state or government intervention in the economy, where decisions about the allocation of resources are taken by a central planning agency on behalf of the government. These decisions are usually taken within the context of a five-year plan.

> ★ **Exam tip**
>
> Despite being called a planned or command economy, there is no country in the world without some form of private sector involvement. It is essentially a question of degree, that is, a planned economy will have a relatively high proportion of decisions taken in the public sector.
>
> The disadvantages of a planned economy, operating through government commands or instructions, are often stressed, but it also has to be understood that such a system can have some advantages, such as the fact that unemployment could be lower than in a market economy and the distribution of income and wealth more equal.

Key terms

Market economy or **market system:** a type of economic system in which decisions about the allocation of resources are taken in the private sector by producers and consumers.

Price mechanism: the process by which changes in price, resulting from changes in demand and/or supply, bring about changes in the allocation of resources in a free market economy.

Key term

Planned economy or **command economy:** a type of economic system in which decisions about the allocation of resources are taken by the state or by government agencies.

Remember

A planned economy can also be known as a command economy, because the government 'commands' or 'controls' the allocation of resources to a large extent.

Mixed economies

It should be clear that both market and planned economies have a variety of advantages and disadvantages, and so most economic systems in the world today can be regarded as **mixed economies**, combining elements of both a market economy and a planned economy.

The balance of a mixed economy is not static and can change over a period of time. For example, in 2008–2009, a number of financial institutions in different countries experienced difficulties and many of these had to be supported by government. In the UK, for example, two of the major banks, Royal Bank of Scotland/NatWest and Lloyds Banking Group, had to be supported by the government to prevent them from going out of existence.

> 💡 **Remember**
>
> Nationalisation and privatisation will change the nature of a mixed economy. Nationalisation increases the size of the public sector relative to that of the private sector with privatisation having the opposite effect.

1.5 Production possibility curves

1.5.1 The nature and meaning of a production possibility curve (PPC)

A **production possibility curve (PPC)** can be used to show the maximum possible output that can be achieved in an economy given the use of a particular combination of resources and technology in a given time period.

> 💡 **Remember**
>
> You need to understand that a production possibility curve can also be called a 'production possibility frontier' or a 'production possibility boundary'.
>
> You also need to understand that a PPC illustrates the total output of two products given the availability of resources in an economy in a given time period. This output of two products is within the constraint of a given level of technology in a given time period.

1.5.2 The shape of the PPC: constant and increasing opportunity costs

If an economy is operating on its PPC, in order to increase the output of one type of product, it will be necessary to reduce the output of the other. This can be seen in Figure 1.1 where a movement from X to Y along the PPC leads to an increase of BD industrial output and a decrease of AC agricultural output. It can be seen that the shape of the PPC is a curve.

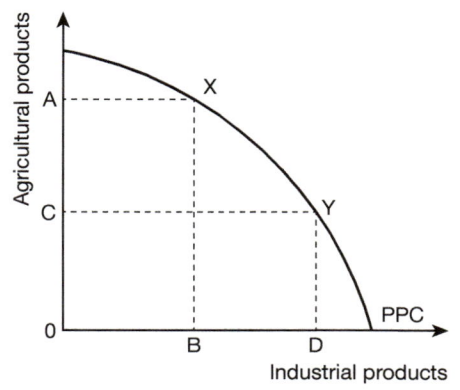

◀ **Figure 1.1** A production possibility curve

Constant and increasing opportunity costs

It has already been pointed out that a PPC is drawn as a curve rather than as a straight line. If there was a situation of constant opportunity costs, then it would be possible to draw a PPC as a straight line. However, it is usually the case that there will be a situation of **increasing opportunity costs**, that is, there will not be an equal sacrifice of resources as there is a movement along a PPC.

> **Key term**
>
> **Increasing opportunity costs:** this occurs when the extra production of one product involves ever-increasing sacrifices of another.

> 💡 **Remember**
>
> You need to understand that a PPC can only be drawn as a straight line, rather than as a curve, when there are constant opportunity costs, that is, when there is a movement along a PPC, the amount of production sacrificed by agricultural products and gained by industrial products are the same.
>
> However, this is unlikely to happen because of the existence of the law of diminishing returns. This stresses that as extra units of a resource are used in production, they will lead to successively smaller increases in output. This is because not all factor inputs are equally suited to the production of different products.
>
> As a position is reached that is closer to either end of a PPC, an ever-increasing amount of one type of product will need to be sacrificed to produce more of the other, because of the fact that different factors of production have different qualities, and that is why a PPC is usually drawn as a curve rather than as a straight line.

1.5.3 The causes and consequences of shifts in a PPC

Figure 1.1 shows a movement from one point on a PPC to another, but it is also possible for there to be a shift of the whole PPC. This is shown in Figure 1.2, where there is a movement of the PPC to the right from PPC$_1$ to PPC$_2$. When this happens, an economy can produce more of both types of good, that is, there can be an increased output of both agricultural products and industrial products.

Of course, it is also possible for there to be a shift of a PPC to the left. In this situation, an economy can produce less of both types of good, that is, there will be a decreased output of both agricultural products and industrial products.

▲ **Figure 1.2** A shift to the right of a PPC

1.5.4 The significance of a position within a PPC

It is important that you clearly understand the significance of a position within a PPC. Figure 1.1 shows a production possibility curve and position X and position Y, on the PPC, showing two positions where an economy is using its resources efficiently.

However, any point inside the production possibility curve would indicate a situation in which an economy is using its resources inefficiently. At such a point, not all of an economy's resources are being fully utilised and the output of both products will therefore be lower than it could be if all resources were being used.

> 💡 **Remember**
>
> If it is possible to shift a PPC to the right, then it becomes possible to produce a greater output of both products. In this situation, the concept of opportunity cost will not apply.

1.6 The classification of goods and services

1.6.1 The nature and definition of free goods and private goods (economic goods)

A **free good** is one which does not involve the basic condition of scarcity, that is, there is a sufficient quantity of it to satisfy demand and so there is no necessity for there to be an **allocative mechanism**. Examples of free goods include sunshine, air and sea water.

> **Key terms**
>
> **Free good:** a good which is not scarce and so therefore does not need a mechanism to allocate it; the demand for a free good is equal to the supply of it at zero price.
>
> **Allocative mechanism:** a method whereby scarce resources are distributed in an economy.

A **private** or **economic good**, on the other hand, is one which does involve the basic condition of scarcity. As a result of such scarcity, there needs to be an allocative mechanism to decide which people are able to consume it and which are not. This will be through the existence of the price mechanism. A private good, such as a bicycle, a car or an item of clothing, will have three essential characteristics. It is:

- rival
- excludable
- rejectable.

★ **Exam tip**

Do not confuse a free good, such as air, with a product that is provided for free by a government. A product such as health care may be free, in that a fee may not be paid directly to a doctor, but it is still an economic good because the resources involved in the provision of the health care have alternative uses.

💡 **Remember**

You need to know that, since free goods are not scarce, there is no cost involved in the consumption of them, unlike the consumption of a private good, so no price is charged. There is no need for there to be a mechanism to allocate a free good because the demand for, and the supply of, the free good are equal at zero price.

Although air may be regarded as an example of a free good, fresh air may be a less helpful example.

💡 **Remember**

You need to understand what characterises a private or economic good:

- It is rival in that when one person consumes a private good, it reduces the quantity that is available to others.
- It is excludable in that potential consumers can be excluded from consuming a product because of the producer charging a price for it.
- It is rejectable in that if a person wishes to reject the opportunity to purchase a private good, they can do this simply by not buying it.

1.6.2 The nature and definition of public goods

Another type of good is that of a **public good**, such as street lighting or a flood control system. Public goods have three essential characteristics, and these are the opposite of those of a private good. They are:

- non-rival
- non-excludable
- non-rejectable.

A particular feature of non-excludability is that it would be impossible to exclude anybody who had not paid for a product, for example, street lighting. This gives rise to the existence of the **free rider** problem, that is, a person who has no incentive to pay for the use of a public good because there can be consumption without any payment being made.

💡 **Remember**

You should understand that the characteristics of a public good are the opposite of those of a private good:

- It is non-rival in that if one person consumes a product, it does not reduce its availability to others.

Continued

Continued

- It is non-excludable in that it is not possible to exclude people from benefiting from the consumption of the good, giving rise to the free rider problem in which it is impossible to charge consumers for the use of a public good.

- It is also non-rejectable in that people cannot reject the security they are afforded by the existence of a police force or a country's armed forces.

It is therefore possible to distinguish between private goods and public goods, but you should understand that in some cases it may not be easy to clearly differentiate between private and public goods and so in this situation, these products are referred to as quasi-public goods ('quasi' meaning 'near' or 'almost').

1.6.3 The nature and definition of merit goods: under-consumption as a result of imperfect information in the market

A **merit good** is a private good and so has the characteristics of being rival, excludable and rejectable. However, it is likely to be under-consumed in a market because of **imperfect information** on the part of consumers. They may not be fully aware of the potential benefit of the product. Examples of merit goods include education, health care, public libraries and museums.

Figure 1.3 shows how a merit good can be under-consumed in a market. The demand curve D_1 represents the demand for a good such as education where imperfect information exists in the market, that is, the good is better for a person than they realise. However, the demand curve D_2 represents the demand for such a good if there was no information failure. The equilibrium position where D_1 and S cross indicates the effect of imperfect information; if this were not the case, the equilibrium position would be at quantity Q_2 and price P_2.

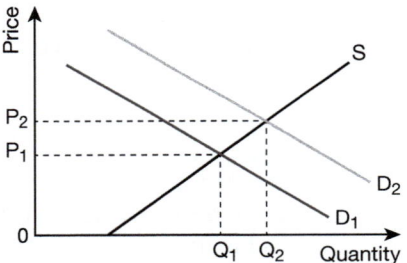

▲ **Figure 1.3** The under-consumption of a merit good in a market

1.6.4 The nature and definition of demerit goods: over-consumption as a result of imperfect information in the market

A **demerit good**, like a merit good, is an example of a private good, but it is likely to be over-consumed in a market because of imperfect information on the part of consumers. They may not be fully aware of the potential damage to themselves of consuming the product. Examples of demerit goods include cigarettes and alcohol.

Figure 1.4 shows how a demerit good can be over-consumed in a market. The demand curve D_1 represents the demand for a good such as tobacco where imperfect information exists in the market, that is, the good is worse for a person than they realise. However, the demand curve D_2 represents the demand for such a good if there was no information failure. The equilibrium position where D_1 and S cross indicates the effect of imperfect information; if this were not the case, the equilibrium position would be at quantity Q_2 and price P_2.

Key term

Free rider: a person who has no incentive to pay for the use of a public good because there can be consumption without any payment being made.

★ **Link**

See Unit 3, section 3.1.1, for details of government intervention in markets to address the non-provision of public goods.

Key term

Merit good: a product which would be under-produced and under-consumed in a market economy as a result of the imperfect information held by consumers.

Key term

Imperfect information: a situation in which people, including both consumers and producers, do not have the full information needed to make rational decisions, reducing the extent of efficiency.

★ **Exam tip**

Make sure you do not confuse a merit good with a free good because some merit goods, such as education, are free at the point of consumption. A free good does not require an allocative mechanism whereas a merit good does.

★ **Link**

See Unit 3, section 3.1.2, for details of government intervention in markets to address the under-consumption of merit goods.

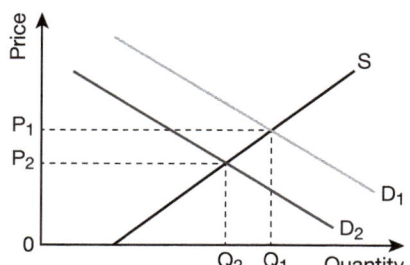

 Figure 1.4 The over-consumption of a demerit good

↑ Raise your grade

Explain what is shown by a production possibility curve and consider why it is usually drawn as a curve rather than as a straight line. [8]

A production possibility curve shows the maximum output that it is possible to produce given the availability of resources in an economy at any one time (1). It shows the output of just two products, one on the vertical axis, such as agricultural output, and one on the horizontal axis, such as industrial output (2).

It could be drawn as a straight line, but this would only apply if there were constant opportunity costs (3). This is not likely to be the case in most situations, and it is more likely that there would be increasing opportunity costs as a movement up or down a PPC is made (4). This is why a PPC is usually drawn as a curve rather than as a straight line.

How to improve this answer

1. The candidate has demonstrated some knowledge and understanding of a production possibility curve, but this could have been developed more fully, for example, by pointing out that the output is also constrained by the technology of a given time period.

2. The candidate could have emphasised how a PPC is a simplified version of what can be produced in an economy with its resources, contrasting this with the reality of production of many different types of products.

3. The candidate refers to the idea of 'constant opportunity costs', but there is no attempt to explain what this actually means.

4. The candidate refers to the idea of 'increasing opportunity costs', but again there is no attempt to explain what this actually means. For example, it would have been helpful if the candidate had brought in the law of diminishing returns to help explain why a PPC is drawn as a curve rather than as a straight line.

Knowledge and understanding:	1/3	Evaluation:	1/2
Analysis:	1/3	Total:	3/8

Worked Example

Explain what is meant by imperfect information and consider how this can be applied to the consumption of merit goods and demerit goods. [8]

Imperfect information refers to the fact that consumers do not always have sufficient information to make an informed decision about the consumption of particular products available in an economy. In particular, the existence of information failure means that consumers are misinformed about the full implications of their decisions.

Consumers may, for example, underestimate the potential benefits to themselves of some products, and underestimate the potential dangers to themselves of other products. Merit goods would be under-consumed and demerit goods would be over-consumed.

In the case of merit goods, consumers may under-consume certain products because they do not fully realise the potential benefits. For example, education can be regarded as an example of a merit good because there is a close link between a person's educational qualifications and the wages or salaries they receive for their work. Other examples of merit goods would be health care, museums or libraries.

In the case of demerit goods, consumers may over-consume certain products because they do not fully realise the potential dangers of such consumption. For example, cigarettes can be regarded as an example of a demerit good because they can seriously damage the health of a person. Alcohol would be another example of a demerit good because of the harm it can cause people.

Exam-style questions

1   Which is the best definition of opportunity cost?

  (a) An alternative that is foregone

  (b) The best alternative foregone by firms

  (c) The next best alternative foregone

  (d) The next best alternative foregone
     by consumers   [1]

2   The term *ceteris paribus* means:

  (a) all other things being equal

  (b) at the margin

  (c) choice is inevitable

  (d) opportunity cost.   [1]

3   Which of the following statements about the short
  run is correct?

  (a) All variables are fixed.

  (b) All variables can change.

  (c) Some variables can change and some are fixed.

  (d) The short run is never more than
     three months.   [1]

4   Which of the following is a positive statement?

  (a) Economic growth is measured through changes
     in Gross Domestic Product.

  (b) Governments should spend more on education.

  (c) The pay of nurses should be doubled.

  (d) Trade unions ought to avoid taking
     industrial action.   [1]

5   The reward to capital is:

  (a) interest

  (b) profit

  (c) rent

  (d) salary.   [1]

6   A transitional economy is one which is:

  (a) in the process of reducing its rate of inflation

  (b) increasing the length of the plan from five to
     ten years

  (c) introducing more nationalisation

  (d) moving from one type of economic system
     to another.   [1]

7   Which of the following will shift a production
  possibility curve to the left?

  (a) An increase in unemployment

  (b) Improved technology

  (c) Improved training of workers

  (d) New mineral deposits   [1]

8   A production possibility curve is likely to be curved
  rather than straight because of:

  (a) *ceteris paribus*

  (b) constant opportunity costs

  (c) inflation

  (d) the law of diminishing returns.   [1]

9   Which of the following will cause an under-
  consumption of merit goods in a market?

  (a) Excludability

  (b) Imperfect information

  (c) Perfect information

  (d) Rivalry   [1]

10 The free rider problem refers to the fact that:

  (a) a demerit good is likely to be over-consumed

  (b) a free good requires some form of allocative
     mechanism

  (c) a merit good is likely to be under-consumed

  (d) it would be impossible to exclude those who
     had not paid for a public good.   [1]

11 (a) Explain what is meant by the concept of
     opportunity cost and consider its
     importance to the decisions of individuals.   [8]

  (b) Assess why some goods and services are
     provided through the private sector and
     some through the public sector in a
     mixed economy.   [12]

12 (a) Explain why enterprise is so important in
     the development of a modern economy.   [8]

  (b) Explain the factor of production enterprise
     and consider why enterprise is so important
     in the development of a modern economy.   [12]

Key topics

- Demand and supply curves
- Price elasticity, income elasticity and cross-elasticity of demand
- Price elasticity of supply
- The interaction of demand and supply
- Consumer and producer surplus

2.1 Demand and supply curves

2.1.1 Effective demand

It is important to stress the distinction between **demand** and **effective demand**. Demand refers to the quantity of a good or service that an individual would like to buy, but effective demand refers to the quantity of a good or service that an individual is willing and able to purchase over a range of prices in a given period of time.

> 💡 **Remember**
>
> You need to be precise in referring to effective demand and not simply to demand, in that there is a clear difference between the desire for a good or service and the demand for a product that is backed by the ability and willingness of consumers to pay for it.
>
> It is important to be able to distinguish between the notional demand for a product, which is where consumers want a product, and effective demand, which is where that want is backed by actual purchasing power.
>
> The definition of effective demand is often supported by a reference to *ceteris paribus*, that is, all other things being equal.

2.1.2 Individual and market demand and supply

Individual demand

An individual **demand curve** shows the quantity of a product that a particular consumer is willing and able to buy at each and every price in a given period of time, other things being equal. The individual demand curve, indicating **individual demand**, will slope downwards from left to right, demonstrating that a consumer is more likely to buy a particular product at a lower price than at a higher price (Figure 2.1). This is known as the **law of demand**.

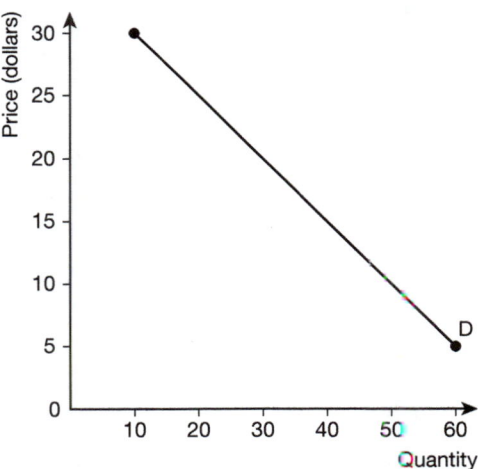

▲ **Figure 2.1** An individual consumer's demand curve for a product

Key terms

Demand: the desire of consumers to purchase goods and services at given prices.

Effective demand: the quantity of a good or service that an individual is able and willing to purchase over a range of prices in a given period of time.

★ **Exam tip**

Make sure you clearly understand the difference between the demand or desire for a product and the effective demand for it.

💡 **Remember**

In a market, effective demand means that consumers are able to afford to pay for particular products.

Effective demand focuses on a situation in which consumers enter into a market with the clear intention of being able to buy a product in that market.

Key terms

Demand curve: a curve showing the relationship between changes in the quantity demanded and changes in prices, other things being equal.

Individual demand: the quantity demanded of a good or service that a particular consumer is willing and able to buy at each and every price in a given period of time, other things being equal.

Law of demand: for most goods and services, the quantity demanded varies inversely with the price.

Market demand

It is possible to derive a **market demand** curve for a product from a number of individual demand curves. This involves bringing together, or aggregating, all the individual consumers of a product to produce market demand, that is, the total quantity of a product that all consumers would be able and willing to buy at a given price in a given period of time (Figure 2.2).

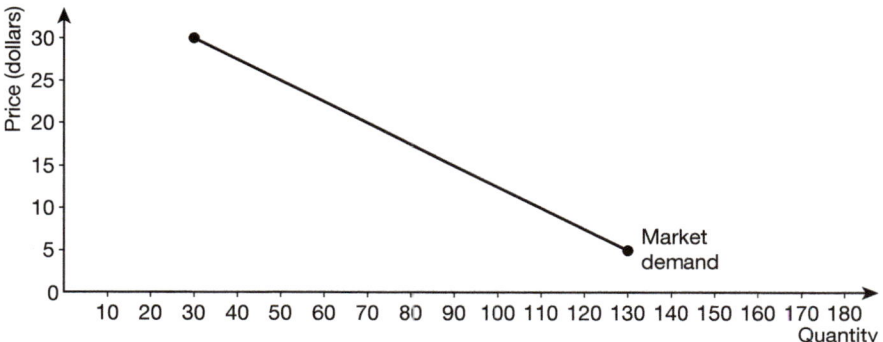

▲ **Figure 2.2** A market demand curve for a product

Individual supply

Whereas an individual demand curve shows the quantity of a product that a particular consumer is willing and able to buy at each and every price in a given period of time, other things being equal, an individual **supply curve** shows the quantity of a product that a particular producer is willing and able to supply at each and every price in a given period of time, other things being equal. The **individual supply** curve will slope upwards from left to right, demonstrating that a producer is more likely to sell a particular product at a higher price than at a lower price (Figure 2.3). This is known as the **law of supply.**

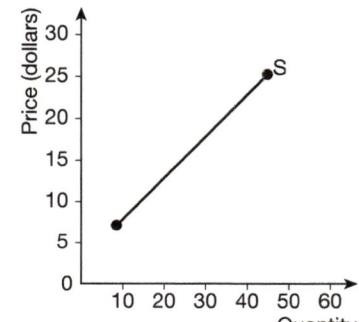

▲ **Figure 2.3** An individual producer's supply curve of a product

Market supply

It has already been stated that it is possible to derive a market demand curve for a product from a number of individual demand curves and it is also possible to derive a **market supply** curve for a product from a number of supply curves of individual producers (Figure 2.4). This involves bringing together, or aggregating, all the individual producers of a product to produce market supply, that is the total quantity of a product that all producers would be able and willing to sell at a given price in a given period of time.

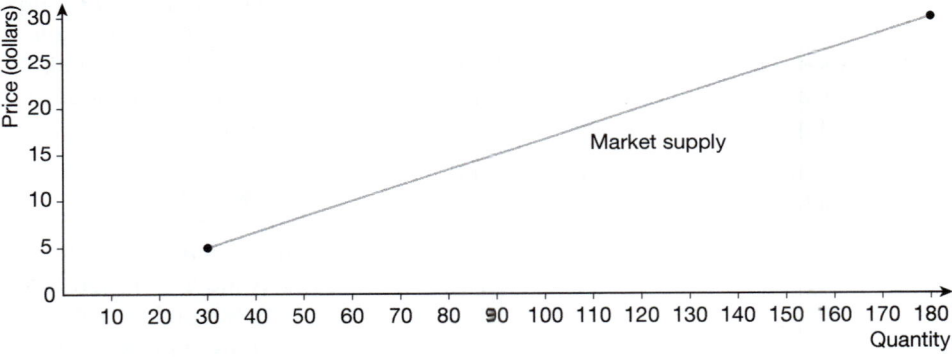

▲ **Figure 2.4** A market supply curve for a product

2.1.3 and 2.1.5 Determinants of demand and causes of a shift in the demand curve

It has already been stated that price has a significant influence on the demand for a product and that there is an inverse relationship between a change in the price of a product and the quantity demanded of a product, all other things being equal.

However, price is not the only factor that can influence the demand for a product. If the assumption of *ceteris paribus* is removed, it is possible to consider a range of other factors that could influence demand. These include:

- a change in the incomes of consumers
- a change in the distribution of income in an economy

- a change in the price of a **substitute**
- a change in the price of a **complement**

- a change in the tastes and preferences of consumers
- an advertising campaign
- a change in the size of the population
- a change in the age or gender distribution of the population
- a change of interest rates
- a change in the weather
- expectations of future prices.

> **Remember**
>
> Make sure you can distinguish between a change in quantity demanded, that is, when demand for a product is influenced by a change in the price of a product, and a change in the conditions of demand, that is when something other than a change in the price of a product causes its demand to change.

> **Remember**
>
> In many cases, an increase in the incomes of consumers will bring about an increase in the demand for a product; this is called a **normal good**. However, it is also possible that an increase in the incomes of consumers will bring about a decrease in the demand for a product; this is called an **inferior good.** It is important you understand that the demand for normal and inferior goods shows the relationship between a change in the quantity demanded of a product and a change in income, not price.
>
> It is not only changes in income that are important, but also changes in the distribution of income in an economy. If the distribution of income becomes more even, the demand for normal goods is likely to increase and the demand for inferior goods is likely to decrease.
>
> The demand for a product can be influenced by changes in the prices of other products; for example, the demand for two substitutes, such as coffee and tea, will be affected by a change in the price of the other. If the price of tea increases and the price of coffee remains constant, there is likely to be an increase in the demand for coffee. The extent of the change in demand as a result of changes in the prices of substitutes will depend on the degree of substitutability of the two products.
>
> The demand for a product can also be influenced by a change in the price of a complement; for example, petrol is a complement to a car and if the price of cars rises considerably, not only may there be a decrease in the demand for cars but also a decrease in the demand for fuel.
>
> A change in the tastes and preferences of consumers could affect demand; for example, over a period of time, the demand for some products could rise while the demand for other products could fall.
>
> The tastes and preferences of consumers could be influenced by an advertising campaign. This could influence the demand for a product; for example, it would be expected that an increase in advertising would be likely to influence the demand for the product being advertised.
>
> A change in the size of the population of an economy could influence the demand for products in that economy, although the increase in a population would need to be relatively large to have any significant effect on demand.
>
> It is not only the size of a country's population that could be significant. There could be changes in the age and gender distribution of a population that influence demand; for example, if a country has an ageing population, this is likely to increase the demand for those products needed by the elderly.
>
> In many countries, a number of purchases are financed by credit, that is consumers buy products over a period of time. The demand for credit will be influenced by the cost of that credit, that is, the rate of interest that needs to be paid. A fall in interest rates will make the cost of borrowing cheaper and this is likely to increase the level of demand for many products.
>
> The demand for certain products could be influenced by changes in the weather, especially where demand is seasonal.
>
> The demand for some products could be influenced by expectations of future prices; for example, if consumers believe that the prices of certain products are likely to rise significantly in the future, this may encourage them to buy the products now rather than to leave it until some time in the future.

2.1.4 and 2.1.6 Determinants of supply and causes of a shift in the supply curve

It has already been stated that price has a significant influence on the supply of a product and that there is a direct relationship between a change in the price of a product and the quantity supplied of a product, all other things being equal.

However, price is not the only factor that can influence the supply of a product. If the assumption of *ceteris paribus* is removed, it is possible to consider a range of other factors that could influence supply. These include:

- costs of production
- the availability of resources
- climate and weather
- technology
- improved management of resources
- changes in the prices of other goods that the producer could supply
- the size of the industry
- taxes and subsidies (these will be considered in Unit 3).

> **Remember**
>
> You need to understand that supply is likely to be influenced by the availability, as well as the cost, of resources. If resources become more readily available, this is likely to lead to an increase in the supply of a product.
>
> Supply, especially of agricultural products, could be influenced by changes in the climate and the weather.
>
> Supply is also likely to be influenced by the level of technological knowledge; for example, an increase in technological knowledge is likely to lead to an increase in supply.
>
> A change in the management of resources could influence supply; for example, a better management structure could improve the productivity of a workforce leading to more product being supplied at each and every price.
>
> If it is possible for a producer to switch from the production of certain goods to other goods, then this decision will be influenced by changes in the prices of other goods that the producer could supply.
>
> The supply of a product in a market is likely to be influenced by the size of the industry; for example, if the barriers to entry into an industry are low or non-existent, new firms may be attracted into an industry, increasing supply.

> **Remember**
>
> If there is an increase in the costs of production of a product, supply will fall and firms will produce less at each and every price. However, if there is a fall in the costs of factors of production, for example, if the cost of labour becomes cheaper, more can be supplied at each and every price.

2.1.7 The distinction between a shift in a demand or supply curve and a movement along these curves

It has already been stressed that it is important to distinguish between a movement along a demand or supply curve and a shift of a demand or supply curve.

Movements along demand and supply curves

A movement along a demand or supply curve occurs when there is a change in the price of a product, but nothing else changes. This means that there is an assumption of *ceteris paribus*, that is, all other influences on demand or supply are assumed to be constant and unchanged.

Shifts of demand and supply curves

If the situation of *ceteris paribus* does not apply, that is, there has been a change in the conditions of demand or supply, then there will be a shift of the demand or supply curve. If the change in the conditions of demand or supply has been favourable, the curve will shift to the right. If the change in the conditions of demand or supply has been unfavourable, the curve will shift to the left.

2.2 Price elasticity, income elasticity and cross-elasticity of demand

2.2.1 The definition of price elasticity, income elasticity and cross-elasticity of demand (PED, YED and XED)

The concept of **elasticity of demand** refers to the responsiveness of demand to a change in one of its determinants, such as price, income or the price of another product.

Price elasticity of demand measures the responsiveness of the demand for a product to a change in its price.

Income elasticity of demand measures the responsiveness of the demand for a product to a change in income.

Cross-elasticity of demand, or cross-price elasticity of demand, measures the responsiveness of the demand for a product to a change in the price of another product.

2.2.2 The formulae for, and calculation of, price elasticity, income elasticity and cross-elasticity of demand

Elasticity is calculated by dividing the percentage change in the quantity demanded of a product by the percentage change in the determinant, such as the percentage change in the price of a product (in the case of price elasticity of demand), the percentage change in income (in the case of income elasticity of demand) or the percentage change in the price of another product (in the case of cross-elasticity of demand).

Price elasticity of demand is calculated by the formula:

$$\frac{\text{percentage change in the quantity demanded of a product}}{\text{percentage change in the price of a product}}$$

Income elasticity of demand is calculated by the formula:

$$\frac{\text{percentage change in the quantity demanded of a product}}{\text{percentage change in income}}$$

Cross-elasticity of demand is calculated by the formula:

$$\frac{\text{percentage change in the quantity demanded of good A}}{\text{percentage change in the price of good B}}$$

2.2.3 The significance of relative percentage changes and the size and sign of the coefficient of price elasticity of demand, income elasticity of demand and cross-elasticity of demand

Price elasticity of demand can range from perfectly inelastic to perfectly elastic.

The income elasticity of demand for most products will be positive, that is, as incomes rise, the demand for products will rise. These are known as normal goods. However, the income elasticity of demand for some products will be negative, that is, as incomes rise, the demand for products will fall. These are known as inferior goods.

> **Remember**
>
> There is usually an inverse relationship between the change in price and the change in demand, so there should really be a minus sign before the PED number as it is a negative number, but the minus sign is usually omitted.
>
> For a Giffen good or a Veblen good, the price elasticity of demand is positive, that is, when price increases, the quantity demand also increases.

> **★ Exam tip**
>
> Make sure you do not confuse a change in demand or supply with a change in the conditions of demand or supply. It is important to be able to distinguish between a change in the price of a product and a change in other possible influences on demand or supply, other than a change in price.

> **Key terms**
>
> **Elasticity of demand:** the responsiveness of demand to a change in one of its determinants.
>
> **Price elasticity of demand (PED):** the responsiveness of demand for a product to a change in its price.
>
> **Income elasticity of demand (YED):** the responsiveness of demand for a product to a change in the incomes of consumers.
>
> **Cross-elasticity of demand (XED):** the responsiveness of the quantity demanded for one product to a change in the price of another product.

> **💡 Remember**
>
> Candidates need to understand that elasticity involves the examination of percentage changes, not absolute changes. Price changes are not usually presented as percentage changes and candidates will therefore need to be able to calculate these.

> **★ Exam tip**
>
> It is important to remember that the percentage change in the quantity demanded of a product goes on top of the formula and what is causing that change on the bottom; many candidates get the formula the wrong way round.

An Engels curve shows the relationship between changes in income and changes in the quantity demanded. This is shown in Figure 2.5.

If two products are substitutes, such as tea and coffee, the cross-elasticity of demand will be positive, that is if there is an increase in the price of good B, many people are likely to switch to the substitute, good A, and so the demand for good A rises.

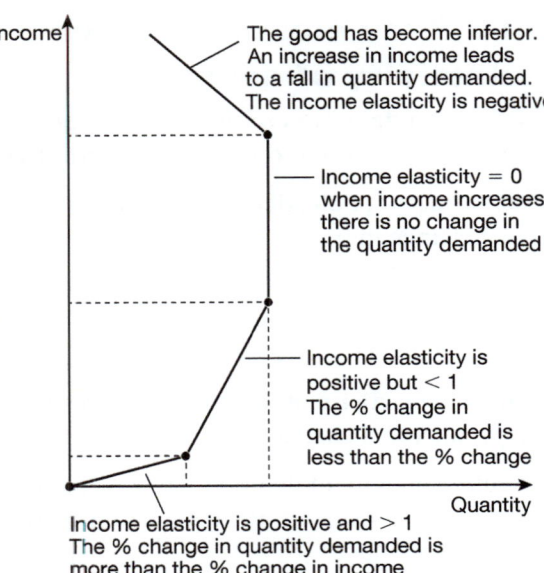

▲ **Figure 2.5** The relationship between changes in income and changes in the quantity demanded

> 💡 **Remember**
>
> It is important that candidates are able to clearly distinguish between normal goods, the demand for which will rise as incomes increase, and inferior goods, the demand for which will fall as incomes increase.
>
> With a normal good, the income elasticity of demand will be positive, that is as incomes rise, the quantity demanded rises. If the value is greater than 1, demand is income elastic, as in the case of luxuries. If the value is less than 1 (but therefore still positive), demand is income inelastic, as in the case of necessities.
>
> With an inferior good, the income elasticity of demand will be negative, that is, as incomes rise, the quantity demanded falls.
>
> You should understand that normal and inferior goods will not always be the same in all economies, that is, it will depend on the economic development of particular economies.
>
> You also need to realise that the size of the YED coefficient, either positive or negative, indicates the strength of the relationship between changes in income and changes in demand; the higher the figure, the greater the relationship between demand and income.

> 💡 **Remember**
>
> You need to appreciate that it is important to distinguish between the cross-elasticity of demand of substitutes and complements; XED will be positive for substitutes and negative for complements.

> 💡 **Remember**
>
> The greater the magnitude of the value of XED for two products, the closer their relationship as substitutes or complements.

If two products are complements, such as DVDs and DVD players, the cross-elasticity of demand will be negative, that is, if there is an increase in the price of good B, fewer people are likely to buy it and so fewer people will buy good A as well.

> ★ **Exam tip**
>
> It is important that you realise that cross-elasticity of demand shows the relationship between changes in the quantity of one product and changes in the price of another product, not changes in the price of the same product.

2.2.4 Descriptions of elasticity values: perfectly elastic, (highly) elastic, unitary elasticity, (highly) inelastic and perfectly inelastic

Elasticity of demand can range from perfectly inelastic to perfectly elastic, that is from zero to infinity. With **elastic demand**, the figure for the elasticity will be greater than 1. If demand is unitary elastic, the figure for the elasticity will be equal to 1. If there is **inelastic demand**, the figure for the elasticity will be less than 1.

> **Key terms**
>
> **Elastic demand:** the percentage (or proportionate) change in demand is greater than the percentage (or proportionate) change in the determinant bringing about the change in demand.
>
> **Inelastic demand:** the percentage (or proportionate) change in demand is less than the percentage (or proportionate) change in the determinant bringing about the change in demand.

★ Exam tip

It is often thought that an inelastic figure, that is one less than 1, is negative; it is, in fact, positive.

Make sure you refer to a particular good as being elastic; it is important to realise, however, that it is not a good or service that is being described as elastic, but the demand for that good or service.

Figure 2.6 illustrates **perfectly elastic demand**, Figure 2.7 illustrates **perfectly inelastic demand** and Figure 2.8 illustrates **unitary elasticity of demand**.

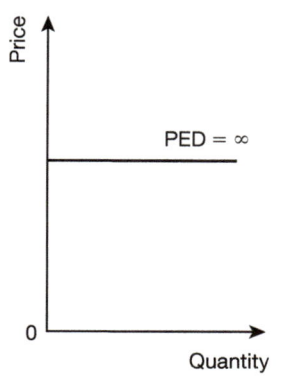

▲ **Figure 2.6** Perfectly elastic demand

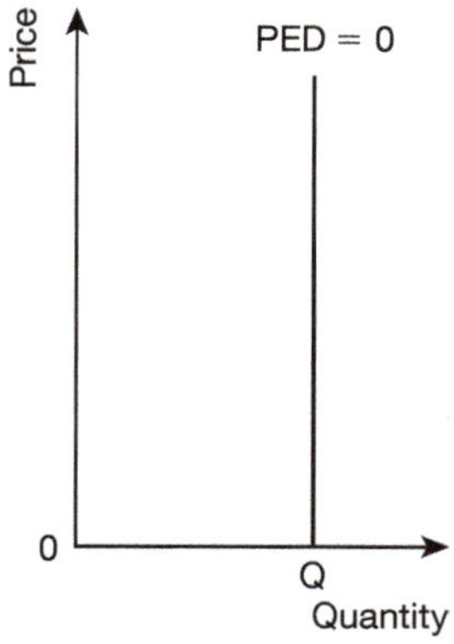

▲ **Figure 2.7** Perfectly inelastic demand

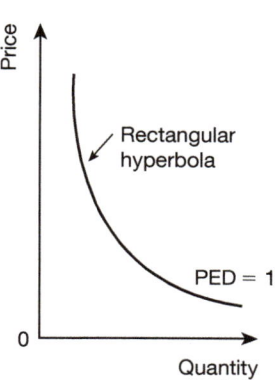

▲ **Figure 2.8** Unitary elasticity of demand

2.2.5 The variation in price elasticity of demand along the length of a straight-line demand curve

Price elasticity of demand will vary along the length of a straight-line demand curve, as can be seen in Figure 2.9. At the midway point, the PED will be equal to 1 and there will be **unitary elastic PED**. When there is a movement up the curve, the PED will become increasingly elastic until it eventually reaches the vertical axis when it becomes **perfectly elastic**. When there is a movement down the curve, the PED will become increasingly inelastic until it eventually reaches the horizontal axis when it becomes **perfectly inelastic**.

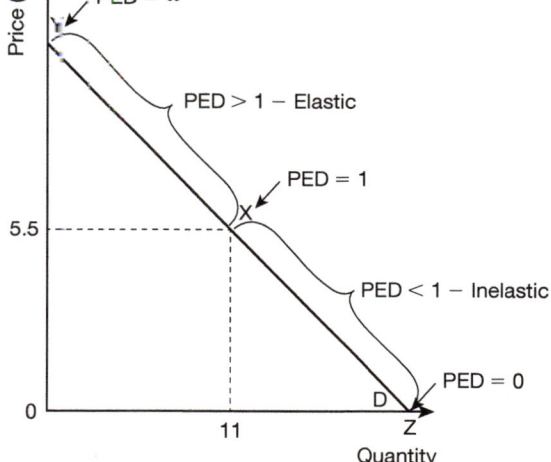

▲ **Figure 2.9** Changes in PED along the length of a straight-line demand curve

Remember

In the case of perfectly elastic PED, shown by a horizontal straight line, perfectly inelastic PED, shown by a vertical straight line, and unitary elastic PED, shown by a rectangular hyperbola, the PED value is constant along the entire length.

In other situations, however, there will be different values of PED along the length of a straight line.

Key terms

Perfectly inelastic PED: demand is totally unresponsive to changes in price; PED is zero.

Inelastic PED: demand is relatively unresponsive to changes in price; PED is more than 0 and less than 1.

Unitary elastic PED: the proportionate change in demand is exactly equal to the proportionate change in price; PED is equal to 1.

Elastic PED: demand is relatively responsive to changes in price; PED is more than 1 and less than infinity.

Perfectly elastic PED: demand is totally responsive to changes in price; PED is equal to infinity.

2.2.6 The factors affecting price elasticity of demand, income elasticity of demand and cross-elasticity of demand

The various factors affecting elasticity of demand can be understood in relation to the three different types of elasticity: that is, price elasticity of demand, income elasticity of demand and cross-elasticity of demand.

The factors affecting price elasticity of demand

There are a number of factors affecting price elasticity of demand, including:

- the number and availability of substitutes
- the width of the definition of a product
- the amount of money spent on a product
- the proportion of income that is spent on a product
- the period of time
- the degree of necessity
- the durability and perishability of products.

> ★ **Exam tip**
>
> It is important not to confuse arc price elasticity of demand, which is a measurement of price elasticity of demand over a range of prices, with point price elasticity of demand, which is a measurement of price elasticity of demand at a particular price.

> 💡 **Remember**
>
> You need to understand that the more substitutes that are available for a particular product, such as different brands of tea or coffee, the more price elastic will be the demand.
>
> It is important to understand that the wider the definition of a product, the more price inelastic will be the demand; for example, the demand for tea or coffee will be more inelastic than the demand for particular brands or types of tea or coffee.
>
> You need to realise that if the amount of money spent on a product is relatively small, the demand is likely to be inelastic; for example, the amount of money spent on newspapers is likely to be a relatively small proportion of total expenditure and so the demand for such a product is likely to be relatively inelastic.
>
> If the proportion of income taken by a product is relatively high, the price elasticity of demand will be more elastic compared to a situation in which the proportion of income spent on a product is relatively low.
>
> The price elasticity of demand for a product is likely to be more inelastic in the short run than in the long run, when it might be possible to think about possible alternatives to a product.
>
> You should understand that the more necessary and essential a product is, the more inelastic the demand for it is likely to be, whereas the demand for luxuries is likely to be more elastic.
>
> The more durable a product is, the more price elastic the demand is likely to be, whereas the demand for more perishable goods is likely to be more price inelastic.

The factors affecting income elasticity of demand

There are a number of factors affecting income elasticity of demand, including:

- the proportion of income that is spent on a product
- the width of the definition of a product
- the economic development of a particular economy.

> 💡 **Remember**
>
> You need to understand that the proportion of income that is spent on a particular good or service will be likely to affect the income elasticity of demand for the product. For example, with products that are inexpensive, the income elasticity of demand will be very low, that is very inelastic.
>
> The width of the definition of a product is likely to influence the income elasticity of demand. For example, the income elasticity of demand for cars is likely to be positive, but it may be negative for cheaper models of car, the demand for which may fall as incomes in an economy rise.
>
> You also need to appreciate that the economic development of a particular economy may influence the income elasticity of demand for a product. For example, in some economies a bicycle may be considered as a normal good, but as the economy develops and incomes rise, more people will be able to afford to buy a car and so the demand for bicycles may fall as incomes rise.

The factors affecting cross-elasticity of demand

There are a number of factors affecting cross-elasticity of demand, including:

- whether the relationship is between substitutes or complements
- whether the substitutes are close or weak substitutes or whether the complements are weak or close complements; the stronger the relationship between two products, the higher is the coefficient of cross-elasticity of demand
- whether there is any relationship at all between two products; unrelated products have a zero cross-elasticity of demand.

2.2.7 The relationship between price elasticity of demand and total expenditure on a product

If price elasticity of demand is less than unitary, that is, it is inelastic, a fall in the price of a product causes a fall in total expenditure on the product and a rise in the price of a product causes a rise in total expenditure on the product. When demand is inelastic, it is clear that price and total expenditure move in the same direction.

If price elasticity of demand is more than unitary, that is, it is elastic, a fall in the price of a product causes a rise in total expenditure on the product and a rise in the price of a product causes a fall in total expenditure on the product. When demand is elastic, it is clear that price and total expenditure move in the opposite direction.

If price elasticity of demand is unitary, that is, equal to one, then a rise or fall in the price of a product leaves total expenditure on the product unchanged.

2.2.8 The implications for decision-making of price, income and cross-elasticity of demand

Price elasticity of demand

Price elasticity of demand is extremely important to an understanding of business decisions, especially in relation to revenue. If the demand for a good or service is price elastic, a firm should lower the price because more products will be bought and this will lead to a higher total revenue. If the demand for a good or service is price inelastic, a firm should raise the price because although fewer items of the product will be sold, the increased revenue from each product will more than compensate for this.

Income elasticity of demand

Income elasticity of demand is also important to an understanding of business decisions. Economic development, especially changes in incomes, can affect the decision making of a firm. For example, if the general level of incomes is rising in an economy, it would be expected that there would be an increase in the demand for normal goods and a decrease in the demand for inferior goods. Firms would need to take account of this in their planning.

> 💡 **Remember**
>
> It is important to understand that if PED for a product is inelastic, total revenue will rise if there is a price increase and fall if there is a price decrease.
>
> If PED for a product is elastic, total revenue will fall if there is a price increase and rise if there is a price decrease.
>
> If the demand for a product is unitary elastic, total revenue will remain constant whether there is a price increase or a price decrease.
>
> Firms can use PED not only to help determine policies on price, but also policies on the number of goods to produce or stock and the number of people to employ.
>
> Firms can also use PED to anticipate the likely impact on their cashflow.

Remember

You need to understand that if an economy is experiencing an increase in the general level of incomes, the demand for normal goods is likely to rise and the demand for inferior goods is likely to fall.

If an economy is experiencing a recession, firms should focus on the production of products with a relatively low income elasticity of demand; for example, people will still buy food in a recession, but they are less likely to buy expensive cars.

Income elasticity of demand can therefore help to inform decisions on production or stocking and on the number of people to employ.

Cross-elasticity of demand

Cross-elasticity of demand is also important to an understanding of business decisions. In the case of substitutes, a firm needs to appreciate that if there is an increase in the price of tea, the demand for coffee is likely to rise and so a retailer would need to take this situation into account when deciding on the quantity of each product to order. In the case of complements, if there is an increase in the price of DVD players, this is likely to lead to a decrease in the demand not only of DVD players but also of DVDs.

Remember

A firm would be able to use the concept of XED to estimate the effect on the demand for their products of a competitor changing the prices of its products.

★ Exam tip

When considering the implications of XED for a firm, you should ensure that you can clearly distinguish between the effects in relation to substitutes and complements and not get these confused.

2.3 Price elasticity of supply

2.3.1 The definition of price elasticity of supply (PES)

Price elasticity of supply measures the responsiveness of the supply of a product to a change in its price.

2.3.2 The formula for, and calculation of, price elasticity of supply

Price elasticity of supply is calculated by the formula:

$$\frac{\text{percentage change in the quantity supplied of a product}}{\text{percentage change in the price of a product}}$$

If the percentage change in supply is greater than the percentage change in price, then supply is price elastic. If the percentage change in supply is less than the percentage change in price, then supply is inelastic.

2.3.3 The significance of relative percentage changes and the size and sign of the coefficient of price elasticity of supply

Price elasticity of supply can range from perfectly elastic to perfectly inelastic, that is, from infinity to zero. If supply is price elastic, the figure for PES will be greater than 1. If supply is price inelastic, the figure for PES will be less than 1.

A perfectly elastic supply curve is drawn as a horizontal straight line, as shown in Figure 2.10.

Key term

Price elasticity of supply (PES): the responsiveness of the quantity supplied of a product to a change in its price.

Remember

You need to understand that elasticity involves the examination of percentage changes, not absolute changes. Price changes are not usually presented as percentage changes and you will therefore need to be able to calculate these.

★ Exam tip

It is important to remember that the percentage change in the quantity supplied of a product goes on top of the formula and what is causing that change on the bottom.

A perfectly inelastic supply curve is drawn as a vertical line, as shown in Figure 2.11.

It is also important to see where a supply curve would intersect with the axes in a price/quantity diagram. Any straight line supply curve, drawn from the

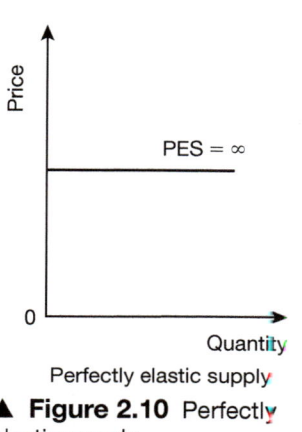

Perfectly elastic supply

▲ **Figure 2.10** Perfectly elastic supply

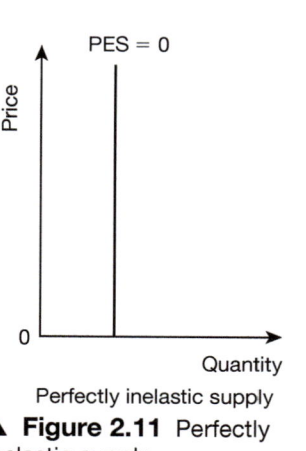

Perfectly inelastic supply

▲ **Figure 2.11** Perfectly inelastic supply

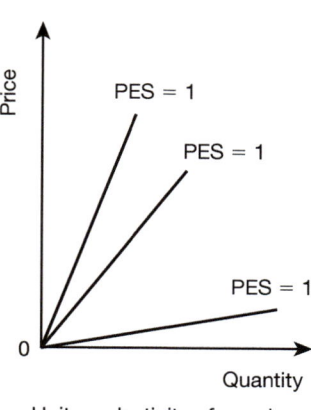

Unitary elasticity of supply

▲ **Figure 2.12** Unitary elasticity of supply

origin, has unitary price elasticity of supply, as shown in Figure 2.12. Any straight line supply curve which intersects with the price axis is price elastic, as shown in Figure 2.13. Any straight line supply curve which intersects with the quantity axis is price inelastic, as shown in Figure 2.14.

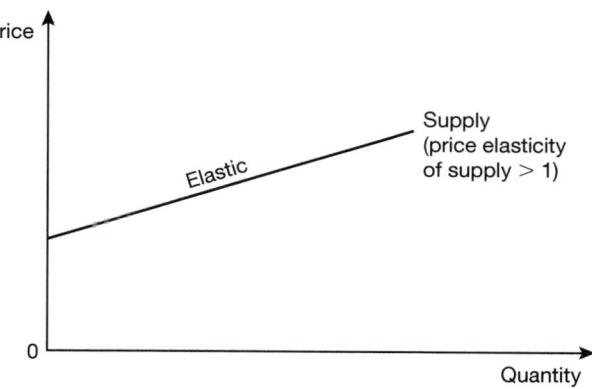

▲ **Figure 2.13** Price elastic supply

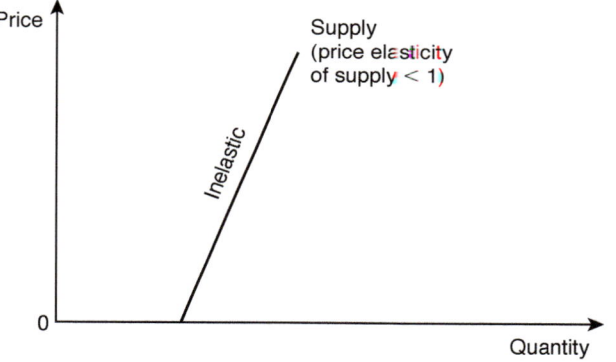

▲ **Figure 2.14** Price inelastic supply

2.3.4 The factors affecting price elasticity of supply

There are a number of factors that can affect the price elasticity of supply, including:

- the number of producers in an industry
- the amount of stock available
- the time period

- the existence of spare capacity
- the length of the production period
- the degree of factor mobility.

You need to understand the greater the number of suppliers in an industry, the easier it will be to increase output in response to a price increase, that is, supply is likely to be relatively elastic. If there are no, or few, barriers to entry for firms into an industry, this will enable production to be increased relatively easily.

If there is an abundance of stock, this will make supply relatively more elastic, whereas where products are perishable or difficult to stock, this will make supply relatively less elastic.

Supply is likely to be more elastic over a longer period of time as this will enable firms to invest in more factors of production and it will also allow more time for new firms to enter into an industry.

If there is a great deal of spare capacity in an industry, this is likely to make supply more elastic.

Supply will usually be more elastic when there is a shorter production period; for example, the supply of manufactured products is likely to be more elastic than the supply of agricultural products.

If it is relatively easy to switch factors of production from one use to another, the more elastic supply is likely to be.

2.3.5 The implications for speed and ease with which firms react to changed market conditions

It should be clear that it is easier for businesses to react to changed market conditions over a relatively long period of time. Figure 2.15 shows how supply tends to be more inelastic in the short run and more elastic in the long run.

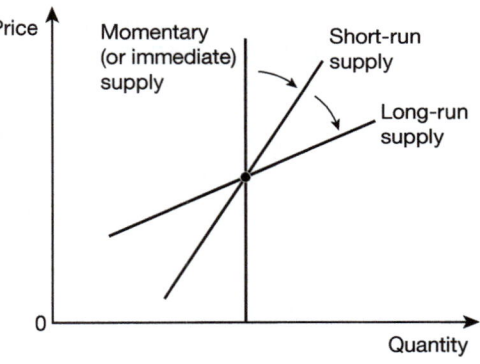

▶ **Figure 2.15** Differences in the speed of reaction of firms to changed market conditions

You need to understand that price elasticity of supply will vary over different periods of time.

Momentary supply refers to the situation of immediate supply when supply is perfectly inelastic.

Short-run supply refers to the situation when there are many constraints on the ability of businesses to substantially increase output, so supply is relatively inelastic.

Long-run supply refers to the situation when all factors of production are variable and so supply is relatively elastic.

You also need to understand that these time periods will vary from one industry to another. For example, the supply of agricultural products tends to be much more inelastic than the supply of manufactured goods because it can take a number of years to bring certain products to the market, depending on the length of the growing season.

In addition to the long run, it is also possible to refer to a period of time, known as the very long run, when there is a change in technological knowledge.

2.4 The interaction of demand and supply

2.4.1 The definition of market equilibrium and disequilibrium

Demand and supply have each been considered and it is now necessary to bring them together to establish **market equilibrium**. This position is where the quantity demanded and the quantity supplied in a market are equal and there is neither excess demand nor excess supply. This position of equilibrium is where there is no tendency to change. If there was a change in the demand and/or supply of a product, the market would be said to be in a state of **market disequilibrium**, although a state of equilibrium will eventually be restored.

Key terms

Market equilibrium: a situation in which demand equals supply, establishing an equilibrium price and an equilibrium quantity.

Market disequilibrium: a situation where demand does not equal supply, leading to a change in price and quantity in a market.

A situation of **excess supply** can be seen in Figure 2.16. If the price is above the equilibrium price of P_0, for example, it is at P_1, there will be a situation of excess supply. That is, the quantity that producers are willing to supply at that price is greater than the quantity that consumers are willing to demand at that price. This can be seen in the diagram by the horizontal distance between Q_1 and Q_2. As a result of the excess supply, the price will fall until equilibrium is reached at a price of P_0 and a quantity of Q_0.

> **Key term**
>
> **Excess supply:** the quantity that producers are willing to supply at a particular price is greater than the quantity that consumers are willing to demand at that price.

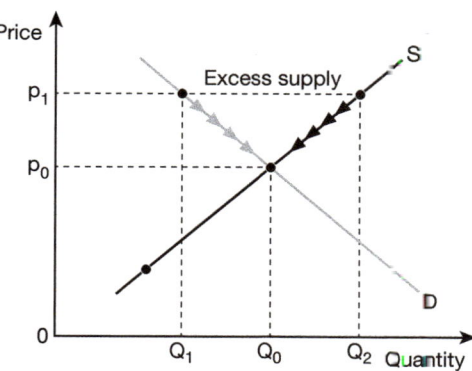

◀ **Figure 2.16** Excess supply bringing about a state of equilibrium in a market

A state of **excess demand** can be seen in Figure 2.17. If the price is below the equilibrium price of P_0, for example, it is at P_3, there will be a situation of excess demand, that is the quantity that producers are willing to supply at that price is less than the quantity that consumers are willing to demand at that price. This can be seen in the diagram by the horizontal distance between Q_3 and Q_4. As a result of the excess demand, the price will rise until equilibrium is reached at a price of P_0 and a quantity of Q_0.

> **Key term**
>
> **Excess demand:** the quantity that producers are willing to supply at a particular price is less than the quantity that consumers are willing to demand at that price.

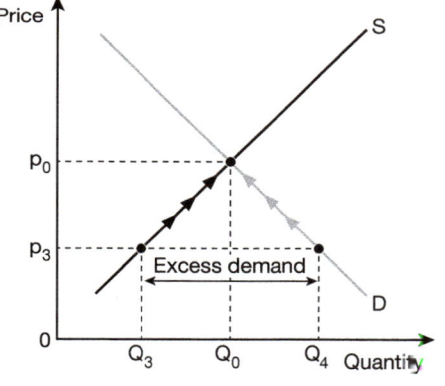

◀ **Figure 2.17** Excess demand bringing about a state of equilibrium in a market

> **Remember**
>
> You need to understand that a state of equilibrium in a market is where there is no tendency to change, that is the market is said to be in a state of rest or balance.

> **Remember**
>
> A situation of excess supply, in which producers are willing to supply more at a given price than consumers are willing to demand, will create disequilibrium in a market. However, a state of equilibrium will be restored in the market by price falling until a point where demand and supply are equal.
>
> A situation of excess demand, in which producers are willing to supply less at a given price than consumers are willing to demand, will create disequilibrium in a market. However, a state of equilibrium will be restored in the market by price rising until a point where demand and supply are equal.

2.4.2 The effects of shifts in demand and supply on equilibrium price and equilibrium quantity

An increase in demand

The effect of an increase in demand for a product can be seen in Figure 2.18. The original equilibrium was at price $0P_1$ and quantity $0Q_1$. If there is a change in the conditions of demand, for example, there is a rise in incomes, the demand curve will shift to the right from D_1 to D_2. There has been an increase in demand and an extension of supply, leading to a new equilibrium position being established at a price of $0P_2$ and a quantity of $0Q_2$.

A decrease in demand

The effect of a decrease in demand for a product can be seen in Figure 2.19. The original equilibrium was at price $0P_1$ and quantity $0Q_1$. If there is a change in the conditions of demand, for example, there is a decrease in the advertising of the product, the demand curve will shift to the left from D_1 to D_2. There has been a decrease in demand and a contraction of supply, leading to a new equilibrium position being established at a price of $0P_2$ and a quantity of $0Q_2$.

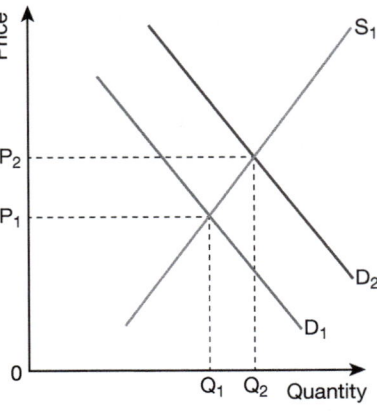

▲ **Figure 2.18** The effect of an increase in the demand for a product

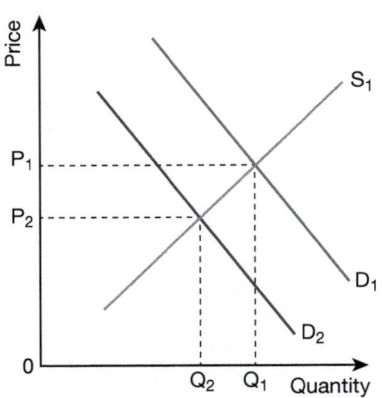

◀ **Figure 2.19** The effect of a decrease in the demand for a product

An increase in supply

The effect of an increase in supply of a product can be seen in Figure 2.20. The original equilibrium was at price $0P_1$ and quantity $0Q_1$. If there is a change in the conditions of supply, for example, there is an improvement in the technology of production, the supply curve will shift to the right from S_1 to S_2. There has been an increase in supply and an extension of demand, leading to a new equilibrium position being established at a price of $0P_2$ and a quantity of $0Q_2$.

A decrease in supply

The effect of a decrease in supply of a product can be seen in Figure 2.21. The original equilibrium was at price $0P_1$ and quantity $0Q_1$. If there is a change in the conditions of supply, for example, there is an increase in the costs of production, the supply curve will shift to the left from S_1 to S_2. There has been a decrease in supply and a contraction of demand, leading to a new equilibrium position being established at a price of $0P_2$ and a quantity of $0Q_2$.

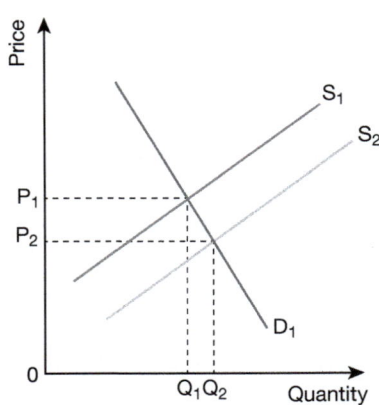

▲ **Figure 2.20** The effect of an increase in the supply of a product

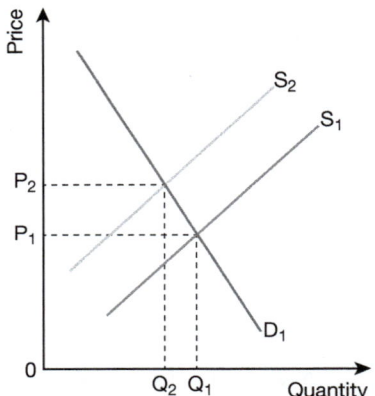

▲ **Figure 2.21** The effect of a decrease in the supply of a product

> 💡 **Remember**
>
> It is important to be able to distinguish between an increase or decrease in demand or supply and an extension or contraction of demand or supply.
>
> If there is a change in the conditions of demand or supply, there will be a shift of the demand or supply curve to the right or to the left.
>
> If there is not a change in the conditions of demand or supply, there will simply be a movement along a demand or supply curve, but not a shift; this is known as an extension or contraction of demand or supply.

> ★ **Exam tip**
>
> Make sure you do not confuse a movement along a demand or a supply curve with a shift of a demand or supply curve.

Applications of demand and supply analysis

There are many different possible applications of demand and supply analysis in a modern economy. For example, if an economy is experiencing an increase in the general level of incomes, there is likely to be an increase in the demand for televisions, shifting the demand curve for televisions to the right. This can be seen in Figure 2.22, where the demand curve has shifted to the right from D_0 to D_1. At the same time, an improvement in the technology of production may have reduced the cost of producing televisions, shifting the supply curve to the right from S_0 to S_1. The effect of these two shifts is that quantity has increased from $0Q_0$ to $0Q_2$. The effect of the shifts of the demand and supply curves on price will depend on the extent of the two shifts. In Figure 2.22, price has returned to the original price of 0P.

2.4.3 Relationships between different markets

It is important to distinguish between **joint demand**, in the case of complements, and **alternative demand**, in the case of substitutes.

Joint demand (complements)

Some products are jointly demanded, that is they are consumed together. Products that are jointly demanded are known as complements. Examples of complementary goods are CDs and CD players or DVDs and DVD players.

Figure 2.23 shows what happens in the case of DVDs and DVD players. The demand for DVD players is shown on the left-hand side. There is an increase in the demand for DVD players shown by a shift of the demand curve to the right from D to D^1. As DVDs and DVD players are complementary goods, there is also a shift of the demand curve to the right for DVDs, shown on the right-hand side.

Alternative demand (substitutes)

Some products, however, are examples of alternative demand, that is they are in competition with each other. Products that are in competition with each other are known as substitutes. Examples of substitute goods are tea and coffee or CDs and vinyl records.

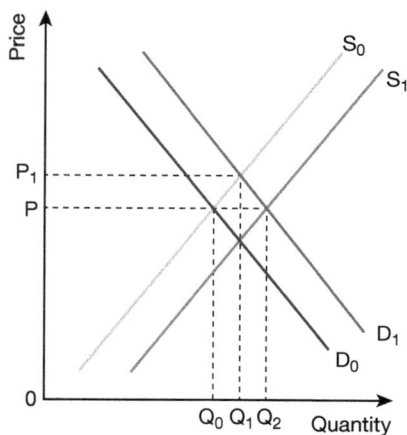

▲ **Figure 2.22** An application of demand and supply analysis to televisions

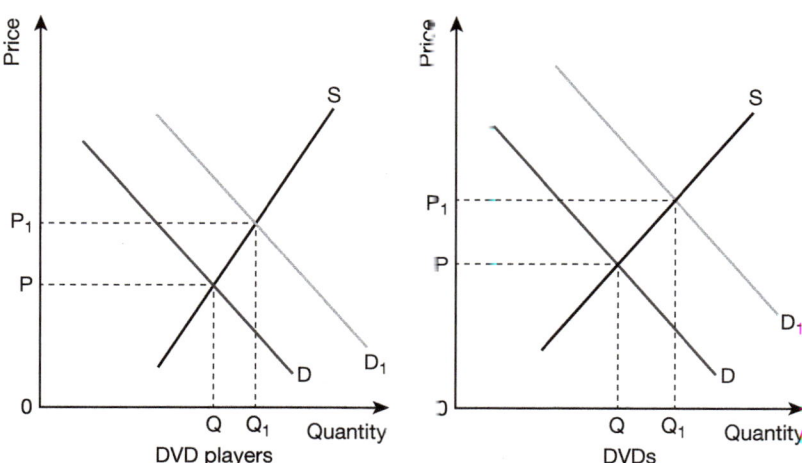

▲ **Figure 2.23** Joint demand for DVD players and DVDs

Figure 2.24 shows what happens in the case of tea and coffee. The demand for tea is shown on the left-hand side. There is an increase in the demand for tea shown by a shift of the demand curve to the right from D to D_1. As tea and coffee are substitute goods, there is a shift of the demand curve to the left for coffee, shown on the right-hand side.

Derived demand

Derived demand refers to the situation in which the demand for a component depends upon the final demand for a product that uses that component. For example, the demand for rubber is derived from the demand for car tyres. The concept of derived demand can also be applied in relation to the demand for particular workers. For example, the demand for train drivers derives from the demand for rail transport.

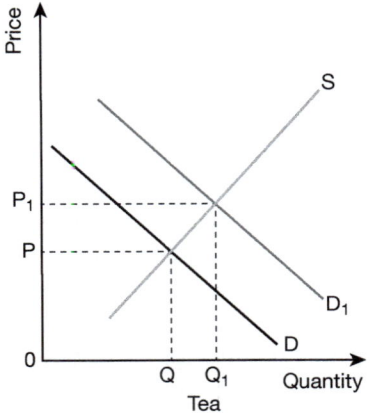
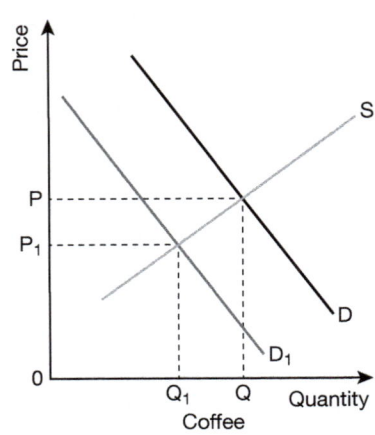

▲ **Figure 2.24** Alternative demand for tea and coffee

Joint supply

Joint supply occurs when the production of one product involves the production of another. For example, this can sometimes happen in the chemical industry where one product may be produced as a by-product of another.

2.4.4 The functions of price in resource allocation; rationing, signalling (the transmission of preferences) and incentivising

The workings of the price mechanism

The price mechanism plays a key role in the allocation of resources in a market. The Scottish economist Adam Smith (1723–1790) stressed the importance of the workings of the price mechanism to a successful economy, describing prices as an 'invisible hand' in allocating scarce resources.

Rationing

Prices also perform a key function as a **rationing** mechanism; for example, if the supply of a product cannot match the demand for it, the price of the product is likely to rise and this will ration the product because only those who are able to pay the higher price will be able to afford it.

Signalling and the transmission of preferences

Changes in the prices of different products, in response to changes in the demand and supply of them, can act as signals, indicating which resources will be needed to produce some products rather than others. In this way, the price mechanism provides a means by which consumers can transmit their preferences for certain products. This is termed **signalling**.

Incentivising

In a competitive market that is working efficiently, all economic agents, for example, individuals and firms, need to be able to respond to incentives within that market. For example, if there is an increase in the demand for a product and the price goes up, firms will know that for selling each product they will receive a higher average level of revenue per unit and so the possibility of earning a higher profit acts as an incentive.

Key term

Derived demand: a demand for a good or service that results from a demand for a related good or service.

Key term

Joint supply: a situation in which the production of one good automatically brings about an increase in the supply of another.

Remember

Products in joint supply are produced together; for example, the production of beef will also lead to the supply of hides for making leather.

Key terms

Rationing: a limit on the amount of a product that can be consumed.

Signalling: the way in which the price mechanism operates by allowing consumers to transmit their preferences for certain products.

Incentivising: a situation in which individuals or firms are encouraged to act in a certain way as a result of higher or lower prices in a market.

2.5 Consumer surplus and producer surplus

2.5.1 The meaning and significance of consumer surplus

Consumer surplus refers to a situation in which consumers are able to obtain a value from consuming a good or service that is above the price that is actually paid for the product. In Figure 2.25, 0P is the equilibrium price and 0Q is the equilibrium quantity. At any price above 0P, consumers would have been willing to pay a higher price than 0P and so the size of the consumer surplus is shown by the triangle PAB.

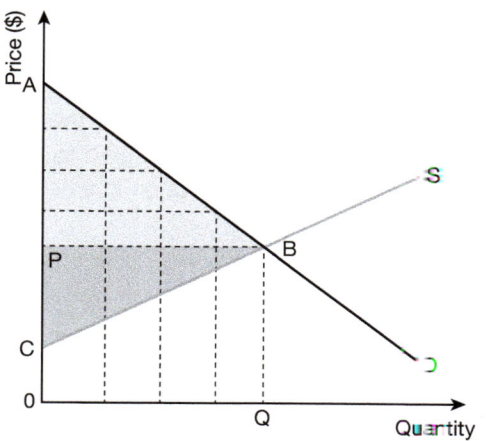

◀ **Figure 2.25** Consumer surplus and producer surplus

2.5.2 The meaning and significance of producer surplus

Producer surplus refers to a situation in which producers would have been willing to accept a lower price for a product but actually received a higher price than this. In Figure 2.25, 0P is the equilibrium price and 0Q is the equilibrium quantity. Producers would have been willing to accept a price below 0P up to point B and so the size of the producer surplus is shown by the triangle PCB.

2.5.3 The causes of changes in consumer surplus and producer surplus

When there is a change in the market price, the consumer surplus will also change. For example, if the equilibrium price was to increase above P in Figure 2.25, and equilibrium quantity was to fall below Q, then the extent of the consumer surplus would be reduced. This is because some consumers would be unwilling to pay the higher price

When there is a change in the quantity supplied of a product, the producer surplus will also change. For example if the quantity supplied falls the extent of the producer surplus will be less. For example, if the equilibrium price was to fall below P in Figure 2.25 and the equilibrium quantity was to decrease below Q, producer surplus would be less.

2.5.4 The significance of price elasticity of demand and of price elasticity of supply in determining the extent of the changes

Price elasticity of demand is significant in influencing the size of the consumer surplus. When the price elasticity of demand is inelastic, consumer surplus will be relatively large. When the price elasticity of demand is elastic, consumer surplus will be relatively small. When the demand for a product is perfectly elastic, consumer surplus is zero because the demand curve is a horizontal line and the price that consumers pay matches exactly what they are willing to pay. On the other hand, when demand is perfectly inelastic, consumer surplus is infinite. In this situation, demand does not respond to a price change.

Price elasticity of supply is also significant in influencing the size of the producer surplus. Price elasticity of supply is inversely related to producer surplus. If price elasticity of supply is perfectly elastic, the supply curve will be a horizontal line and producer surplus will be zero. On the other hand, when supply is perfectly inelastic, it is shown as a vertical line and producer surplus is infinite.

Key term

Consumer surplus: the difference between the maximum price an individual is prepared to pay for a product and the price that is actually paid.

💡 **Remember**

You need to understand that consumer surplus refers to a situation in which there is a difference between the maximum price that consumers are willing to pay for a product and the price prevailing in a market that they actually pay. This is shown by the triangle between the price line and the demand curve.

Key term

Producer surplus: the difference between the minimum price a producer is prepared to accept for a product and the price that is actually received.

💡 **Remember**

You need to understand that producer surplus is the difference that producers are willing to accept for what is sold and the price that is actually received. This is shown by the triangle between the price line and the supply curve.

↑ Raise your grade

Assess the usefulness of price elasticity of demand, income elasticity of demand and cross-elasticity of demand to a car manufacturer. [12]

There are three different types of elasticity of demand. Price elasticity of demand is defined as the relationship between the change in demand for a product and the price of that product (1). Income elasticity of demand is defined as the relationship between the percentage change in the demand for a product and the change in incomes in an economy (2). Cross-elasticity of demand is defined as the relationship between the percentage change in demand for a product and the percentage change in price (3).

In the case of a car manufacturer, if the demand for a car is price elastic, the firm should increase the price of the cars to raise total revenue (4). If incomes in an economy are rising, this is likely to lead to an increase in total revenue (5). If the price of fuel is increasing, this is likely to lead to a reduction in sales of cars and therefore a decrease in total revenue (6).

How to improve this answer

1. The candidate needs to make it clear that PED is defined as the percentage change in the quantity demanded of a product divided by the percentage change in its price; there is no reference in this first sentence to percentage or proportionate changes. Also, the candidate has written very little on the concept of PED; the answer could have been developed more fully, such as in relation to analysing the difference between elastic and inelastic demand.

2. The candidate has referred to the percentage change in the quantity demanded of a product, but has not referred to the fact that it is the percentage change in incomes that needs to be considered, not simply the change in incomes. The treatment of YED is very limited; for example, there is no reference to the contrast between normal goods and inferior goods.

3. The candidate has referred to both changes in terms of percentage changes, but has not made it clear that the change in price is not in terms of the same good, but that of another good. The analysis of XED is again limited, with no distinction between substitutes and complements.

4. The candidate has made a significant error here. If the demand for a car is price elastic, the manufacturer should reduce the price of the cars to increase total revenue, not increase it.

5. The candidate could have developed this evaluation more fully, for example, by commenting on the significance of the extent of the increases in income, perhaps in terms of whether the firm is producing cheaper car models or more expensive types.

6. It needs to be made clear that fuel and cars are complements.

Knowledge and understanding and analysis:	Level 2	3/8
Evaluation:	Level 1	1/4
Total:		4/12

Worked Example

Explain what is meant by a situation of market equilibrium and consider how market equilibrium can arise. [8]

A situation of market equilibrium is said to exist when there is no tendency to change. This means that the quantity demanded in a market is exactly equal to the quantity supplied in a market and there is a state of rest or balance. This situation will be at a particular price and a particular quantity.

A situation of market disequilibrium can occur when there is a change in this situation. This could come about through either excess demand or excess supply. In the case of excess demand, the price will eventually rise to restore a state of equilibrium in the market. In the case of excess supply, the price will eventually fall to restore a state of equilibrium in the market. A new equilibrium position will eventually be reached at a new equilibrium price and a new equilibrium quantity.

The new situation of market equilibrium will be at a market clearing position where demand is equal to supply and there is no excess demand or excess supply in the market.

Exam-style questions

1 Effective demand is defined as demand that is:

(a) adjusted to take account of the rate of inflation in an economy

(b) backed by the ability and willingness of consumers to pay

(c) the outcome of the dreams of all consumers in a market

(d) what consumers would like to purchase. [1]

2 Which of the following will cause the shift of the demand curve for a product to the right?

(a) A decrease in the price of a substitute

(b) A decrease in the price of the product

(c) An increase in the price of a complement

(d) An increase in the price of a substitute [1]

3 Which of the following will cause the shift of the supply curve of a product to the left?

(a) A decrease in the costs of production

(b) An improvement in the technology of production

(c) An increase in the costs of production

(d) An increase in the productivity of factors of production [1]

4 Which of the following is drawn as a rectangular hyperbola?

(a) Elastic price elasticity of demand

(b) Perfectly elastic price elasticity of demand

(c) Perfectly inelastic price elasticity of demand

(d) Unitary price elasticity of demand [1]

5 The income elasticity of demand is negative for:

(a) a luxury

(b) a necessity

(c) a normal good

(d) an inferior good. [1]

6 Any straight line supply curve, drawn through the origin, will have:

(a) elastic price elasticity of supply

(b) inelastic price elasticity of supply

(c) perfectly inelastic price elasticity of supply

(d) unitary price elasticity of supply. [1]

7 Which of the following will cause a movement along a demand curve for a product?

(a) A change in incomes

(b) A change in the price of a complement

(c) A change in the price of a substitute

(d) A change in the price of the product [1]

8 Which of the following are examples of alternative demand?

(a) Beef and hides

(b) CDs and CD players

(c) DVDs and DVD players

(d) Tea and coffee [1]

9 Adam Smith described the price mechanism as:

(a) an invisible hand

(b) *ceteris paribus*

(c) normal

(d) ostentatious. [1]

10 Consumer surplus is shown in a diagram by:

(a) half of the area between the demand curve and the supply curve

(b) the triangle between the demand curve and the supply curve

(c) the triangle between the price line and the demand curve

(d) the triangle between the price line and the supply curve. [1]

11 (a) Explain the difference between a change in price and a change in the conditions of demand, and consider why it is important to distinguish between the changes in prices of cars and changes in the conditions of demand for cars. [8]

(b) Assess why income elasticity of demand is elastic for some models of cars and inelastic for others. [12]

12 (a) Explain what is meant by market equilibrium and consider why a market may be in a state of disequilibrium for only a short period of time. [8]

(b) Assess how effective the price mechanism is likely to be in the transmission of consumer preferences. [12]

3 Government microeconomic intervention

Key topics
- Reasons for government intervention in markets
- Methods and effects of government intervention in markets
- Addressing income and wealth inequality

3.1 Reasons for government intervention in markets

3.1.1 Addressing the non-provision of public goods

Public goods have already been discussed in section 1.6.2. It was pointed out there that it would not be possible to provide a public good, such as street lighting, through a market because it would be impossible to prevent someone who had not paid from benefiting from the service. This is known as the free rider problem and comes about as a result of public goods having the characteristics of non-rivalry and non-excludability. Therefore, a major reason for government intervention in a market is to address the problem of the non-provision of public goods. This is an example of market failure because of the impossibility of charging a price for them.

3.1.2 Addressing the over-consumption of demerit goods and the under-consumption of merit goods

Merit goods

Another reason for government intervention in markets is to address the problem of the under-consumption of merit goods. Merit goods have already been discussed in section 1.6.3. It was pointed out there that merit goods, such as education and healthcare, would be under-consumed in a market as a result of imperfect information. The problem is that there is information failure and people do not fully understand and appreciate the value of a merit good. Therefore, a major reason for government intervention in a market is to address the problem of market failure in the form of the under-consumption of merit goods.

Demerit goods

Governments also intervene in markets to address the problem of the over-consumption of demerit goods. Demerit goods have already been discussed in section 1.6.4. It was pointed out there that demerit goods, such as alcohol and tobacco, would be over-consumed in a market as a result of imperfect information. The problem is again that there is information failure and people do not fully understand the potential dangers associated with the consumption of products such as alcohol and tobacco. Therefore, a major reason for government intervention in a market is to address the problem of market failure in the form of the over-consumption of demerit goods.

★ **Exam tip**

Make sure that you are able to explain what is meant by the free rider problem, using appropriate examples to support your explanation.

★ **Link**

See Unit 1, section 1.6.2, for details of the nature and definition of public goods.

★ **Link**

See Unit 1, section 1.6.3, for details of the nature and definition of merit goods and of the under-consumption of merit goods as a result of imperfect information in the market.

💡 **Remember**

You need to understand the importance of information failure in relation to the over-consumption of demerit goods and the under-consumption of merit goods.

★ **Link**

See Unit 1, section 1.6.4, for details of the nature and definition of demerit goods and of the over-consumption of demerit goods as a result of imperfect information in the market.

3.1.3 Controlling prices in markets

Another reason for government intervention in markets is to control prices. This intervention can be due to three possible situations:

- High prices: the price of certain essential goods in a market, such as bread or rice, could rise so high, without maximum price controls, that poorer sections of a community would not be able to afford them. This could have detrimental effects on their health and standard of living. A government might therefore decide to intervene in a market to prevent the price from rising above a certain level.

- Low prices: the price of certain goods in a market could fall so low, without minimum price controls, that certain producers could go out of business. One example would be intervention in certain agricultural markets to help producers maintain their incomes. A minimum price could also be established in a market for demerit goods, such as tobacco and alcohol, to discourage consumption.

- Unstable prices: if left to free market forces, there is always a chance that prices will fluctuate widely in those markets where there can be great variations in supply over a period of time due to the weather. This is especially the case with agricultural markets, where supply is relatively fixed in the short run, and in such a situation a government might need to intervene in a market.

3.2 Methods and effects of government intervention in markets

3.2.1 The impact and incidence of specific indirect taxes

Impact and incidence

It is important to distinguish between the **impact of a tax** and the **incidence of a tax**.

The impact of a tax refers to the person, company or transaction on which a tax is levied, that is, it is essentially the legal responsibility for the payment of tax. The incidence of a tax, however, refers to the burden of a tax, that is, who actually pays a tax.

Specific indirect taxes

A **specific tax**, such as an excise duty, is where a fixed amount has to be paid. This is shown by a parallel shift to the left of the supply curve so that the vertical distance between the two supply curves remains constant, as in Figure 3.1.

3.2.2 The impact and incidence of subsidies

A **subsidy** is where a government gives money to a producer, shifting the supply curve to the right. This can be seen in Figure 3.2. The vertical distance between S_1 and S_2 indicates the extent of the subsidy.

> **Remember**
>
> You need to remember that governments intervene in markets to control prices in relation to three situations: high prices, low prices and unstable prices.

> ★ **Link**
>
> See Unit 8, section 8.1.1, for further information on price controls.

> **Remember**
>
> Producers will try to pass the increased cost, in the form of the tax, on to the consumer. The ability of producers to do this depends on the relative elasticities of demand and supply. If demand is more inelastic than supply, the consumers will pay the greater proportion of the tax, that is, the greater incidence of the tax will be placed on them. If supply is more inelastic than demand, the producers will pay the greater proportion of the tax, that is, the greater the incidence of the tax will be placed on them. If demand and supply are equally inelastic, the incidence of the tax will be equally shared by the producers and the consumers.

> ★ **Link**
>
> See Unit 5, section 5.2.4, and Unit 8, section 8.1.1, for further information on taxation.

Key terms

Impact of a tax: the person, company or transaction on which a tax is levied.

Incidence of a tax: how the burden of taxation is shared between the producer and the consumer.

Indirect tax: a tax levied on expenditure.

Specific tax: a specific amount of money has to be paid in taxation.

Subsidy: the amount of money paid by a government to a producer so that the price to the consumer will be lower than it otherwise would have been.

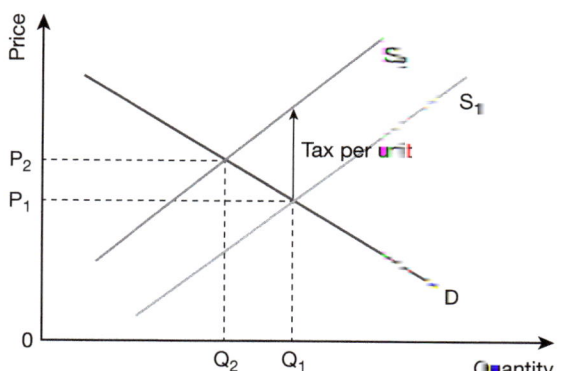

◀ **Figure 3.1** The imposition of a specific tax

The impact of a subsidy in a market will be a reduction in price and an increase in output. The incidence of a subsidy relates to who is made better off by the subsidy and by how much. The vertical distance between the two supply curves in Figure 3.2 indicates the size of the subsidy, but the price that the consumer pays does not fall by the full amount of the subsidy. This is because the producer gains some of the benefit in terms of extra revenue that they can keep. The effect of the subsidy is that there will be both a gain to the consumer and a gain to the producer. The extent of the different gains will depend on the price elasticity of demand for, and the price elasticity of supply of, the product.

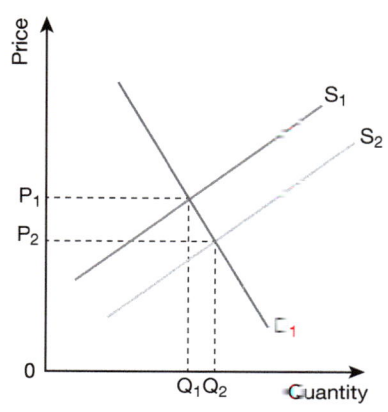

▲ **Figure 3.2** The effect of a subsidy

Remember

The impact and incidence of a subsidy will depend on the elasticity of demand for, and the elasticity of supply of, a product.

★ **Link**

See Unit 8, section 8.1.1, for further information on subsidies.

Remember

If the demand for a product is relatively elastic, the provision of a subsidy would lead to a relatively small reduction in price, but a relatively large increase in consumption.

If the demand for a product is relatively inelastic, the provision of a subsidy would lead to a relatively large reduction in price, but a relatively small increase in consumption.

3.2.3 The direct provision of goods and services

Another way in which a government could intervene in a market is through the **direct provision of goods and services**. Although a government could intervene in a market to discourage the production of goods and services, such as through the use of taxation, or to encourage the production of goods and services, such as through the use of subsidies, it could also intervene in a market by directly providing goods and services itself, often alongside the provision of such goods and services by the private sector.

Such direct provision in a market would increase the size of the public sector and reduce the size of the private sector in an economy. It could have a number of advantages, such as saving an industry from collapse, but it could also have a number of disadvantages, such as being less efficient.

Key term

Direct provision of goods and services: a situation in which a government decides to provide particular goods and services itself.

⭐ **Link**

See Unit 8, section 8.1.1, for further information on the direct provision of goods and services.

3.2.4 Maximum and minimum prices

Maximum price control

The price and quantity in a market are usually determined by market forces, that is, by demand and supply. However, a government could decide to intervene in a market by establishing a **maximum price** that acts as a ceiling, ensuring that price cannot go any higher than this maximum price. The effect of imposing a maximum price in a market can be seen in Figure 3.3.

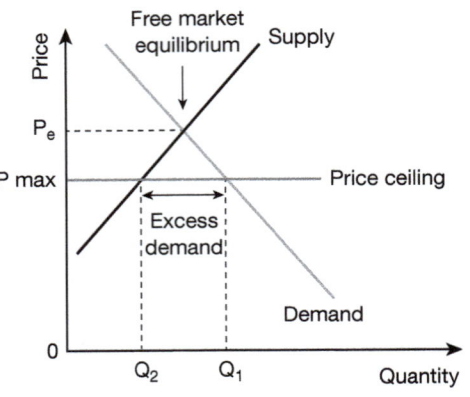

▲ **Figure 3.3** Maximum price control in a market

Key term

Maximum price: a situation in which a maximum price, or price ceiling, is established in a market below what would have been the equilibrium price without government intervention.

Minimum price control

A government could also decide to intervene in a market by establishing a **minimum price** that acts as a floor, ensuring that price cannot go any lower than this minimum price. The effect of imposing a minimum price in a market can be seen in Figure 3.4.

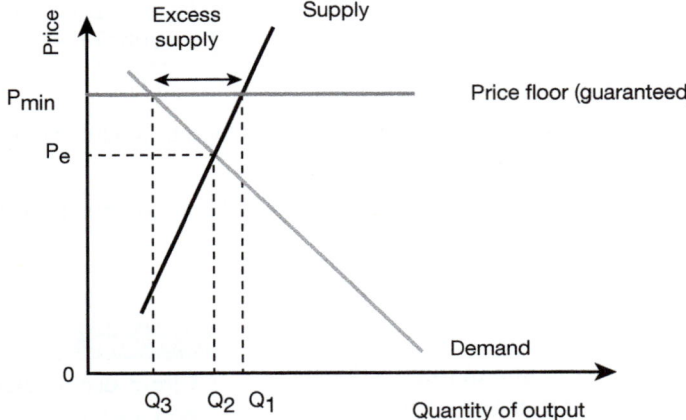

▲ **Figure 3.4** Minimum price control in a market

Key term

Minimum price: a situation in which a minimum price, or price floor, is established in a market above what would have been the equilibrium price without government intervention.

3.2.5 Buffer stock schemes

If a market is characterised by wide fluctuations in prices, such as agricultural markets, a government could try to bring about **price stabilisation** by intervening through what is called a **buffer stock scheme**.

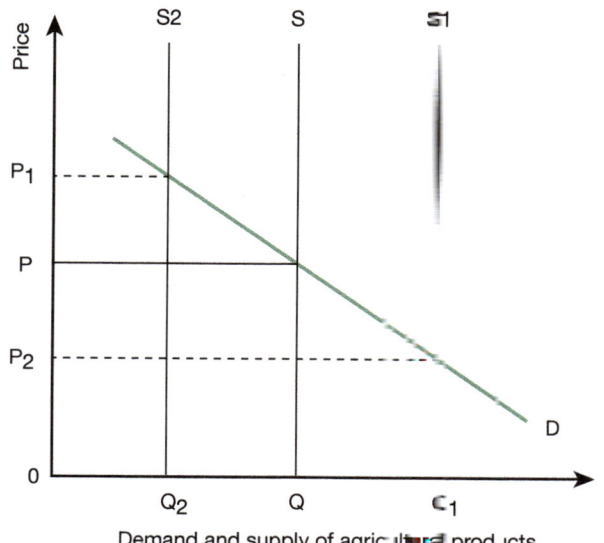

Demand and supply of agricultural products

◀ **Figure 3.5** The operation of a buffer stock scheme

★ **Link**

See Unit 8, section 8.1.1, for further information on price controls.

Key terms

Price stabilisation: an arrangement whereby a government prevents excessive volatility of prices by intervening to purchase stocks of a commodity when the supply is high and to sell stocks of a commodity when the supply is low.

Buffer stock scheme: a scheme which allows stocks of a commodity to be held back from a market during periods of high production and released onto a market during periods of low production.

A government may decide to intervene in a market to stabilise prices. This is known as a buffer stock system. Figure 3.5 shows what happens with such a system. When supply is high, as with S_1, the government purchases some of the stock and prevents it from entering the market. The effect of this intervention is to prevent the price falling too low, that is, it is kept at 0P rather than being allowed to fall to $0P_2$. When supply is low, as with S_2, the government releases some of the stock and allows it to enter the market. The effect of this intervention is to prevent the price rising too high, that is, it is kept at 0P rather than being allowed to rise to $0P_1$. Government intervention through a buffer stock scheme brings about price stabilisation in a market, with price maintained at or close to 0P and quantity maintained at or close to 0Q.

💡 **Remember**

A buffer stock scheme can have a number of possible advantages:

- It can overcome the problem of wide fluctuations in the prices in a market from one year to another.
- If price stabilisation can be brought about in a market, it will also help to bring about greater stability in the incomes received by the producers.
- The greater stability of prices and incomes will make medium-term and long-term planning easier.

However, a buffer stock scheme can also have a number of possible disadvantages:

- It might not be easy for a government to decide what the stable price in a market should be and this will affect the amount of stock that is stored or released.
- There will be a cost involved in running a buffer stock scheme, such as the cost of storage, and if a government pays for this, there will be an opportunity cost involved, that is the other goods or services that the money could have been spent on.
- The scheme may become very difficult to operate if there is either a succession of good harvests or a succession of bad harvests.

3.2.6 The provision of information

Market failure can be caused by inadequate information. A government could therefore aim to increase the availability of appropriate information to consumers in order to try to influence their economic behaviour.

It is assumed that consumers will always aim to maximise their utility or satisfaction, but they will only be able to achieve this objective if they are in possession of the necessary information. If this information is not available, it is unlikely that they will be able to make rational decisions.

Key term

Information failure: a situation in which people lack the full information that would allow them to make the best decisions about consumption.

Information failure is a major cause of market failure and so a government will need to take measures to improve the accuracy and availability of information that consumers need. This will help them make rational decisions and ensure that scarce resources are allocated as efficiently as possible. For example, a government could aim to make people as well informed as possible about the potential advantages of the consumption of merit goods, such as education and healthcare. It could also aim to make people as well informed as possible about the potential disadvantages of demerit goods, such as alcohol and tobacco. A particular example of such an approach in relation to the consumption of demerit goods is 'nudge' theory.

⭐ **Link**

See Unit 8, section 8.1.1, for further information on the provision of information.

3.3 Addressing income and wealth inequality

3.3.1 The difference between income as a flow concept and wealth as a stock concept

Income is not the same as wealth. There are clear differences between income and wealth and one of the most important is the idea of income as a flow and wealth as a stock.

Income is a flow of money going to factors of production, including:

- wages and salaries: these are paid to people for the work they have carried out
- welfare benefits: money paid to people receiving benefits, such as a state pension and a tax credit
- profits: these are received by businesses
- dividends: payments distributed to shareholders
- rental income: this is a flow to people who own, and rent or lease out, property
- interest: money paid to people who hold money in interest paying accounts with financial institutions.

Wealth is a stock of money or assets, including:

- savings: these can be held in various forms of accounts
- shares: ownership of shares issued by limited companies
- property: ownership of property
- bonds: money held in bonds
- pension schemes: wealth held in occupational pension schemes and life assurance schemes.

Key terms

Income: money received, usually on a regular basis.

Wealth: all assets that have a monetary value.

💡 **Remember**

Income and wealth can be clearly distinguished because income is a flow concept and wealth is a stock concept.

3.3.2 Measuring income and wealth inequality

A number of policies can be used to bring about a redistribution of income and wealth in an economy. However, it is necessary to consider how that distribution can be measured.

Gini coefficient

A **Gini coefficient** is a way of measuring the extent of inequality in the distribution of income in an economy. It is measured by the ratio of the area between the diagonal line of total equality and the Lorenz curve to the total area under the diagonal line (see section 11.4.2 for a discussion of the Lorenz curve). The bigger this area, the more unequal the distribution of income.

In this way, the Gini coefficient measures the extent to which the distribution of income in an economy diverges from the position of total equality. The lower the value of the coefficient, the more even the distribution of income. The higher the value of the coefficient, the less even the distribution of income.

Key term

Gini coefficient: a statistical measurement of the extent of inequality of income in an economy.

⭐ **Exam tip**

You will not be required to calculate the Gini coefficient in the AS examination.

⭐ **Link**

See Unit 11, section 11.4.2, for details of the calculation of the Gini coefficient.

3.3.3 Economic reasons for the inequality of income and wealth

There are a number of different possible economic reasons for the inequality of income and wealth, including:

- employment: a major cause of income equality is the ability of people to obtain well paid employment. When there is a decrease in employment in an economy, there will be fewer people receiving wages and salaries and more people receiving benefits. When there has been a decrease in full-time employment and an increase in part-time employment, income inequality will widen because rates of pay are likely to be lower in part-time than in full-time employment

- government policy: if an economy is experiencing difficulties, there could be a 'wage freeze' or lower-than-inflation wage rises. This is especially the case with public sector workers who may have experienced a fall in their real standard of living where increases in wages have been below increases in prices

- taxation: a government may decide to raise the levels of taxation in order to increase public revenue. It might also make tax more regressive when a higher proportion of tax is taken from people on relatively lower incomes than those on relatively higher incomes.

3.3.4 Policies to redistribute income and wealth

Minimum wage

A government could decide to establish a minimum wage rather than allow wages to be determined by the demand for, and the supply of, labour in particular markets. The actual wage paid to workers will often depend on their age.

However, one problem with a minimum wage is that it could be argued that it could lead to income becoming more unequal because some employers may not be able to pay all their workers the minimum wage and so some of them will become unemployed and be forced to live on benefits.

> ★ **Link**
>
> See Unit 8, section 8.3.8, for details of the influence of government on wage determination and employment in a labour market using a national minimum wage.

Transfer payments

A government could intervene in a market through the provision of **transfer payments**. This is where revenue received by a government, such as through the proceeds from taxation, is used to provide financial support for people, particularly those who are less well off. Examples of transfer payments include pensions and social security payments.

The provision of transfer payments could have an effect on the market. For example, unemployment benefit is paid in many countries to those people who are unemployed. This can be seen as advantageous to those who have been unable to find employment, but it could also be argued that it has a distorting effect on the labour market. For example, if the unemployment benefit is relatively high, it may make some people unwilling to seek employment.

> 💡 **Remember**
>
> Although transfer payments can be seen as worthwhile, transferring money from one group of people to another, they can also be seen as potentially having a distorting effect on a market.

Key term

Minimum wage: the lowest wage permitted by law in a country.

💡 **Remember**

Although the establishment of a minimum wage can have some advantages, there are also some potential disadvantages.

Key term

Transfer payments: a situation in which revenue is received from one part of society, such as taxpayers, and paid to another part of society, such as pensioners.

★ **Exam tip**

Make sure you do not confuse transfer payments with transfer earnings in relation to wage determination.

Progressive income taxes and inheritance and capital taxes

A **progressive tax** is one where not only the amount of tax paid rises when there is an increase in income, but the rate of tax increases. For example, rates of income tax could start at 10% and then increase to 20%, 30%, 40%, 50% and even higher as income rises. In this situation, the marginal rate of taxation increases with a rise in income and the marginal rate of tax will be higher than the average rate of tax.

A government could also decide to intervene in an economy with the aim of bringing about a more equitable distribution of wealth, as well as income. Examples of such taxes include inheritance and capital taxes.

> ★ **Link**
>
> See Unit 5, section 5.2.4, for further details on progressive taxation.

Key terms

Progressive tax: a situation in which the proportion of income paid in tax increases as income increases.

Income tax: this is a tax on earned incomes.

Inheritance tax: this is a tax on income in the form of property, money and possessions, also known as the 'estate', of someone who has died.

Capital tax: this is a tax, also called a capital gains tax, on income in the form of an increase in the value of possessions, such as a second home, antiques or shares, during the time that a person has owned them.

State provision of essential goods and services

State provision of essential goods and services helps to redistribute income and wealth because the money to pay for the provision of the essential goods and services comes from the money received from taxation. This helps to lessen inequality because the money received by the government pays for the goods and services that poorer people are unable to afford. State provision of healthcare is an example of this.

> ★ **Link**
>
> See Unit 8, section 8.1.1, for further information on state provision of essential goods and services.

 # Raise your grade

Assess to what extent the establishment of a maximum price in a market is likely to be effective. [12]

Instead of allowing an equilibrium price to be established in a market by the intersection of demand and supply, a government could intervene in a market by establishing its own price (1). This would be especially important as a way of keeping down the prices of certain products (2).

However, such an initiative by a government could lead to certain problems and difficulties. For example, a maximum price could lead to excess demand (3) and this could create some form of queue or waiting list (4). Such a situation could possibly lead to an element of corruption and bribery. It is also possible that the imposition of a price ceiling in the official market for the product could lead to the creation of an informal market (5) and the price in this market is likely to be different from that in the legal or official market (6).

↑ Continue

How to improve this answer

1. The candidate has implied that the price would be different as a result of government intervention but has not made it clear that the imposition of a maximum price control would establish a price below the equilibrium price. The candidate could have included a diagram to show this and to support the answer.

2. The candidate has referred to keeping down the prices of certain products, but it would have been helpful if some appropriate examples had been included, such as important food items, the amount of rent paid for housing or in the transport market, for example the cost of rail transport.

3. The candidate has referred to the situation of excess demand but has not really made it clear how this would come about as a result of the price being lower than it would have been without government intervention.

4. The candidate has referred to the possible existence of a queue or a waiting list, but this point could have been developed further by reference to the need for an alternative allocative mechanism, such as through the use of rationing.

5. The candidate has referred to the existence of an informal, in contrast to a formal, market, but there could also have been a reference to such markets also being known as black markets.

6. The candidate has stated that the price in the informal market would be different from that in the formal market, but has not made it clear that this price would likely be higher.

Knowledge and understanding and analysis:	Level 1	2/8
Evaluation:	Level 1	2/4
Total:		4/12

Worked Example

Assess the likely effectiveness of policies to redistribute income and wealth.

One of the aims of government is to bring about a greater degree of equality in the distribution of income and wealth.

One policy that could be used to achieve this objective is the introduction of a minimum wage below which nobody in an economy is paid. However, the effectiveness of such a policy will depend on the level of pay it is established at, whether there are some exceptions to the minimum wage and the degree to which it is actually enforced.

Another policy that could be used is the use of transfer payments. These cover a range of benefits that can be paid to the poorer people in an economy. However, the effectiveness of such a policy will depend on the amount of money that is paid in the form of benefits, and this will depend on a government's fiscal policy. For example the size of benefits is likely to be constrained if a government was planning for a budget surplus or a balanced budget rather than a budget deficit.

Progressive taxes could also be used to redistribute income and wealth, where those on higher incomes and with more wealth could be taxed in such a way that an increasing proportion of their income or wealth is taken in tax as their income or wealth increases. However, the effectiveness of this policy will depend on the degree to which any particular tax is progressive.

Finally, a government could decide to provide essential goods and services through the state. This will ensure that people have access to such services as education and health care irrespective of their income and wealth. However, the effectiveness of such a policy will depend on the degree to which a government has the necessary resources to provide an effective service.

Exam-style questions

1   A maximum price control in a market will establish a price:

   (a) above the equilibrium price

   (b) at the equilibrium price

   (c) below the equilibrium price

   (d) that creates a price floor.   [1]

2   A minimum price control in a market will establish a price:

   (a) above the equilibrium price

   (b) at the equilibrium price

   (c) below the equilibrium price

   (d) that creates a price ceiling.   [1]

3   The incidence of a tax refers to the:

   (a) eventual burden of a tax

   (b) person on which a tax is levied

   (c) rate at which the average rate of tax increases

   (d) rate at which the marginal rate of tax increases.   [1]

4   A tax which involves a particular amount of money to be paid on a product is known as:

   (a) a marginal tax

   (b) a specific tax

   (c) an *ad valorem* tax

   (d) an average tax.   [1]

5   Which of the following is a reason for government intervention in markets?

   (a) Over-consumption of free goods

   (b) Over-consumption of merit goods

   (c) Under-consumption of demerit goods

   (d) Under-consumption of merit goods   [1]

6   Which of the following is an advantage of a buffer stock scheme?

   (a) It encourages producers to be efficient.

   (b) It encourages the over-supply of products.

   (c) It helps to maintain the incomes of farmers.

   (d) It requires taxes to be raised to pay for it.   [1]

7   Which of the following is an example of wealth?

   (a) Dividend payments

   (b) Property ownership

   (c) Salary payments

   (d) Welfare benefits   [1]

8   A subsidy will:

   (a) lead to a higher price in a market

   (b) lead to a lower quantity in a market

   (c) shift the supply curve to the left

   (d) shift the supply curve to the right.   [1]

9   Which of the following is an example of a transfer payment?

   (a) Gini payment

   (b) Minimum wage

   (c) Pension

   (d) Salary   [1]

10 A progressive tax is one where:

   (a) the marginal rate of tax is always 10% lower than the average rate of tax

   (b) the marginal rate of tax is higher than the average rate of tax

   (c) the marginal rate of tax is lower than the average rate of tax

   (d) the marginal rate of tax is the same as the average rate of tax.   [1]

11 (a) Explain why a government might decide to intervene in a market, and consider whether such intervention is likely to be effective.   [8]

   (b) Assess whether the provision of a subsidy is likely to be effective in substantially reducing the price of a product charged to consumers.   [12]

12 (a) Explain what is meant by a transfer payment and consider why some such payments can have a distorting effect on a market.   [8]

   (b) Assess whether the state provision of essential goods and services is always in the public interest.   [12]

Key topics

- National income statistics
- Introduction to the circular flow of income
- Aggregate demand and aggregate supply analysis
- Economic growth
- Unemployment
- Price stability

4.1 National income statistics

4.1.1 The meaning of national income

National income statistics actually involve a variety of different statistics. National income is often used as a generic term, but there are three different forms of the statistics:

- Gross Domestic Product (GDP)
- Gross National Income (GNI)
- Net National Income (NNI)

4.1.2 The measurement of national income

Gross Domestic Product (GDP)

Gross Domestic Product (GDP) refers to all that is produced within the geographical boundaries of a country over a particular period of time – usually a year. It does not matter whether the productive assets are owned within the country or are foreign owned.

There are three different ways of measuring the value of a country's GDP:

- The **output method**
- The **income method**
- The **expenditure method**

However, all three methods will produce the same value because they all measure the flow of income in an economy over a particular period of time.

Net domestic product (NDP) is obtained by deducting depreciation, or capital consumption, from GDP.

Gross National Income (GNI)

Gross National Income (GNI) is the sum of a country's Gross Domestic Product and its net income (positive or negative) from abroad. It represents the value produced by a country's economy in a given year, regardless of whether the source of the value created is domestic production or receipts from abroad.

Net National Income (NNI)

Net National Income (NNI) refers to Gross National Income minus the depreciation of fixed capital assets, such as buildings, machinery and equipment through wear and tear and obsolescence.

4.1.3 The adjustment of measures from market prices to basic prices

It is important to distinguish between nominal value and real value. If a country is experiencing inflation, the value of its GDP will rise, but this increase could be due solely to the rise in prices – in other words, there may not have been a real increase in value if the effect of inflation is eliminated from the figures. This is a limitation of any data that is expressed at **current market prices**.

Economists usually produce national income statistics at **constant prices** or basic prices, so that changes in real output can be identified rather than changes in value that are purely due to the inflation that exists in a country.

The **GDP deflator** is a price index that is used to convert the figures into real GDP. It measures the prices of products produced in a country and not the prices of products consumed. It therefore includes the value not just of consumer products but also of the capital used in the production of the products. It includes the prices of exports, but not the prices of imports.

> **Key terms**
>
> **Current market prices:** data at current prices have not been corrected to take account of inflation.
>
> **Constant prices:** data at constant prices have been corrected to take account of inflation.
>
> **GDP deflator:** a price index that is used to remove the effect of price changes, so that statistics can show changes in real output in an economy.

> 💡 **Remember**
>
> It is important to distinguish between nominal and real National Income statistics. If the statistics are nominal, that is, they are at current prices, no adjustment would have been made to take into account the effects of inflation. If the statistics are real, that is, they are at constant prices, an adjustment would have been made to take into account the effects of inflation. A GDP deflator is used to convert nominal National Income statistics into real GDP.

4.1.4 The adjustment of measures from gross values to net values

Gross values are adjusted to net values by the deduction of **depreciation** or capital consumption.

Net Domestic Product (NDP)

Net Domestic Product (NDP) is obtained by deducting depreciation, or capital consumption, from GDP.

Net National Product (NNP)

Net National Product (NNP) is obtained by deducting depreciation, or capital consumption, from GNP. As with net domestic product, this is done to take into account the money that will need to be spent on replacing machinery and equipment that has been worn out during the course of the year.

> 💡 **Remember**
>
> The figure for net income from abroad tends to be positive for developed countries and negative for developing countries. This means that in developed countries, the GNI is likely to be greater than the GDP, whereas in developing countries, the GDP is likely to be greater than the GNI.

> ★ **Exam tip**
>
> Gross National Income (GNI) is now being used more extensively than in the past. For example, the World Bank now uses GNI rather than GNP or GDP. The Human Development Index (HDI) now uses GNI rather than GDP.

> ★ **Exam tip**
>
> It is important that you are able to demonstrate an understanding of the difference between nominal National Income statistics, which do not take inflation into account, and real National Income statistics, which do take inflation into account.

> **Key terms**
>
> **Net domestic product:** the gross domestic product of a country minus depreciation or capital consumption.
>
> **Net national product:** the gross national product of a country minus depreciation or capital consumption.
>
> **Depreciation:** the fall in value of the capital stock of a country as a result of equipment and machinery that has become worn out in the production process; it is also known as capital consumption.

4.2 Introduction to the circular flow of income

4.2.1 The circular flow of money in a closed and an open economy

The circular flow of income

The **circular flow of income** refers to movements of income around an economy.

Closed economy

A **closed economy** is one where it is assumed that a country does not engage in trade with any other countries in the world. If there is a movement of incomes between households and firms, then this form of closed economy is known as a two sector economy. If a government is then added, in addition to households and firms, then this form of closed economy is known as a three sector economy.

Open economy

A more realistic approach, however, would be to assume that a country does engage in trade with other counties in the world. In this case, it would be described as an **open economy**. If the trade in goods and services that are exported from, and imported to, a country is added to the households, firms and government, then it is described as a four sector economy.

The circular flow of income between households, firms, government and the international economy

If the trade in goods and services that are exported from, and imported to, a country is added to the households and firms and to the government, then it is described as a four sector economy.

4.2.2 Injections and leakages

As has already been stated in section 4.2.1, the circular flow of income refers to movements of income around an economy. At any one time, there will be a number of injections into the economy and a number of withdrawals or leakages out of the economy.

Injections

There are three types of injection into the circular flow of income:

- Investment spending by private sector firms (I)
- Government spending (G)
- Income received from exports sold abroad (X)

Leakages

There are three types of withdrawal or leakage out of the circular flow of income:

- Savings (S)
- Taxation (T)
- Income spent on imports bought from abroad (M)

4.2.3 Equilibrium and disequilibrium

One way of showing equilibrium in an economy is through the withdrawal/injection approach. For income to be in equilibrium in an economy, the injections into the circular flow of income need to be equal to the withdrawals from the circular flow of income.

Equilibrium occurs when there is no change in the circular flow of income. It is therefore defined as a situation in which there is no tendency for the levels of income, expenditure and output to change. The condition for equilibrium in the macroeconomy is when injections equal leakages.

Disequilibrium occurs when injections are not equal to withdrawals. When injections are more than withdrawals, that is, the additions from I, G or X are more than the withdrawals from S, T or M, there will be a disequilibrium and this will cause the level of national income to rise. If the withdrawals are more than the injections, that is, the additions from I, G or X are less than the withdrawals from S, T or M, this will cause the level of national income to fall.

4.3 Aggregate Demand (AD) and Aggregate Supply (AS) analysis

4.3.1 The definition of Aggregate Demand (AD)

Aggregate demand refers to the total demand for all the goods and services in an economy.

4.3.2 The components of AD and their meanings

Aggregate demand is made up of four elements:

- C: consumer spending
- I: investment by firms, such as expenditure on machinery and equipment
- G: government expenditure
- X – M: the net effect of trade, that is, exports minus imports

Aggregate demand can therefore be expressed as equal to $C + I + G + (X - M)$.

💡 **Remember**

In the determination of aggregate demand in an economy, it is the net effect of international trade that needs to be taken into account, that is, exports minus imports.

4.3.3 The determinants of AD

A change in any of the four components of aggregate demand will bring about a change in aggregate demand. These changes could come about as a result of a number of possible factors, including:

- changes in interest rates, that is. the price of money

- changes in the money supply, that is, the quantity of money

- changes in taxes

- changes in expectations of future economic conditions

- changes in degrees of confidence, for example, optimism or pessimism

- changes in exchange rates

- changes in the accumulation of income/wealth

- changes in technology.

4.3.4 The shape of the AD curve

The AD curve reflects the four determinants of C + I + G + (X − M). It is downward sloping from left to right. This is shown in Figure 4.1. If the price level rises from $0P_1$ to $0P_2$, real output falls from $0Y_1$ to $0Y_2$.

4.3.5 The causes of a shift in the AD curve

In Figure 4.1, a movement along the AD curve is determined by a change in the price level. However, if there is a change in AD other than as a result of a change in the price level, then there will be a shift of the AD curve.

A shift of the AD curve, from AD_1 to AD_2, is shown in Figure 4.2, causing an increase in the price level from $0P_1$ to $0P_2$ and an increase in real output from $0Y_1$ to $0Y_2$.

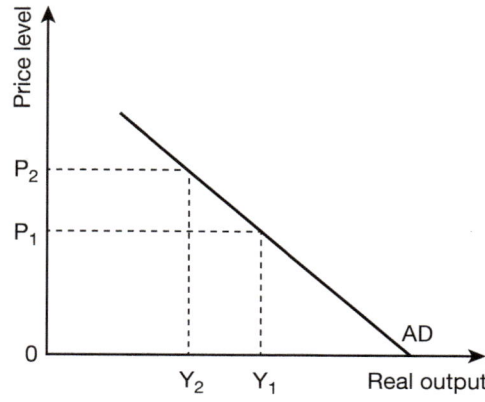

▲ **Figure 4.1** The AD curve

4.3.6 The definition of Aggregate Supply (AS)

Aggregate supply refers to the total output that the firms in an economy are able and willing to supply at different price levels in a given period of time.

4.3.7 The determinants of Aggregate Supply (AS)

Changes in aggregate supply could come about as a result of a number of possible factors including:

- changes in the state of technology

- changes in the cost and productivity of capital

- changes in the cost and productivity of labour

- changes in the cost of raw materials

- changes in taxation

- changes in exchange rates

- changes in government policy, for example, rules and regulations.

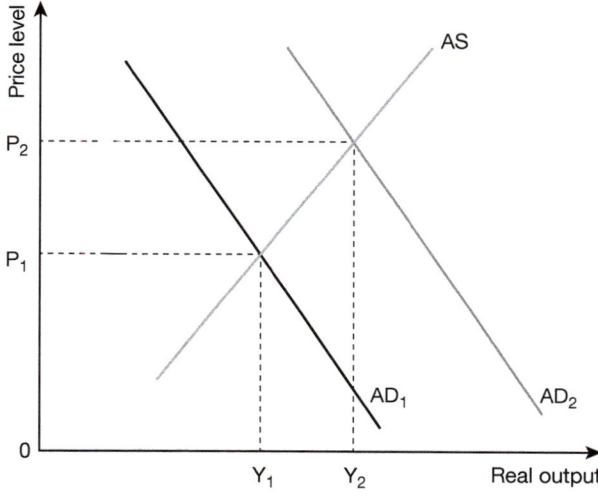

▲ **Figure 4.2** A shift of the AD curve to the right

Key term

Aggregate supply: the total value of goods and services produced in an economy.

4.3.8 The shape of the AS curve in the short-run (SRAS) and in the long-run (LRAS)

The AS curve is an upward sloping line or a sweeping curve from left to right. This is shown in Figure 4.3. If the price level rises from $0P_1$ to $0P_2$, real output rises from $0Y_1$ to $0Y_2$.

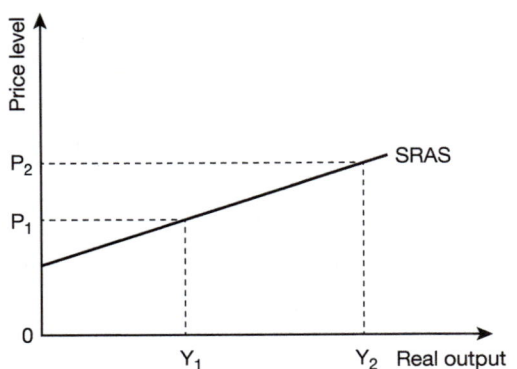

◀ **Figure 4.3** The AS curve in the short-run

However, this is the situation in the short run (SRAS) and it is important to distinguish between aggregate supply in the short run and in the long run. In the long run it is possible that the AS curve becomes vertical, that is, supply is perfectly inelastic. This is shown in Figure 4.4, where at the full employment level of real output, the AS curve is vertical.

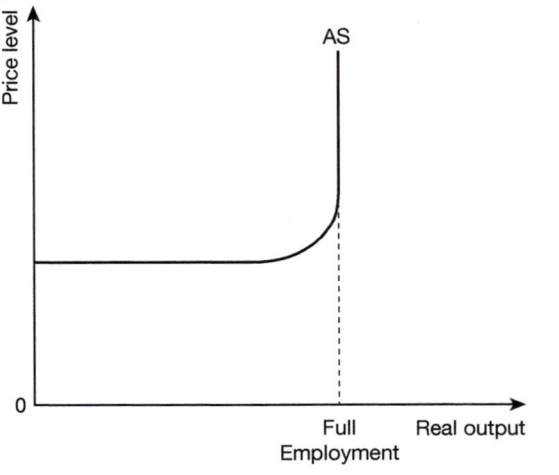

◀ **Figure 4.4** The AS curve in the long run

4.3.9 Causes of a shift in the AS curve in the short run (SRAS) and in the long run (LRAS)

If there is a change for any reason other than price, the SRAS curve will shift. If there is an increase in aggregate supply, the curve will shift to the right. If there is a decrease in aggregate supply, the curve will shift to the left.

In the long run, however, the shape of the LRAS curve will change. At low levels of output, the AS curve can be horizontal, indicating that it is perfectly elastic. At high levels of output, the AS curve can be vertical, indicating that it is perfectly inelastic. Indeed, some economists argue that the long-run AS curve is perfectly inelastic, indicating that an economy will operate at full capacity.

4.3.10 The distinction between a movement along and a shift in AD and AS

In Figures 4.1 and 4.3, a movement along the curve will be determined by a change in the price level. However, if there is a change in AD or AS other than as a result of a change in the price level, then there will be a shift of the AD or AS curve.

A shift of the AD curve, from AD_1 to AD_2, is shown in Figure 4.2, causing an increase in the price level from $0P_1$ to $0P_2$ and an increase in real output from $0Y_1$ to $0Y_2$. There is a movement along, but not a shift of, the AS curve.

A shift of the AS curve, from AS_1 to AS_2 is shown in Figure 4.5, causing an increase in the price level from $0P_1$ to $0P_2$ and a decrease in real output from $0Y_1$ to $0Y_2$. There is a movement along, but not a shift of, the AD curve.

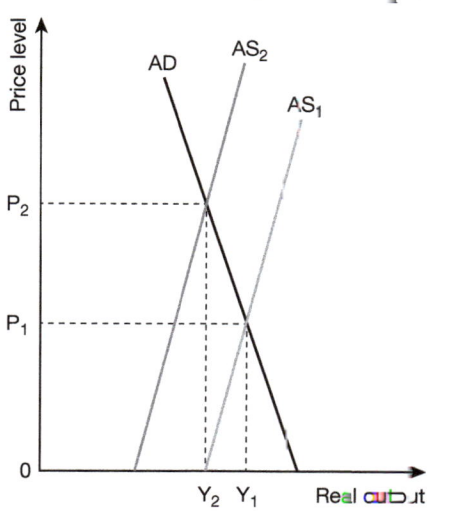

◀ **Figure 4.5** A shift of the AS curve to the left

★ **Exam tip**

Be careful not to confuse a change in the price level, which only causes a movement along an AD or an AS curve, with changes in other possible influences on AD or AS, which causes a shift of the AD or AS curve. Favourable changes in these other influences will cause a shift to the right of an AD or AS curve, whereas unfavourable changes will cause a shift to the left of an AD or AS curve.

💡 **Remember**

It is important to be able to distinguish between a movement along an AD or an AS curve, and a shift of an AD or an AS curve. The important difference is that movements along an AD or an AS curve can only be caused by a change in the price level, whereas shifts of an AD or an AS curve can be caused by any other factor affecting AD or AS apart from price. For example, in Figure 4.5, the shift of the AS curve to the left could have been caused by an increase in the price of imported materials, a decline in technology, less incentives to work, higher money wages, less capital, higher rates of interest or a smaller population of working age.

4.3.11 The establishment of equilibrium in the AD/AS model and the determination of the level of real output, the price level and employment

Levels of output, price and employment in an economy are determined by the interaction of AD and AS. For example, in Figure 4.6, the initial equilibrium position is where the AD_1 and AS curves intersect at a price level of P_1 and a real output level of Y_1.

4.3.12 The effects of shifts in the AD curve and the AS curve on the level of real output, the price level and employment

A shift of the AD curve and/or the AS curve can affect the level of real output, the price level and employment in an economy. For example, in Figure 4.6, there has been a shift of the AD curve to the right.

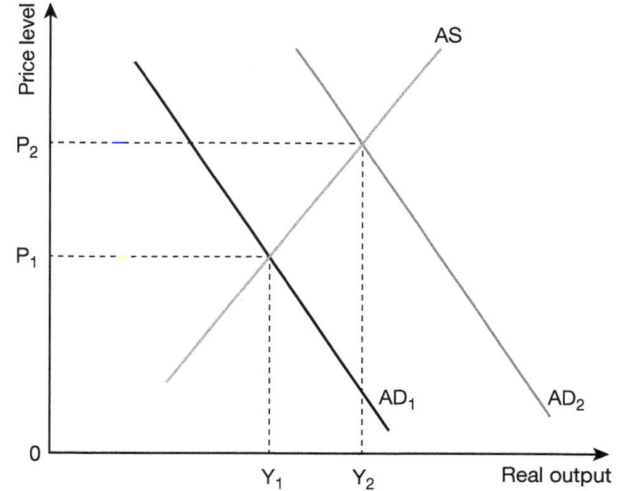

▲ **Figure 4.6** Changes in the level of output, price and employment in an economy

The effect on the level of output, prices and employment in this economy is as follows:

Effect on the level of output	There is a rise in the level of output from $0Y_1$ to $0Y_2$
Effect on the level of employment	There is a rise in the level of employment as more workers will be required to produce this increased level of output
Effect on the price level	There is a rise in the price level from $0P_1$ to $0P_2$

★ **Exam tip**

Be careful not to label the axes on an AD/AS diagram the same as on a demand and supply diagram, that is, P and Q. In an AD/AS diagram, the vertical axis should be labelled 'price level' and the horizontal axis 'real output'.

4.4 Economic growth

4.4.1 The meaning of economic growth

Economic growth is defined as the increase in the national output of a country over a period of time.

4.4.2 The measurement of economic growth

Economic growth is usually measured in terms of a change in gross domestic product.

4.4.3 The distinction between growth in nominal GDP and real GDP

Economic growth is the increase in the production of goods and services in an economy over a specific period, but to be accurate the measurement must remove the effects of inflation. **Nominal GDP** is GDP that has not been adjusted to take into account the effects of inflation, whereas **real GDP** is GDP that has been adjusted to take into account the effects of inflation.

4.4.4 The causes of economic growth

Economic growth can be brought about in an economy by a number of factors, including:

- an increase in the number of workers
- an improvement in the quality of labour, for example, the acquisition of new or improved skills, as a result of improved education and training, leading to a higher level of productivity
- a greater commitment to research and development, in terms of both **invention** and **innovation**
- an improvement in the state of technology
- an increase in investment in capital stock, for example, machinery and equipment; this can also be called an increase in gross fixed capital formation
- a reduction in taxes on the profits of businesses to allow firms to keep more funds that can be used to finance investment
- encouragement given to saving, that is, to bring about an increase in the savings ratio, because a high level of savings will provide the necessary funds to finance investment
- a move towards more capital-intensive, and away from labour-intensive, production
- increased mobility and flexibility of factors of production
- a more efficient allocation of resources
- the development of new markets, for example, for exports
- an upturn or recovery in the business, or trade, cycle.

> **Key term**
>
> **Economic growth:** an increase in the national output of an economy over a period of time, usually measured through changes in real gross domestic product.

> **Key terms**
>
> **Nominal GDP:** the measurement of the value of all the goods and services produced by a country in a given period at current market prices.
>
> **Real GDP:** the measurement of a country's total economic output in a given period, adjusted for the effects of price changes.

> **Remember**
>
> It is important to understand that the increase in output needs to be an increase in real output, that is, the increase in output needs to have taken inflation into account.

> **Key terms**
>
> **Invention:** the discovery of new products and new methods of production.
>
> **Innovation:** the bringing of inventions to the market place.

> ★ **Exam tip**
>
> Economic growth comes about in an economy not only from an increase in the quantity of factors of production used in the production process, but also from an increase in the quality of those economic resources.

4.4.5 The consequences of economic growth

Economic growth clearly has benefits for a country, but it is also important to recognise that there can also be costs of growth.

Link

See Unit 9.2 for further information on economic growth.

Remember

The **benefits** of economic growth include:

- an increase in the number of goods and services produced in a country, leading to an increase in the standard of living and a reduction in poverty

- economic growth is an indication that an economy is doing well and this could lead to greater confidence and optimism in the long-term prospects of an economy, encouraging investment decisions

- it could lead to a decrease in the level of unemployment in an economy

- the increase in output, if exported, could lead to a reduction of a deficit in the current account of a country's balance of payments

- increased tax revenue could lead to an improvement in an economy's infrastructure, for example, in relation to education and health care.

The **costs** of economic growth include:

- it can sometimes involve a shift away from consumer goods to capital goods, which will be good in the long-run but not necessarily in the short-run

- it may lead to a depletion of natural resources and possible damage to the environment, for example, in relation to pollution, and so a certain rate of economic growth could be regarded as unsustainable

- the benefits of economic growth may not always be shared evenly in an economy

- there could be a reduction in the quality of life of people, for example, if working hours are longer, this will reduce leisure time.

4.5 Unemployment

4.5.1 The meaning of unemployment

Unemployment refers to the situation which occurs when people are able and willing to work, but are unable to find employment.

4.5.2 Measures of unemployment, with reference to possible difficulties in measurement

It is important to be able to distinguish between the number of people who are unemployed in a country and the **unemployment rate**. The unemployment rate refers to the total number of people who are unemployed in a country divided by the labour force.

The size and components of a labour force

The **labour force** of a country refers to all the people who are employed or who are actively looking for work. It therefore consists of both the employed and the unemployed in an economy, that is, it is the number of people in an economy who are available for work.

Exam tip

If a question requires a discussion of the consequences of economic growth, remember to refer to both the costs and benefits of growth.

Key terms

Unemployment: a situation in which a number of people in an economy are able and willing to work but are unable to gain employment.

Unemployment rate: the number of unemployed people in an economy divided by the labour force.

Labour force: the number of people in a country who are available for work.

Another way of expressing the number of people in a country who are available to work is to refer to the **working population**. The **participation rate** refers to the proportion of the population that is employed or officially registered as unemployed.

The size of a country's labour force depends on a number of factors, including:

- the total size of a country's population
- the birth rate
- the death rate
- the school leaving age
- the number of people who stay in full-time education after leaving school
- the retirement age
- the availability and value of transfer payments to those who do not have a job
- the availability and cost of childcare
- the attitudes in a country to women working
- the economic state of a country.

The components of the labour force refer to the sector of employment, for example, the primary, secondary or tertiary sectors, and the classification of workers by age and gender.

Difficulties involved in measuring unemployment

There are various difficulties involved in measuring unemployment and this is why there are two different ways of measuring it.

One method is the **claimant count**. This is where the number of people who officially register as unemployed is counted. One difficulty of this method is that not everybody who is able and willing to work actually register as officially unemployed. Another difficulty is that some people who register do so in order to receive certain transfer payments, for example, unemployment benefits, and yet have no intention to work.

Another method is the **labour force survey**. This is where a survey is conducted to find out the people who are able and willing to work, but who have not officially registered themselves as unemployed, and this number is then added to the claimant count. The difficulty of this method is that not all of those who are able and willing to work, and who have not officially registered as unemployed, will necessarily be identified in the labour force survey. Another difficulty, like any survey, is that it uses a sample of households and there is no guarantee that this sample will be entirely representative.

★ Exam tip

Make sure you indicate that there are a number of potential difficulties involved in measuring unemployment and that there are two different methods involved in the process of measurement: the claimant count and the labour force survey.

Key terms

Working population: the number of people in a country who are currently working or who are actively seeking work.

Participation rate: the proportion of a country's population that is either employed or officially registered as unemployed.

★ Exam tip

Make sure you understand that 'labour force' or 'working population' do not only refer to those people in employment. In fact, the two terms include **both** the employed and the unemployed, that is, all the people in a country who are in work or who are available for work.

Key terms

Claimant count: the number of people in an economy who officially register as unemployed.

Labour force survey: this includes not only those who are officially registered as unemployed in the claimant count, but those who have not registered, including those who do not qualify for any transfer payment given by the state.

💡 Remember

The labour force survey will give a higher figure of the unemployed people in an economy than the claimant count.

4.5.3 The causes and types of unemployment

The causes of unemployment

It is possible to distinguish between two distinct explanations of the cause of unemployment in an economy.

The Monetarist school states that the cause of unemployment is external interference in the labour market which leads to a situation where the supply of labour does not equal the demand for labour in the labour market. For example, minimum wage laws, restrictive trades union practices, taxes on companies, transfer payments in the form of unemployment benefits, occupational immobility, geographical immobility and various rules and regulations all prevent the labour market from clearing.

The Keynesian school states the unemployment in an economy is largely caused by the trade, or business, cycle. The lack of aggregate demand for goods and services reduces the demand for workers to produce these goods and services.

> **Remember**
>
> It is important to be able to distinguish between these two explanations of the causes of unemployment of these two schools of thought, with the Monetarists explaining unemployment as the result of excessive interference in the labour market and Keynesians emphasising the cyclical nature of unemployment.

The types of unemployment

Just as it is possible to distinguish between different causes of unemployment, it is also possible to distinguish between different types of unemployment. These include:

- **structural unemployment**: changes in the conditions of demand in an economy can lead to some industries declining and so unemployment occurs as a result of such changes in the structure of an economy

- **regional unemployment**: this occurs as the result of structural changes in an economy taking place in particular areas or regions of a country

- **cyclical unemployment**: this is where unemployment is more widespread in an economy, resulting from a downturn or recession in an economy; this is therefore called cyclical as it is related to changes in the trade, or business, cycle, although it is also known as **demand-deficient** unemployment

- **frictional unemployment**: a situation in which at any one moment in time, some people will be between jobs, that is, they are only unemployed for a relatively short period of time. It is possible to distinguish between three different types of frictional unemployment: **search**, **casual** and **seasonal**

- **technological unemployment**: a situation in which some people lose their jobs as a result of a move away from labour-intensive methods of production towards capital-intensive methods of production

- **real wage unemployment**: a situation in which some people are unemployed in an economy because real wages are too high, for example, as a result of the negotiating strength of trades unions; this is also known as **classical unemployment**.

Key terms

Structural unemployment: a situation in which unemployment occurs as a result of changes in the structure of an economy.

Regional unemployment: a situation in which unemployment is much higher in particular regions of a country.

Cyclical unemployment: a situation in which unemployment occurs as a result of adverse changes in the trade, or business, cycle.

Demand-deficient unemployment: another name for cyclical unemployment, stressing the lack of aggregate demand in an economy.

Frictional unemployment: a situation in which unemployment occurs for a relatively short period of time, when people are between jobs.

Search unemployment: a situation in which people are prepared to spend time searching for the best possible job available rather than taking the first one offered.

Casual unemployment: a situation in which employment in certain occupations is irregular, causing unemployment at certain times.

Seasonal unemployment: a situation in which people are unemployed because of a lack of demand for them in certain seasons of the year, such as in the agriculture or tourism industries.

Technological unemployment: a situation in which some people lose their jobs as a result of a greater use of technology compared with labour.

Real wage unemployment: a situation in which some people are unemployed in an economy because real wages are too high.

Classical unemployment: this is another term for real wage unemployment.

★ **Exam tip**

Although it is possible to consider unemployment in a generic sense, it is also important to be able to distinguish between different types of unemployment that could occur in an economy and to give appropriate examples to indicate that these differences have been understood.

💡 **Remember**

It is important to understand that frictional unemployment can actually be regarded as a positive sign in an economy, indicating dynamic change, with some sectors expanding while others are declining.

4.5.4 The consequences of unemployment

Unemployment can have a number of consequences in an economy, including:

- economic resources are scarce and so any unemployment will involve a waste of scarce resources

- an economy with a relatively high level of unemployment will be underperforming because the level of national output produced will be lower than would otherwise have been the case

- this will mean that the standard of living and quality of life will be lower than would have been the case if there had been a lower level of unemployment

- tax revenue will be less than it would otherwise have been, both in terms of direct taxes, such as income tax, and indirect taxes, such as a goods and services tax

- government expenditure is likely to be more, for example, as a result of spending on transfer payments in the form of unemployment benefits and on the provision of training schemes to give the unemployed the necessary skills to enable them to gain employment

- the budget deficit is likely to increase as a result in the fall in revenue and the rise in expenditure.

★ **Exam tip**

Make sure that you read any question in the exam on the topic of unemployment very carefully, especially in terms of distinguishing between the 'causes' and the 'consequences' of unemployment. It is easy to confuse the two words.

★ **Link**

See Unit 9.3 for further details on unemployment.

4.6 Price stability

4.6.1 The definition of inflation, deflation and disinflation

Inflation

Inflation can be defined as a sustained increase in the general or average level of prices in an economy over a given period of time.

Degrees of inflation

There are varying degrees of inflation, both in one economy at different times and in various economies at the same time. It is possible to distinguish between:

- **creeping inflation**, where the rate of inflation is relatively low and relatively stable over a period of time and so is not a major problem in an economy

- **accelerating inflation**, where the rate of inflation is getting significantly higher and is becoming a major problem in an economy

- **hyperinflation**, where the rate of inflation has reached such a high level that it affects confidence in an economy and may even lead to the collapse of the country's currency, as happened in Germany in 1923 and in Zimbabwe in 2008.

Deflation

Deflation can be defined as a general decrease in the average level of prices in an economy over a period of time.

Disinflation

A general increase in the level of prices in an economy over a period of time, but where the rate of increase of these prices is slowing down.

Key terms

Inflation: a persistent rise in the general price level of an economy leading to a fall in the value of money.

Creeping inflation: a situation in which the rate of inflation is relatively low, say 3-4%.

Accelerating inflation: a situation in which the rate of inflation is rising and is beginning to become a serious problem in an economy.

Hyperinflation: a situation in which the rate of inflation in an economy is becoming so high, for example, over 100% or 1000%, that confidence in the currency is decreasing.

Targeted inflation: a rate of inflation that is set by a government and policies are implemented to maintain that rate.

Deflation: a general decrease in the average level of prices in an economy over a period of time.

Disinflation: a situation in which there is a fall in the rate of inflation in an economy.

★ Exam tip

Make sure you understand that if there is a fall in the rate of inflation in an economy, it does not mean that the general level of prices is falling. It simply means that prices are still rising, but at a slower rate than previously. This is known as disinflation.

★ Exam tip

It is sometimes thought that hyperinflation is determined when inflation reaches a certain level in an economy, but this is not so. There is no precise point at which inflation becomes hyperinflation.

Deflation is a term that can be confusing because it actually has two meanings. It can refer to a general decrease in the average level of prices in an economy over a period of time, but it can also refer to a reduction in the level of aggregate demand in an economy.

Make sure that you do not think that disinflation refers to a situation of a decrease in the general level of prices in an economy, as this is not the case. When an economy is experiencing disinflation, there is still inflation, that is, the general level of prices is still increasing, but it is increasing at a lower rate of increase than was previously the case.

4.6.2 The measurement of changes in the price level

The consumer price index (CPI)

The level of inflation in an economy is measured through the use of a price index, such as a consumer price index. Different goods and services are included in a **basket** that would be bought by people in an economy and each of these products is given a **weight** in relation to the proportion of total expenditure spent on particular products. A base year is chosen, which is given a value of 100, and the general level of prices is compared with that base year.

> **Remember**
>
> To calculate a price index, it is necessary to compare the price of a representative basket of goods and services today compared to the base year using the following equation:
>
> $$\frac{\text{present cost of a basket of goods and services}}{\text{cost of the basket of goods and services in the base year}} \times 100$$
>
> You need to remember that the various goods and services in the representative basket are given weights to reflect their relative importance in relation to total expenditure.

Possible difficulties in measurement

There are a number of possible difficulties in the measurement of changes in the price level, including:

- The base year (= 100) needs to be one in which there are not particularly wide fluctuations in prices.

- Any particular basket of goods and services may not be representative of the spending patterns of all people in an economy.

- The basket of goods and services will need to be updated on a regular basis, leaving out some products and bringing in others so as to reflect changes in spending patterns.

- The relative importance of different goods and services may change and so the weights will need to change to reflect these changes in spending patterns.

> **Key terms**
>
> **Basket:** a selection of goods and services that would be purchased by a representative sample of people in an economy.
>
> **Weight:** a value that is given to products in a basket to reflect the proportion of income spent on such products by people in an economy.

> **Key term**
>
> **Consumer price index:** a method of measuring changes in the prices of a number of products in an economy over a given period of time.

4.6.3 The distinction between money values (nominal) and real data

It is important to be able to distinguish between money values and real data.

Money values

A **money value** is one that does not take into account the effects of inflation. It can also be known as the nominal value of a given amount of money.

> **Key term**
>
> **Money value:** this refers to the value of a given sum of money that has not taken into account the effects of inflation.

Real data

Real data refers to the value of something that has taken the effects of inflation into account. The real value of a given sum of money is one where it is assumed that the prices of goods and services in an economy have remained constant over a period of time that is, the effect of inflation has been eliminated.

4.6.4 The causes of inflation: cost-push and demand-pull inflation

Cost-push inflation

Cost-push inflation in an economy arises as a result of an increase in the costs of production, such as the cost of labour, and these increased costs are passed on to consumers in the form of higher prices. Where the increase in costs is largely due to the increase in the cost of imported raw materials or component parts, it is called **imported inflation**.

Cost-push inflation can be seen in Figure 4.7 where the price level has increased from $0P_0$ to $0P_1$ as a result of changes in the costs of production.

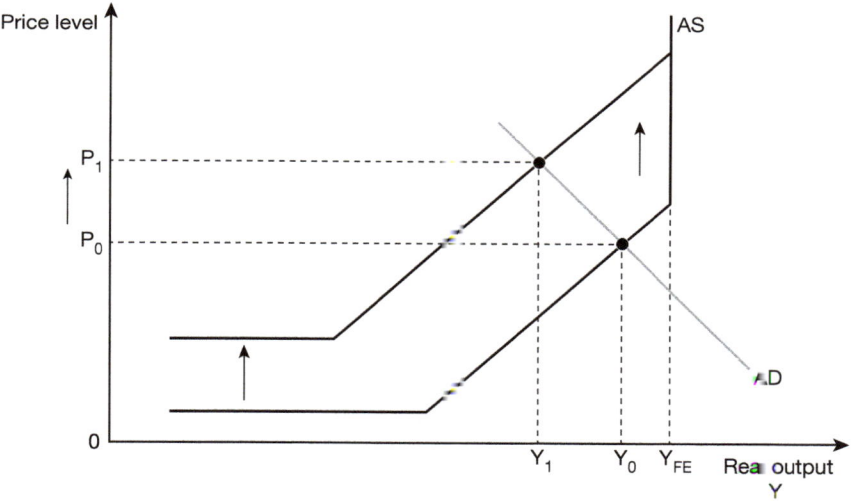

▲ **Figure 4.7** Cost-push inflation

Demand-pull inflation

Another possible cause of inflation in an economy is when there is too much demand in an economy, that is, aggregate demand is greater than aggregate supply. This is likely to be the case when an economy is at a situation of full employment, and in this case prices are pulled upwards as a result of the excess demand. This emphasis on the demand side of an economy is often linked with monetary explanations, that is, it is the increase in the money supply, making the increase in demand possible, which is important. This situation is known as monetary inflation.

Demand-pull inflation can be seen in Figure 4.8 where the price level has increased from $0P_0$ to $0P_1$ as a result of changes in demand.

> **Key terms**
>
> **Demand-pull inflation:** a rise in the general level of prices in an economy that is primarily caused by too much demand for goods and services, that is, aggregate demand is greater than aggregate supply causing excess demand.
>
> **Monetary inflation:** a rise in the general level of prices in an economy that is primarily caused by too much money chasing too few goods.

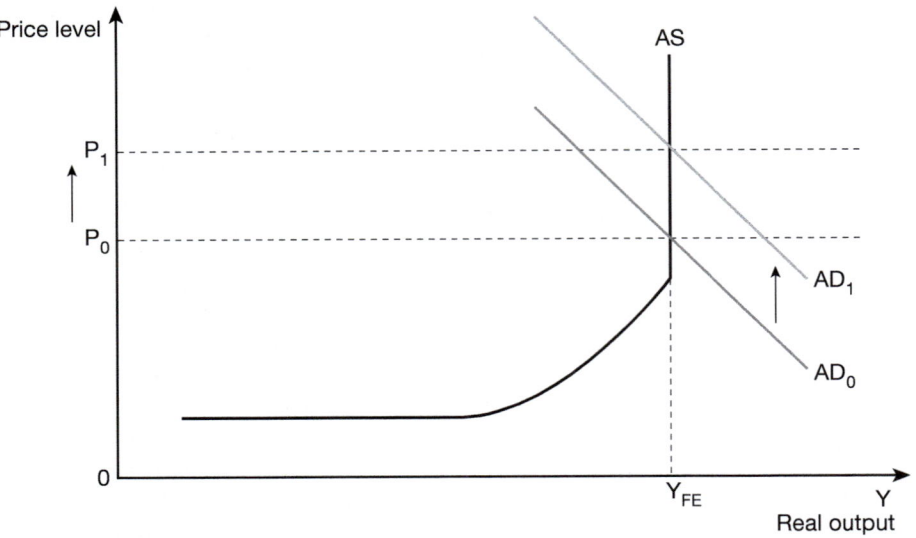

◀ **Figure 4.8** Demand-pull inflation

> **Key terms**
>
> **Menu costs:** the costs of continually having to change the prices of products.
>
> **Shoe leather costs:** the costs of continually having to search for the best returns, involving time and effort.
>
> **Fiscal drag:** a situation in which more people are dragged into the 'tax net' as a result of tax allowances not increasing in line with inflation.

4.6.5 The consequences of inflation

Inflation is regarded as potentially a serious economic problem as there are a number of negative consequences, including:

* the purchasing power of a nominal sum of money will fall in real terms

* a country's exports could become uncompetitive

* there will be a redistribution of income in an economy, with some people adversely affected, such as those on fixed incomes and savers

* **menu costs**, that is, the need to keep changing the advertised products, can be expensive

* **shoe leather costs**, that is, the need to continually search for the best returns, involving time and effort

* a greater degree of uncertainty in an economy, making planning more of a problem

* a situation of **fiscal drag** could occur, with more people caught in the 'tax net' if tax allowances do not rise in line with inflation.

However, inflation can have a number of positive consequences in an economy, including:

* the profits of firms could increase if prices rise by more than costs, and in this situation they could be encouraged to expand, reducing the level of unemployment in an economy

* the redistribution of income in an economy could be advantageous to some people, such as borrowers as their debt will be less in real terms.

> ★ **Link**
>
> See Unit 9.4 for further details on inflation.

> ★ **Exam tip**
>
> If an examination question requires you to discuss the consequences of a relatively high rate of inflation, remember to include both the positive consequences and the negative consequences in your answer.

> 💡 **Remember**
>
> You need to understand that the effects of inflation will depend on a number of possible factors, including whether the inflation is anticipated or not, what the extent of the increase in prices is, whether the inflation rate is accelerating, stable or falling and the extent to which other countries are experiencing inflation.

Raise your grade

Explain the differences between demand-pull and cost-push inflation in an economy, and consider which of these two causes is likely to be more significant. [8]

It is important to distinguish between demand-pull and cost-push inflation.

Demand-pull inflation occurs where there is too much demand in an economy (1). It is sometimes described as a situation in which too much money is chasing too few products (2).

Cost-push inflation occurs where higher prices are caused by higher costs of production, such as when there is a wage-price spiral (3).

The key difference between these two explanations of inflation is related to the source of the price increases, that is, whether they originate from the demand or the supply side (4).

How to improve this answer

1. The candidate has referred to a situation of too much demand in an economy, but this could have been developed more fully. For example, the candidate could have referred to the fact that this situation comes about when aggregate demand is greater than aggregate supply, causing a situation of excess demand. The candidate could have added that this would be more likely as an economy approached full employment. An appropriate diagram would have helped the explanation.

2. There is a reference here to a situation of too much money chasing too few products, but this could have been taken further by a reference to the idea of monetary inflation.

3. The candidate has referred to the existence of a wage-price spiral, but has not really explained what is meant by this term. It would also have been helpful if the candidate had also explored the idea of a price-wage spiral.

4. The candidate has made an attempt to explain how the differences in the two types of inflation could be applied to an economy, but this really needed to be developed more fully. For example, the candidate could have included an AD/AS diagram to contrast the two causes of inflation.

Knowledge and understanding:	2/3	Evaluation:	0/2
Analysis:	1/3	Total:	3/8

Worked Example

Assess the consequences of unemployment. (12)

One of the main consequences of unemployment is that the output of an economy will be lower than would otherwise be the case. This would involve a waste of scarce resources and would mean that an economy was operating within its production possibility curve.

Unemployment would also have negative consequences on a government in terms of both its revenue and expenditure. Revenue is likely to be lower because the income from both direct and indirect taxes will be lower than expected. In addition, a government would need to pay out more money in the form of unemployment benefits to those out of work. A government might also need to increase its expenditure on retraining schemes so that those unemployed had a better chance of finding employment.

The standard of living of people would be lower than would otherwise be the case and a prolonged period of relatively high unemployment could negatively impact a country's economic growth.

However, there could be positive consequences of unemployment for an economy if there was a fall in aggregate demand as this could lead to a reduction in the rate of inflation in an economy, especially if that inflation was caused by excess demand in the economy.

Exam-style questions

1 Net Domestic Product is obtained by:

(a) adding depreciation, or capital consumption, to GDP

(b) adding net property income to GDP

(c) deducting depreciation, or capital consumption, from GDP

(d) deducting the rate of inflation from GDP.   [1]

2 Which of the following is a leakage from the circular flow of income?

(a) government spending

(b) investment

(c) net exports

(d) taxation   [1]

3 Aggregate demand consists of:

(a) consumption, government and net exports

(b) consumption, investment, government and exports

(c) consumption, investment, government and net exports

(d) investment, government and imports.   [1]

4 Real GDP takes into account changes in:

(a) exchange rates

(b) inflation

(c) international trade

(d) unemployment.   [1]

5 When people are between jobs, it is known as:

(a) cyclical unemployment

(b) demand-deficient unemployment

(c) frictional unemployment

(d) structural unemployment.   [1]

6 Disinflation refers to a situation of:

(a) a fall in the general level of prices

(b) an annual inflation rate of over 10%

(c) the price level neither rising nor falling

(d) the price level rising at a decreasing rate.   [1]

7 Which of the following is a cause of demand-pull inflation?

(a) Higher energy prices

(b) Increased consumer spending

(c) Increases in the cost of raw materials

(d) Wage increases not linked to higher productivity   [1]

8 Menu costs refer to:

(a) increases in the prices of restaurant meals

(b) increases in the wages of workers

(c) the costs of changing the prices of products

(d) the costs of searching for good returns.   [1]

9 Which of the following would cause an increase in the labour force of a country?

(a) A decrease in the retirement age

(b) An increase in the birth rate

(c) An increase in the death rate

(d) An increase in the school leaving age   [1]

10 Which of the following is added to GDP in order to arrive at a figure for GNI?

(a) Capital consumption

(b) Government spending

(c) Net income from abroad

(d) Taxation   [1]

11 (a) Explain the distinction between a movement along and a shift of an AD curve, and consider the potential impact of a shift in an AD curve on the price level in an economy.   [8]

(b) Assess whether the consequences of inflation will always be negative.   [12]

12 (a) Explain the different types of unemployment that can exist, and consider why unemployment can be difficult to measure accurately.   [8]

(b) Assess whether the consequences of economic growth will always be positive.   [12]

5 Government macroeconomic intervention

Key topics
- Government macroeconomic policy objectives
- Fiscal policy
- Monetary policy
- Supply-side policy

5.1 Government macroeconomic policy objectives

There are a number of different macroeconomic objectives. Three of these will be covered in this chapter:

- Price stability
- Low unemployment
- Economic growth

5.2 Fiscal policy

5.2.1 The meaning of a government budget

Fiscal policy refers to the use of revenue and expenditure decisions by a government to influence economic activity in a country. In particular, these decisions are taken to influence the level of aggregate demand in an economy. Slight changes in policy in relation to revenue and/or expenditure can have significant economic effects, and so the term **fine-tuning** has been used to describe what is happening when a government takes policy decisions on revenue and/or expenditure.

A **government budget** is a financial document that gives details of a government's proposed income and expenditure for a particular period of time.

5.2.2 The distinction between a government budget deficit and a government budget surplus

In each economy in the world, the government will produce a summary of its income and expenditure.

A government can deliberately plan for one of three financial positions to achieve its objectives:

- A budget deficit
- A budget surplus
- A balanced budget

It might be thought that a government would deliberately aim to achieve a **balanced budget** by ensuring that revenue was equal to expenditure. This can happen, but governments frequently decide to aim for a **budget deficit** or a **budget surplus**.

Budget deficit

If an economy is facing a relatively high level of unemployment and a relatively low rate of economic growth, a government may decide to stimulate the economy by deliberately aiming to achieve a budget deficit, that is, more money will go into the economy than goes out. Examples of instruments to bring such a situation about include reductions in taxation and increases in public expenditure.

Budget surplus

On the other hand, if an economy is facing a relatively high rate of inflation, a government may decide to deflate the economy by deliberately aiming to achieve a budget surplus, that is, more money will go out of an economy than goes in. Examples of instruments to bring such a situation about include increases in taxation and decreases in public expenditure.

5.2.3 The meaning and significance of the national debt

The **national debt** refers to the total of all debt that has been accumulated over a period of time by the government or the public sector of a country. It is therefore a government's stock of outstanding debt.

If there is a relatively high rate of unemployment in an economy, a government may decide to plan for a budget deficit and the effect of this will be to increase the size of the national debt. On the other hand, if there is a high rate of inflation in an economy, a government may decide to plan for a budget surplus and the effect of this will be to reduce the size of the national debt.

> ★ **Exam tip**
>
> Don't think that if there is a reduction in the size of a country's budget deficit in one year, then the size of the national debt will decrease. This is not the case. If a country's budget deficit falls, money will still need to be borrowed to pay for this debt, so the size of the country's national debt will continue to rise, even if it increases at a slower rate than before.

5.2.4 Taxation

Types of taxes

It is important to be able to clearly distinguish between the following two types of taxes:

- Direct/indirect taxes
- Progressive/regressive/proportional taxes

Direct and indirect taxes

A **direct tax** is a tax imposed on the incomes of individuals and firms. Examples of direct taxes include:

- income tax (on the incomes of individuals)
- corporation tax (on the profits of companies)
- inheritance tax (on the wealth of individuals).

Key terms

Balanced budget: a budget where revenue is equal to expenditure.

Budget deficit: a budget where expenditure is greater than revenue.

Budget surplus: a budget where revenue is greater than expenditure.

Key term

National debt: the total of all debt accumulated by a government; it is the amount of money that a government, or public sector, owes both domestically and abroad which has accumulated over a number of years.

★ **Exam tip**

Make sure you understand that a budget deficit only applies to a particular period of time and is brought about by the excess expenditure over revenue within a financial year, whereas the national debt refers to debt that has accumulated over centuries.

Key term

Direct tax: a tax levied on income or wealth.

Income tax is a direct tax on the incomes of individuals. There is usually a personal allowance, which is tax-free, and then different tax rates for different levels of income over the tax-free allowance.

An **indirect tax**, on the other hand, is a tax imposed on expenditure. Examples of indirect taxes include:

- value added tax (VAT)
- goods and services tax (GST).

Progressive, regressive and proportional taxes

It is important to be able to distinguish between progressive, regressive and proportional taxes.

A **progressive tax** is one where not only the amount of tax paid rises when there is an increase in income, but the rate of tax increases. For example, rates of tax could start at 10% and then increase to 20%, 30%, 40%, 50% and even higher as income rises. In this situation, the marginal rate of taxation increases with a rise in income and the marginal rate of tax will be higher than the average rate of tax.

A **regressive tax** is the opposite of a progressive tax. This occurs where a fixed percentage of tax is imposed on expenditure, as with VAT (value added tax). In this case, the marginal rate of taxation falls as income increases.

A **proportional tax**, also known as a flat tax, has a constant marginal rate of taxation irrespective of any changes in the income level. With a proportional tax, the marginal rate of tax and the average rate of tax are the same.

> **Key terms**
>
> **Progressive tax:** a situation where the proportion of income paid in tax increases as income increases.
>
> **Regressive tax:** a situation where the proportion of income paid in tax falls as income increases.
>
> **Proportional tax:** a situation where the proportion of income paid in tax remains constant regardless of the level of income.

> **Remember**
>
> With a proportional tax, the marginal rate of taxation is constant when there is a rise in income. With a progressive tax, the marginal rate of taxation increases when there is a rise in income. With a regressive tax, the marginal rate of taxation decreases when there is a rise in income.

Rates of tax: marginal and average rates of taxation

It is important to be able to distinguish between marginal and average rates of taxation.

The **average rate of tax** (ART) refers to the average percentage of total income which is paid in taxes. The **marginal rate of tax** (MRT) refers to the proportion of any increase in income that is paid in tax.

> **Exam tip**
>
> Make sure that you are able to clearly distinguish between a person's average rate of tax and their marginal rate of tax.

> **Key term**
>
> **Indirect tax:** a tax levied on expenditure.

> ★ **Link**
>
> See Unit 3, section 3.2.1, for further information on indirect taxes.

> ★ **Exam tip**
>
> You need to be able to clearly distinguish between a direct and an indirect tax and you may be required to provide appropriate examples of each type of tax.

> ★ **Exam tip**
>
> Make sure you understand that with a progressive tax, it is not only that a person pays more in tax as income rises, but that they pay an increasing proportion of income in tax as their income rises above a certain income threshold at which a higher rate of tax has to be paid.

> **Remember**
>
> It is important to distinguish between average rates of taxation and marginal rates of taxation.

> ★ **Link**
>
> See Unit 3, section 3.3.4, for further information on progressive taxation.

> **Key terms**
>
> **Average rate of tax (ART):** the average percentage of total income that is paid in tax.
>
> **Marginal rate of tax MRT):** the proportion of additional income that is taken in tax.

The canons of taxation

The **canons of taxation** refer to a number of principles that should apply to taxation. They include:

- equity or fairness
- certainty or transparency
- convenience
- cost
- efficiency.

The reasons for taxation

There are a number of possible reasons for taxation. These are to:

- provide revenue for a government: taxation is used to enable a government to finance its expenditure on a number of different goods and services, such as the provision of public goods, for example, street lighting and national defence, or the provision of merit goods, for example, education and healthcare

- achieve government macroeconomic policy objectives: taxation is used to influence the level of aggregate demand in an economy, for example, if there is a high rate of unemployment, taxes could be lowered to stimulate the level of demand in an economy in an attempt to reduce the level of unemployment

- redistribute income and wealth from the rich to the poor: taxation is used to finance the provision of a range of transfer payments to those people in society who are relatively less well off

- avoid negative externalities: taxation is used to discourage firms from causing environmental damage, for example, taxes on firms can be used to reduce the level of pollution in an economy

- discourage the consumption of demerit goods: taxation is used in an attempt to lower the level of demand for demerit goods, such as tobacco or alcohol.

5.2.5 Government spending

Types of spending

It is important to distinguish between two types of government spending:

- capital (investment) spending
- current spending

Capital (investment) spending refers to government expenditure on fixed assets, such as expenditure on building a new road or extra defence equipment.

Current spending is expenditure on the day to day running costs of a government, such as expenditure on the wages and salaries of public sector workers.

The reasons for government spending

There are a number of reasons for government spending, including the following:

- It is an important component of aggregate demand: it has already been pointed out in 4.3.2 that government spending is one of the components of aggregate demand, so an increase in government spending (assuming the other components stay constant) will increase aggregate demand in an economy.

- It is important in providing public goods and merit goods: governments can spend on public goods, such as street lighting and national defence, because these goods would not be provided in the private sector and so governments are required to provide them; governments can also spend on merit goods, such as education and health care, because although these goods could be provided in the private sector, they are likely to be under-consumed and so governments spend money on them to encourage their consumption.

- It helps to achieve greater equity in an economy: governments could decide to spend money on a range of benefits and transfer payments as a way of achieving greater equity, for example, expenditure on state pensions and unemployment benefits.

★ **Link**

See Unit 9, section 9.1.2, for further information on government spending.

5.2.6 The distinction between expansionary and contractionary fiscal policy

It has already been pointed out in 5.2.1 that fiscal policy is the use of public revenue and/or public expenditure to influence the level of aggregate demand in an economy. However, it is important to distinguish between **expansionary** and **contractionary fiscal policy**.

Expansionary fiscal policy

This is where a government decides to increase its expenditure and/or lower taxes to boost the level of aggregate demand in an economy. This approach would be appropriate if the objective is to encourage economic growth, lower the rate of unemployment or lower the rate of inflation.

Contractionary fiscal policy

This is where a government decides to lower its expenditure and/or increase taxes to reduce the level of aggregate demand in an economy. This approach would be appropriate if the objective is to lower economic growth or the rate of inflation.

5.2.7 AD/AS analysis of the impact of expansionary and contractionary fiscal policy

AD/AS analysis can be used to assess the impact of expansionary fiscal policy and contractionary fiscal policy on equilibrium national income in relation to:

- the level of real output
- the price level
- the employment level.

The impact of expansionary fiscal policy

In section 4.3.5, it was pointed out that if there is a change in any of the components of aggregate demand, such as a change in consumption expenditure (C), investment expenditure (I), government expenditure (G) or net expenditure on exports (X-M), the AD curve will shift. If there is an increase in aggregate demand, the curve will shift to the right. This can be seen in Figure 4.4 where the AD curve shifts from AD_1 to AD_2. There is an increase in employment and in the level of real output from Y_1 to Y_2 and an increase in the price level from P_1 to P_2.

An expansionary fiscal policy could bring this about in a number of ways. For example, if a government decides to raise its expenditure, this will increase G. If it decides to lower income tax, this will increase C.

The impact of contractionary fiscal policy

If there is a decrease in aggregate demand the AD curve will shift to the left. This will cause a decrease in the level of employment, real output and the price level.

A contractionary fiscal policy could bring this about in a number of ways. For example, if a government decides to lower its expenditure, this will reduce G. If it decides to increase income tax, this will reduce C.

 Link

See Unit 10, section 10.3, for further information on fiscal policy.

💡 **Remember**

In terms of fiscal policy, it is important to distinguish between discretionary fiscal policy and automatic stabilisers. When a government deliberately decides to change taxation and/or public expenditure to bring about a particular change in an economy, this is known as discretionary fiscal policy. However, with automatic stabilisers, this is where changes in an economy take place without deliberate government action.

5.3 Monetary policy

5.3.1 Definition of monetary policy

Monetary policy refers to use of decisions by a government to influence economic activity in a country in relation to the price of money and the quantity of money.

5.3.2 The tools of monetary policy

There are three main tools of monetary policy:

- Interest rates
- Money supply
- Credit regulations

The **interest rate** is concerned with the price of money. An increase in the interest rate will raise the cost of borrowing and a decrease in the interest rate will lower the cost of borrowing.

The **money supply** refers to the amount of money that is available in the banking system. An increase in the money supply will be likely to encourage borrowing and a decrease in the money supply will be likely to discourage borrowing.

Credit regulations refer to laws that relate to borrowing money on credit. They are concerned with loans and/or hire purchase agreements. The regulations cover the information consumers should be provided with before they enter into a credit agreement, the content and form of credit agreements, the method of calculating the rate of interest and the procedures relating to default, termination and early settlement.

5.3.3 The distinction between expansionary and contractionary monetary policy

If an economy is facing a relatively high rate of unemployment and a relatively low rate of economic growth, a government may decide to use expansionary monetary policy to stimulate the economy by reducing the rate of interest and/or increasing the money supply. Slight changes in policy in relation to the price or the supply of money can have significant economic effects and so the term fine-tuning (already referred to in the context of fiscal policy) has been used to describe what is happening when a government takes policy decisions on interest rates and/or the money supply

On the other hand, if an economy is facing a relatively high rate of inflation, a government may decide to use contractionary monetary policy to deflate the economy by increasing the rate of interest and/or decreasing the money supply.

★ **Link**

See Unit 10, section 10.3, for further information on monetary policy.

5.3.4 AD/AS analysis of the impact of expansionary and contractionary monetary policy

AD/AS analysis can be used to assess the impact of expansionary monetary policy and contractionary monetary policy on equilibrium national income in relation to:

- the level of real output
- the price level
- the employment level.

The impact of expansionary monetary policy

In section 4.3.5, it was pointed out that if there is a change in any of the components of aggregate demand, such as a change in consumption expenditure (C), investment expenditure (I), government expenditure (G) or net expenditure on exports (X-M), the AD curve will shift. If there is an increase in aggregate demand, the curve will shift to the right. This can be seen in Figure 4.4 when the AD curve shifts from AD_1 to AD_2. There is an increase in employment and in the level of real output (from Y_1 to Y_2) and an increase in the price level (from P_1 to P_2).

An expansionary monetary policy could bring this about in a number of ways. For example, if a government decides to increase the money supply and/or reduce the interest rate, this will increase consumption expenditure (C). A reduction in the interest rate is also likely to increase investment (I).

The impact of contractionary monetary policy

If there is a decrease in aggregate demand, the AD curve will shift to the left. This will cause a decrease in the level of employment, real output and the price level.

A contractionary monetary policy could bring this about in a number of ways. For example, if a government decides to lower the money supply and/or increase the interest rate, this will decrease consumption expenditure (C). An increase in the interest rate is also likely to decrease investment (I).

5.4 Supply-side policy

5.4.1 The meaning of supply-side policy

In particular, such policies are often taken in an attempt to improve the efficiency of markets.

In particular, **supply-side policy** is designed to have an effect on LRAS (long run aggregate supply) curves. The policies are aimed at making markets and industries operate more efficiently so that they contribute to a faster rate of growth of real national output. Successful supply-side policies will have the effect of shifting the LRAS curve to the right leading to a rise in the productive potential output of an economy. The advantage of an improved supply-side performance in an economy is that sustained economic growth can be achieved without causing a rise in inflation.

Key term

Supply-side policy: policies that are designed to allow markets to work more efficiently and flexibly.

5.4.2 The objectives of supply-side policy

The objectives of supply-side policy can include:

- increasing **productivity**: supply-side policies, with their emphasis on bringing about greater efficiency in the production process, can contribute to a greater rate of output, that is, products produced, per unit of input, for example, labour and capital

- increasing **productive capacity**: supply-side policies can contribute to an increase in the maximum possible output of an economy.

Key terms

Productivity: the measurement of output per unit of input.

Productive capacity: the maximum potential output of an economy.

💡 **Remember**

Labour productivity is the measurement of the efficiency of labour in terms of the output per worker per period of time, such as 1 hour, 1 day or 1 week.

The productivity of workers can vary for a number of reasons, including differences in:

- education, training, skills, experience, technical knowledge, level of capital available
- working methods and practices and the level of motivation.

5.4.3 The tools of supply-side policy

Examples of supply-side policies include:

- increasing incentives to work through the lowering of income tax and unemployment benefits, the idea being that this will encourage more people to seek employment

- increasing expenditure on education and training to improve the quality of the labour force, the idea being that this will improve the productivity and flexibility of the labour force

- reforming trade unions so that their power is reduced, the idea being that fewer working days will be lost as a result of industrial action, such as strikes

- encouraging privatisation so that the size of the private sector in an economy increases and the size of the public sector decreases, the idea being that firms in the private sector are likely to be more efficient than those in the public sector, especially when there is intense competition in an industry

- encouraging deregulation which will allow greater competition, the idea being that a reduction of barriers into an industry will enable more firms to enter

- providing more information about job vacancies, the idea being that greater knowledge of what is available in the labour market could encourage a greater degree of occupational and geographical mobility of labour in an economy

- encouraging infrastructure development, such as the construction of new road and rail links to improve transport and so reduce the costs of production

- supporting technological improvement, such as by providing financial incentives for research and development.

> **Remember**
>
> In terms of supply-side policy, it is important to distinguish between market-orientated supply-side policies and interventionist supply-side policies. Examples of market-orientated supply-side policies include privatisation and deregulation. Examples of interventionist supply-side policies include the direct provision of infrastructure and funding for training schemes.

> **★ Link**
>
> See Unit 10, section 10.3, for more information on supply-side policy, including both market-based and interventionist policies.

5.4.4 AD/AS analysis of the impact of supply-side policy

AD/AS analysis can be used to assess the impact of supply-side policy on equilibrium national income in relation to:

- the level of real output

- the price level

- the employment level.

In section 4.3.9, it was pointed out that equilibrium national income can be affected by changes in the AS curve as well as the AD curve. If there is an increase in aggregate supply, as a result of supply-side policies, the AS curve will shift to the right. If there is a decrease in aggregate supply, the AS curve will shift to the left.

In the long run, the shape of the LRAS curve will change. At low levels of output, the AS curve can be horizontal, indicating that it is perfectly elastic. At high levels of output, the AS curve can be vertical, indicating that it is perfectly inelastic. Indeed, some economists argue that the long-run AS curve is perfectly inelastic, indicating that an economy will operate at full capacity. That is why it is important that supply-side policy shifts the LRAS curve to the right, allowing for an increase in the productive capacity of an economy.

A shift to the right of the LRAS curve will increase the level of real output and the level of employment, but will decrease the price level. A shift to the left of the LRAS curve will decrease the level of real output and the level of employment and increase the price level.

↑ Raise your grade

Explain, with the use of examples, the differences between progressive and regressive taxes, and consider which of these will help to bring about a greater degree of equality of income in an economy. [8]

A progressive tax is one where not only the amount of income paid in tax rises as incomes rise, but also the rate of tax on income increases (˙). An example of such a tax is income tax (2).

A regressive tax is one where the rate of tax remains the same for all people irrespective of their income (3). In this situation, a person's income is not taken into account (4).

How to improve this answer

1. The candidate clearly understands what is meant by a progressive tax, but the answer could have been developed more fully by referring to the fact that there will be an increase in both marginal and average rates of tax as incomes rise.

2. The candidate has given an appropriate example of a progressive tax, that is, income tax, but could have written more about what happens in many countries in relation to income tax, that is, that the marginal rate of tax will rise as incomes rise above a particular threshold, for example, 10%, 20%, 30%, 40% and 50%.

3. The candidate correctly states what happens in relation to a regressive tax, but the answer could have been developed further by referring to the fact that there will be a decrease in both marginal and average rates of tax as incomes rise.

4. The candidate has not actually given an example of a regressive tax, despite the fact that the question explicitly requires the candidates to do so. Examples could include VAT (value added tax) or GST (goods and services tax)

Knowledge and understanding:	2/3
Analysis:	1/3
Evaluation:	0/2
Total:	3/3

Worked Example

Explain what is meant by productivity and consider how it can be increased through supply-side policies. [8]

Productivity refers to the efficiency of a factor of production. For example, in relation to labour, this efficiency can be measured in terms of the output of a worker over a specific period of time.

Supply-side policies can be used to increase productivity in a number of ways. For example, in relation to labour, a government can decide to increase expenditure on education and training in order to make the labour force better qualified and more skilful. A reduction in the powers of trade unions could also lead to an increase in the productivity of labour if fewer days are lost as a result of industrial action.

The productivity of capital could also be increased if a government decided to provide financial assistance to firms to encourage them to buy more advanced technology. The productivity of capital could also be increased if firms were encouraged to increase expenditure on research and development.

The productivity of enterprise could be increased if a government decided to reduce the number of laws and regulations required when starting up a business, making it relatively easier for entrepreneurs to establish an enterprise.

Exam-style questions

1 A sales tax of a fixed percentage is an example of a:

   (a) progressive tax

   (b) proportional tax

   (c) regressive tax

   (d) transfer tax. [1]

2 The average rate of tax and the marginal rate of tax are the same in the case of a:

   (a) progressive tax

   (b) proportional tax

   (c) regressive tax

   (d) transport tax. [1]

3 Which of the following is not a canon of taxation?

   (a) certainty

   (b) convenience

   (c) disincentive

   (d) equity [1]

4 Which of the following would stimulate demand in an economy?

   (a) A decrease in the money supply

   (b) An increase in government expenditure

   (c) An increase in taxation

   (d) An increase in the interest rate [1]

5 Slight changes in fiscal or monetary policies to affect the level of economic activity in a country are known as:

   (a) balanced

   (b) deregulation

   (c) fine-tuning

   (d) targeting. [1]

6 When a government deliberately decides to change public revenue and/or public expenditure to achieve an objective, it is known as:

   (a) automatic fiscal policy

   (b) automatic monetary policy

   (c) discretionary fiscal policy

   (d) discretionary monetary policy [1]

7 Which of the following is an example of a market-orientated supply-side policy?

   (a) Direct provision of infrastructure

   (b) Funding for training

   (c) Grants for research and development

   (d) Privatisation [1]

8 Which of the following is an example of deflationary monetary policy?

   (a) A reduction in public expenditure

   (b) An increase in the interest rate

   (c) An increase in the money supply

   (d) An increase in taxation [1]

9 A policy to encourage spending in an economy is called:

   (a) deflationary

   (b) disinflationary

   (c) reflationary

   (d) regulatory. [1]

10 Providing more information about job vacancies is likely to:

   (a) contribute to a lower rate of inflation in an economy

   (b) encourage greater occupational and geographical mobility of labour

   (c) increase the amount of money paid out through unemployment benefits

   (d) lead to the privatisation of industries in an economy [1]

11 (a) Explain the distinction between fiscal policy and monetary policy, and consider which of these is likely to be more effective in an economy. [8]

   (b) Assess whether a budget deficit should always be avoided. [12]

12 (a) Explain the difference between market-orientated and interventionist supply-side policies, and consider which are likely to be more effective. [8]

   (b) Assess whether supply-side policies are guaranteed to correct inflation. [12]

6.1 The reasons for international trade

6.1.1 The distinction between absolute and comparative advantage

International trade between countries is based on the concept of specialisation, where one country is more efficient at producing a product than another country. This gives rise to two different types of advantage: absolute and comparative advantage.

Absolute advantage

A situation of **absolute advantage** occurs where one country is able to produce a particular good with fewer resources than another country. As a result of this absolute efficiency, the country will enjoy a cost advantage.

Comparative advantage

Whereas absolute advantage is based on the idea that one country has an absolute efficiency in the production of a good, **comparative advantage** is based on the relative efficiency of one country compared to another. In this way, a country could produce a good in which it does not have an absolute advantage, but it could be relatively more efficient in producing this good than another good.

> **Key terms**
>
> **Absolute advantage:** the ability to produce more of a product than another country can produce that has the same amount of resources.
>
> **Comparative advantage:** the ability of a country to produce a product at a lower opportunity cost than another country.

> ★ **Exam tip**
>
> Make sure that you understand the difference between the absolute advantage of a country in producing a particular good and the comparative or relative advantage of a country in producing a certain good.

> 💡 **Remember**
>
> You need to understand that the concept of comparative or relative advantage can best be explained by stating that this occurs where a product is produced at a lower opportunity cost. This means that a country will concentrate on producing a good where it has to give up less production of another good. This is another example of the importance of opportunity cost in economic analysis. Two countries will trade at a ratio somewhere between their two opportunity costs. It is important that you understand that specialisation and trade will only take place if the opportunity cost ratios are different. If this was not the case, there would be no advantage in specialising and trading.

> 💡 **Remember**
>
> There are a number of assumptions that have to be made in relation to the principle of comparative advantage. It is assumed that there are only two goods involved, that there is perfect competition in both factor and product markets, that there are no transport costs, that no capital movements take place which could affect the exchange rate, that production is subject to constant returns to scale and that there are no restrictions on trade.

6.1.2 The benefits of specialisation and free trade (trade liberalisation), including the trading possibility curve

The benefits of free trade

There are a number of potential benefits of free trade, including:

- an increase in world output
- the more efficient allocation of resources
- a wider range of products for consumers to choose from
- an increase in a country's economic growth

- an improvement in the standard of living and quality of life of people
- the possibility of economies of scale resulting from increased output through specialisation
- lower prices resulting from increased efficiency and economies of scale.

⭐ **Link**

See Unit 1, section 1.3.4, for more information on specialisation.

The trading possibility curve

A trading possibility curve can be used to show the gains from trade. A trading possibility curve shows the maximum possible quantities of each good that each country could produce, given the terms of trade between the two countries following specialisation. If two countries specialise in the production of goods in which they have a comparative advantage, that is, a lower opportunity cost, it is possible for both countries to produce outside of their production possibility curve.

In Figure 6.1, Country A has a comparative advantage in the production of cars and Country B has a comparative advantage in the production of toys. If each country specialised in what it was most efficient at producing, both countries would produce on their trading possibility curve rather than on their production possibility curve. This can be seen in Figure 6.1 where the TPC is to the right of the PPC for both countries.

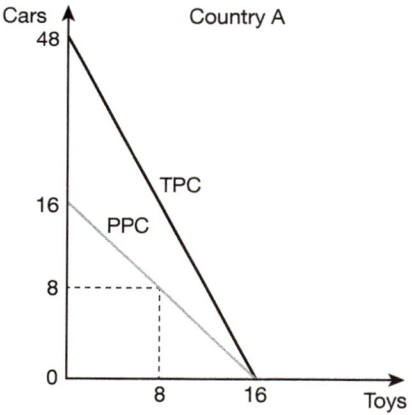 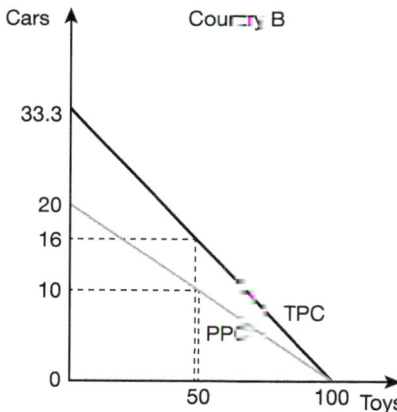

▲ **Figure 6.1** The trading possibility curve showing the gains from trade

Key terms

Free trade: trade between countries that is not restricted or limited by various types of import control.

Trading possibility curve: a curve that shows the advantages of two countries trading with each other, taking advantage of the fact that the opportunity costs of production in the two countries are different.

💡 **Remember**

You need to understand that the benefits of **free trade** can lead to countries producing on their **trading possibility curve** rather than on their production possibility curve, leading to gains from trade in the form of increased output.

6.1.3 Exports, imports and the terms of trade

The measurement of the terms of trade

The **terms of trade** refer to the relative changes of export prices and import prices. They are calculated by:

$$\frac{\text{index of export prices}}{\text{index of import prices}} \times 100$$

> **Key term**
>
> **Terms of trade:** the ratio of export prices to import prices.

> **Remember**
>
> An increase in the terms of trade index indicates that more imports can be purchased with a given quantity of exports. In this situation, the terms of trade are said to have improved or to have become more favourable. On the other hand, a decrease in the terms of trade indicates that fewer imports can be purchased with a given quantity of exports. In this situation, the terms of trade are said to have deteriorated or worsened.

> **Remember**
>
> The terms of trade and the balance of trade are not the same. The terms of trade show changes in the relative prices of exports and imports. The balance of trade shows a country's trading position with other countries in the world.

> **Exam tip**
>
> Be careful not to confuse the terms of trade with the balance of trade. The terms of trade simply show the relationship between changes in the prices of exports and changes in the prices of imports. They do not indicate changes in the quantity or value of exports and imports traded between different countries.

The causes of changes in the terms of trade

Changes in the terms of trade can be caused by a number of different factors, including the following:

- A fall in the price of manufactured goods will cause the terms of trade of those countries producing such goods to worsen.

- The increased demand for natural resources has pushed up their prices, benefiting those countries exporting such products.

- If the prices of a country's exports rise significantly more than the price of imports into the country, then the terms of trade will increase.

- If a country's exchange rate depreciates or is devalued, its terms of trade will have worsened because export prices will have fallen and import prices will have risen.

- If a country has a monopoly in the production of a good, it will be better able to raise the prices of such goods, causing an improvement in its terms of trade.

The impact of changes in the terms of trade

When there is a worsening in a country's terms of trade, this is regarded as an unfavourable change because more exports will need to be sold to buy the same number of imports. However, if exports have become relatively cheaper than imports, this will help to improve a country's balance of trade situation as long as the price elasticity of demand for both exports and imports is elastic.

When there is an improvement in a country's terms of trade, this is regarded as a favourable change because fewer exports will need to be sold to buy the same number of imports. However, if exports have become relatively more expensive than imports, this is likely to worsen a country's balance of trade situation, assuming that the price elasticity of demand for both exports and imports is elastic.

> **Exam tip**
>
> Be careful not to regard a fall in the terms of trade index as being unhelpful in terms of a country's trading position. A fall in the terms of trade means that export prices have become relatively cheaper, and if the price elasticity of demand for both exports and imports is elastic, this will help to improve, not worsen, a country's balance of trade position.

6.1.4 Limitations of the theories of absolute and comparative advantage

The theories of absolute and comparative advantage are helpful in explaining how total world output can be increased as a result of specialisation, but there are a number of real-world limitations. These include the following:

- It is assumed that there are no transport costs involved in international trade, but this is unrealistic; transport costs may actually offset any cost advantages arising from applying the theories.

- It is assumed that there are constant returns to scale and constant costs of production, but it is always possible that an increase in output leads to diseconomies of scale and a situation of rising costs of production.

- It is assumed that there is free trade between countries, but in reality, there are many import restrictions which exist in different parts of the world.

- It is assumed that exchange rates are stable and that the benefits of international trade will not be affected by exchange rates, but movements in exchange rates can help to make trade more or less advantageous to a country in the real world.

- It is assumed that factor inputs can switch between different products easily and work with the same efficiency, but this may not necessarily happen.

6.2 Protectionism

6.2.1 The meaning of protectionism in the context of international trade

Protectionism refers to those policies taken by countries to protect domestic producers from international competition, or to give support to them. It is the opposite of free trade and comes about because countries are worried that without trade barriers, domestic firms will not be able to compete effectively with firms in other countries.

> **Key term**
>
> **Protectionism:** actions taken by a country to protect domestic producers from international competition.

6.2.2 The different tools of protection and their impact

There are a number of different tools of protection.

Tariffs

A **tariff** is a tax that is imposed on products that are imported into a country. They are designed to make the imported products more expensive, leading to a reduction in the demand for them. The impact of a tariff, however, will depend on the price elasticity of demand for the imported goods.

> **Key term**
>
> **Tariff:** a tax that is imposed on imported goods to make them more expensive and so reduce the demand for them.

The impact of the imposition of a tariff on an imported good can be seen in Figure 6.2. S_w shows the world supply of a product before the imposition of a tariff and S_w + tariff shows the world supply of a product after the imposition of a tariff. The vertical distance between P_1 and P_2 shows the size of the specific tariff. S_h shows the home or domestic supply of the product. The quantity of imports coming into the country has been reduced from Q_1Q_4 to Q_2Q_3.

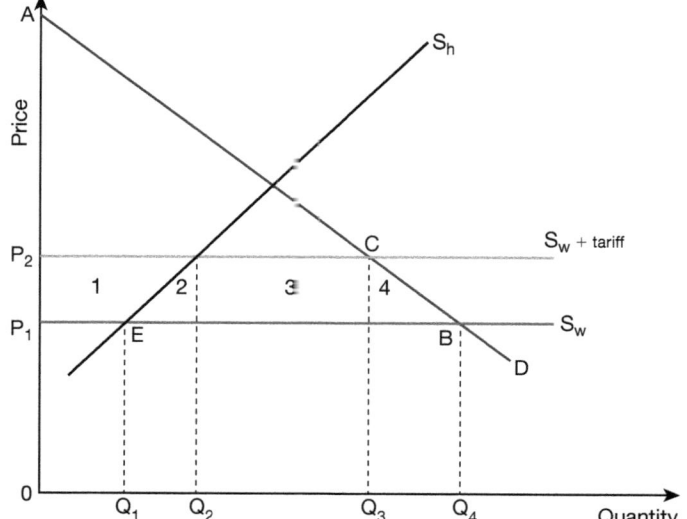

▲ **Figure 6.2** The impact of a tariff

Import quotas

Whereas tariffs involve trying to reduce the demand for imported goods by making them more expensive, a **quota** is a restriction on imports into a country. A quota can be expressed in one of three ways: a limit on the quantity of goods that can be imported into a country, a limit on the value of goods that can be imported into a country or a limit on the proportion of market share that they represent.

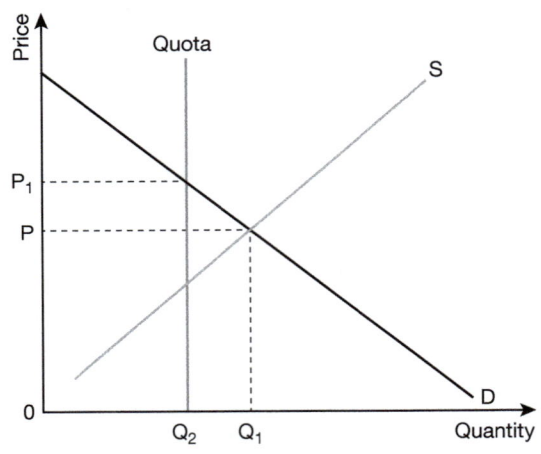

▲ **Figure 6.3** The imposition of a quota

Figure 6.3 shows the impact of a quota in a market. The original quantity demanded and supplied in the market was $0Q_1$, but once a quota has been established, the quantity available is only $0Q_2$. This amount is priced at $0P_1$.

Export subsidies

As has already been indicated in Unit 3, a subsidy is a payment by a government to firms to keep down the costs of production, enabling a lower price to be charged to consumers. If such subsidies are given to firms that are intending to export their goods, this should increase the demand for such products, assuming that demand is price elastic.

Embargoes

An **embargo** is a complete ban on the imports of certain products from particular countries. An embargo is usually imposed largely for political, rather than economic, reasons.

Excessive Administrative Burdens

Such burdens are often described as 'red tape'. The paperwork that is involved in the importation of goods into a country is made particularly difficult. The aim of such a measure is to discourage imports by making the process of importation much more time consuming and complex.

> **Key term**
>
> **Excessive administrative burdens:** this is often referred to as 'red tape' and it occurs when paperwork is made excessive in an attempt to make the importing process so complex and time-consuming that imports will be discouraged.

> **Remember**
>
> Make sure you understand that the imposition of a tariff has an effect on the size of the consumer surplus and producer surplus. In Figure 6.2, the original consumer surplus, before the tariff was introduced, was represented by the area P_1AB. After the imposition of the tariff, this has fallen to P_2AC. Some of this has been lost to producers in the form of an increased producer surplus and some to the government as revenue from the tariff. There has therefore been a redistribution of welfare from consumers to producers. Similarly, the imposition of a quota will involve a welfare loss to consumers.

> **Key term**
>
> **Quota:** a limit on the imported products that are allowed into a country. A quota can take the form of a limited quantity, a limited value or a limited market share.

> **Key term**
>
> **Export subsidies:** a payment by a government to domestic firms to keep down the costs of production and therefore the prices of the products, making their exports more competitive in international markets.

> ★ **Link**
>
> See Unit 3, section 3.2.2, and Unit 8, section 8.1.1, for more information on subsidies.

> **Key term**
>
> **Embargo:** a ban on imports from particular countries, either in relation to certain products imported from those countries or, in some cases, on all products.

> ★ **Exam tip**
>
> Make sure that you understand the various benefits and drawbacks of the different methods of protectionism. For example, a tariff or import duty will provide government revenue, but this will not be the case with a quota.

6.2.3 Arguments for and against protectionism

The arguments for protectionism

A number of arguments can be put forward in favour of protectionism. These include:

- specific protection for **infant or sunrise industries** to enable such firms to compete with more established firms from other countries

- specific protection for **declining or sunset industries** to give sufficient time for factors of production to be transferred to other uses

- a strategic industry may need to be protected, such as military equipment, to provide a country with an appropriate defence

- to provide protection against firms that are **dumping** products in another country, that is, they are selling below the cost of production

- protectionism may be necessary to help a country reduce a deficit on the current account of the balance of payments

- certain protectionist methods, such as tariffs and duties, are a form of raising government revenue.

> **Remember**
>
> The impact of a tariff, an import duty or an export subsidy will depend on the price elasticity of demand for the products being traded.

The arguments against protectionism

Economists emphasise that there are a number of arguments against protectionism. These include the following:

- When trade barriers are established, it can lead to trade diversion – a certain amount of trade will be lost as a result of the establishment of the barriers.

- Protectionism can encourage industries to remain inefficient because they are protected from tough foreign competition and so there is an inefficient allocation of resources.

- Protectionism can also allow monopolies to be created as foreign competition is reduced or eliminated.

- Protectionism involves the distortion of markets, whereby there is a deadweight loss of consumer and producer surplus, reducing economic welfare through higher prices and restricted consumer choice.

- Trade barriers reduce world production.

- Protectionist barriers encourage consumers to buy domestically produced goods, but these may be of inferior quality.

- Protectionism can reduce the potential benefits of free trade and this is why it is strongly discouraged by the World Trade Organisation.

Key terms

Infant or sunrise industry: a newly established industry that will need protection, at least temporarily.

Declining or sunset industry: an industry that is declining and which will need protection, at least temporarily, to enable factors of production to be reallocated.

Dumping: the practice of selling a product that is below the cost of producing it.

★ **Exam tip**

Make sure you appreciate that although there are certain arguments in favour of protectionism, these do go against the principle of free trade.

 Remember

Make sure you understand that although a case can be made for the protection of infant/sunrise industries and/or declining/sunset industries, these should only be temporary, otherwise it is possible that protectionist methods are used to support inefficient industries, especially in the case of declining/sunset industries. You also need to realise that protectionism to reduce a deficit in a country's current account will not overcome the underlying reasons for that deficit.

6.3 The current account of the balance of payments

6.3.1 The components of the current account of the balance of payments

The current account

The **current account** of the **balance of payments** consists of the following four parts:

- The **trade in goods**, that is, the balance of trade in relation to the **exports** and **imports** of goods.

- The **trade in services**, that is, the balance of trade in relation to the exports and imports of services.

- Net primary income, that is, incomes from interest, profits and dividends resulting from investment.

- Net secondary income, that is, contributions to international organisations and overseas development aid.

> **Key terms**
>
> **Current account:** this account is made up of four parts: the trade in goods, the trade in services, net primary income and net secondary income.
>
> **Balance of payments:** a set of accounts that shows the payments and receipts arising from the transactions of one country with the rest of the world. It consists of the current account, the capital account, the financial account and a balancing item.
>
> **Trade in goods:** the balance of trade in relation to the export and import of goods.
>
> **Exports:** goods and/or services that are sold to other countries.
>
> **Imports:** goods and/or services that are brought into a country.
>
> **Trade in services:** the balance of trade in relation to the export and import of services.

> ★ **Exam tip**
>
> The composition of the current account of the balance of payments has changed in recent years and now comprises the balance of trade in goods, the balance of trade in services, net primary income and net secondary income.

The definition of balances and imbalances (deficit and surplus) in the current account of the balance of payments

Balances in the current account of the balance of payments

A balance in the current account of the balance of payments refers to a situation in which the current account as a whole is balanced, either in a given year or over a period of time, and there is neither a **deficit** nor a **surplus**.

Imbalances in the current account of the balance of payments

An imbalance in the current account of the balance of payments refers to a situation in which the current account as a whole is not balanced, either in a given year or over a period of time, and there is either a deficit or a surplus. It usually means that a country is experiencing a persistent deficit or surplus over a period of time.

> **Key terms**
>
> **Deficit:** a negative balance in the balance of payments of a country when outflows exceed inflows.
>
> **Surplus:** a positive balance in the balance of payments of a country when inflows exceed outflows.

> ★ **Exam tip**
>
> Be careful not to confuse a deficit or a surplus in the balance of payments with a deficit or a surplus in the budgetary position of a country, for example, when a deficit occurs as a result of public expenditure exceeding government revenue. To avoid this confusion, it is better to refer to the balance of payments as an external balance to distinguish it from a government's fiscal situation.

6.3.2 The calculation of the balance of trade in goods, the balance of trade in goods and services, the balance of trade in goods and services and the current account balance (CAB)

The balance of trade in goods

The balance of trade in goods has already been defined in section 5.3.1 as the difference in value of exports and imports of goods (sometimes called visibles) over a given period.

An example of a calculation is:

Value of exports	US$440 billion
Value of imports	− US$620 billion
Balance of trade in goods	− US$180 billion

The balance of trade in services

The balance of trade in services has already been defined in section 5.3.1 as the difference in value of exported services and imported services (sometimes called invisible inflows and invisible outflows) over a given period.

An example of a calculation is:

Value of exported services	US$550 billion
Value of imported services	− US$470 billion
Balance of trade in services	US$ 80 billion

The balance of trade in goods and services

The balance of trade in goods and services is the sum of the balance of trade in goods and the balance of trade in services.

An example of a calculation is:

Balance of trade in goods	− US$180 billion
Balance of trade in services	US$ 80 billion
Balance of trade in goods and services	− US$ 100 billion

The current account balance (CAB)

The current account balance has already been defined in section 6.3.1 as the sum of the balance of trade in goods, the balance of trade in services, the primary income and the secondary income.

An example of a calculation is:

Balance of trade in goods	− US$180 billion
Balance of trade in services	US$ 80 billion
Primary income	US$300 billion
Secondary income	− US$ 50 billion
Current account balance	US$150 billion

The causes of imbalances in the current account of the balance of payments

The current account of the balance of payments could be negative, that is, there is a deficit, as a result of the value of imports exceeding the value of exports. This could apply to the balance of trade in goods account and/or the balance of trade in services account.

There are a number of possible reasons why a country might be experiencing a persistent imbalance in the current account of the balance of payments. In relation to a persistent deficit, reasons could include the following:

- The foreign exchange rate could be too high, causing exports to be more expensive than they should otherwise be; if demand for these exports is price elastic, this could have a significant effect on the current account of the balance of payments.

- Consumers in a country could have begun to increase their demand for imported products, that is, as incomes have risen, there has been an increase in the **marginal propensity to import**. This could also lead to a deficit in the current account of the balance of payments.

- There could be changes in consumer tastes and preferences within the country and/or abroad which reduce the demand for a country's exports and increase the demand for imports.

- Low competitive strength in world markets, such as resulting from relatively low levels of productivity or low levels of spending on research and development, will adversely affect a country's exports.

> **Key term**
>
> **Marginal propensity to import:** the proportion of any change in income that is spent on imports.

The current account of the balance of payments could be positive, that is, there is a surplus, as a result of the value of exports exceeding the value of imports. This could apply to the balance of trade in goods account and/or the balance of trade in services account.

There are a number of possible reasons why a country might be experiencing a persistent disequilibrium in the form of imbalances in the current account of the balance of payments in the form of a persistent surplus. These reasons could include the following:

- Technological changes in methods of production in domestic industries may lead to lower costs, lower prices and an improvement in the quality of products.

- A tightening of import restrictions will make it more difficult to import products from other countries.

- A low level of inflation in an economy, which makes exports more price competitive in world markets, may increase the demand for them.

The consequences of imbalances in the current account of the balance of payments on the domestic and external economy

It is important to be able to distinguish between the consequences of a disequilibrium or imbalance in the current account of the balance of payments for the domestic economy and the external economy.

> **★ Exam tip**
>
> Make sure you understand that a persistent disequilibrium or imbalance in the current account of a country's balance of payments can arise from either a deficit or a surplus. It is easy to think that a state of disequilibrium or imbalance only applies to deficits, but it can refer to either deficits or surpluses.

Domestic economy

A disequilibrium or imbalance in the current account of the balance of payments can affect a domestic economy in various ways. These include the following consequences of a persistent current account deficit:

- There will be an increase in unemployment if there has been a decrease in the demand for exports and an increase in the demand for imports, creating a deficit in the current account.

- A persistent deficit in the current account could lead to a reduction in business confidence, leading to a fall in the level of investment in the domestic economy.

- If corrective action is taken in an attempt to reduce, and hopefully eliminate, the deficit, consumers will either have a restricted range of imported products to choose from (if quotas have been introduced) or have to pay much more for the imported products (if tariffs have been introduced).

- This increase in prices could have an inflationary effect on the economy.

- A current account deficit means that expenditure will be leaving an economy.

- A current account deficit may lead to a depreciation in the value of a country's exchange rate, although this would help to restore a country's competitiveness in world markets.

- A deficit may indicate an unbalanced economy, focused on short-term consumption rather than on long-term investment, although a deficit can enable an economy to have a higher standard of living.

There are also consequences of a persistent current account surplus:

- It increases a country's net assets by the amount of the surplus.

- A relatively high level of exports could lead to an increase in employment in the export sector of the domestic economy.

- Lower import spending may mean consumers are spending more on domestic products rather than buying foreign ones and this greater demand for domestic goods could increase domestic employment.

External economy

In addition to the possible effects of a disequilibrium or imbalance in the current account of the balance of payments on a domestic economy, there are also possible consequences for the external economy. These could include the following:

- If the disequilibrium is a deficit, there is likely to be a move towards greater protectionism in the international economy, reducing the extent of the benefits that would otherwise have been obtained from trade.

- If the disequilibrium is a surplus, a country will be able to accumulate foreign assets around the world, for example, China's investment in many African countries.

- Another issue with a persistent current account surplus is that it could cause less output and less employment in those countries experiencing a deficit in their current account balance.

★ **Exam tip**

Be sure you understand that a disequilibrium in the current account of the balance of payments can have consequences for both a domestic economy and an external economy.

★ **Link**

See Unit 11, section 11.1, for further information on the current account of the balance of payments.

6.4 Exchange rates

6.4.1 The definition of an exchange rate

An **exchange rate** refers to the value of one currency in relation to the value of another; that is, it is the price of one currency expressed in terms of another.

Key term

Exchange rate: the value of one currency in relation to another.

★ **Exam tip**

Be careful not to confuse the internal value of money with the external value of a currency. Exchange rates are concerned with the external value of a currency, that is, what it is worth when compared with other currencies.

6.4.2 The determination of a floating exchange rate

A **floating exchange rate** is a type of exchange rate system where the external value of a currency is determined through a market, the foreign exchange market. The value of a currency is determined, like any other price in a market, through the forces of demand and supply.

Figure 6.4 shows an increase in the value of a currency as a result of a shift in the demand curve to the right. The value of the currency has gone up from 0P to 0P$_1$.

Key term

Floating exchange rate: an exchange rate system where the value of a currency is allowed to float up or down, determined by the market forces of the demand for, and the supply of, the currency.

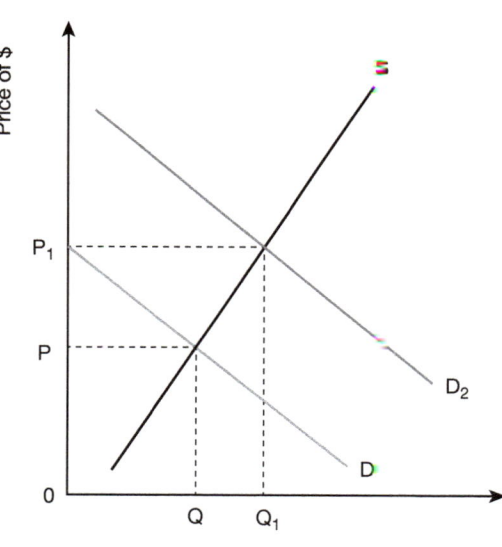

▲ **Figure 6.4** A floating exchange rate

The advantages and disadvantages of a floating exchange rate

Advantages	Disadvantages
No need for a central bank to hold foreign currency reserves to use to intervene to maintain a particular exchange rate	Speculation may affect the value of the exchange rate
The value of an exchange rate will be an accurate price, determined by the demand for, and the supply of, the currency; that is, the value automatically adjusts	A floating exchange rate may be volatile, making economic planning and forecasting more difficult; this causes instability, which can discourage investment and trade
Changes in the exchange rate will reflect, and put right, disequilibrium in the balance of payments. For example, when there is a deficit, the exchange rate will depreciate, which should encourage exports and discourage imports	A significant fall in the exchange rate can be a major cause of a rise in the rate of inflation
A floating exchange rate means that interest rates can be set to meet domestic economic aims rather than to maintain a particular exchange rate value	

6.4.3 The distinction between the depreciation and appreciation of a floating exchange rate

If an exchange rate falls in a floating exchange rate system, it is called a **depreciation**. If the rate rises in a floating exchange rate system, it is called an **appreciation**.

6.4.4 The causes of changes in a floating exchange rate system: demand and supply of the currency

There are a number of possible factors that can cause changes in exchange rates. These include:

- the demand for a country's exports from other countries

- the demand for imports into a country from other countries

- relative inflation rates in different countries, affecting the international competitiveness of goods and services that are traded between different countries

- the quality and reliability of products that are traded internationally

- relative interest rates in different countries, which can be a major factor in the movement of **hot money** from one country to another

- changes in the costs of production in different countries

- changes in the levels of productivity in different countries

- differences in the state of technology in different countries.

6.4.5 AD/AS analysis of the impact of exchange rate changes on the domestic economy's equilibrium national income and the level of real output, the price level and employment

It has already been stated that AD = C + I + G + (X − M). Exports and imports are therefore a part of AD and so any change in exports and/or imports is likely to have an effect on AD. If a country's currency rises so that exports are more expensive and imports are less expensive, and demand for both is elastic, the value of net exports, that is, the value of exports after allowing for the value of imports, is likely to fall in an economy, and this will shift AD to the left. This can be seen in Figure 6.5 where the level of real output will fall from $0Y_2$ to $0Y_1$, causing a fall in employment. The price level will fall from $0P_2$ to $0P_1$.

Key terms

Depreciation: a situation where an exchange rate decreases in value in a floating exchange rate system.

Appreciation: a situation where an exchange rate increases in value in a floating exchange rate system.

★ Exam tip

Make sure that you clearly understand the difference between a depreciation and an appreciation of an exchange rate.

Key term

Hot money: inflows and outflows of money between countries, largely as a result of the different interest rates in various countries.

★ Link

See Unit 11, section 11.2, for further details on exchange rates.

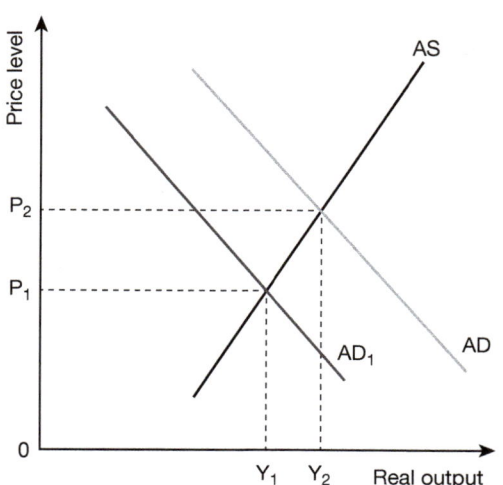

◀ **Figure 6.5** The effect of a changing exchange rate on an economy

6.5 Policies to correct disequilibrium in the current account of the balance of payments

6.5.1 and 6.5.2 Government policy objective of stability of the current account and the effect of fiscal, monetary, supply-side and protectionist policies on the current account

Three macroeconomic objectives of a government were identified in section 5.1.1. It is now possible to add a fourth objective: the achievement of stability of the current account of the balance of payments over a period of time. The aim is for an equilibrium over time in the account so that deficits and surpluses are approximately equal. However, this may not be possible and so a government may need to take action to correct an imbalance or disequilibrium in the current account, whether that is a deficit or a surplus.

Fiscal policy

If a country is experiencing a deficit on the current account of its balance of payments, it may use fiscal policy instruments to try to reduce this deficit. For example, to reduce the demand for imports, a government could increase income tax and/or reduce government spending. This will reduce aggregate demand in an economy, reducing expenditure on imports. A government could also use fiscal policy to discourage the consumption of imported goods by imposing a tariff on the imports, making them more expensive.

The effectiveness of fiscal policy to correct a balance of payments disequilibrium will depend on a number of factors. For example, the effect of imposing a tariff on imported goods will depend on the price elasticity of demand for imports. If demand is price elastic, consumers will be likely to reduce the demand for the imports and buy domestically produced goods instead, but if demand is price inelastic, it will not have a very significant effect in reducing the demand for imports. There is also the danger that the imposition of tariffs on imports into a country could lead to retaliation by the country producing those goods and this could lead to a decrease in a country's exports to that country. Also, an increase in income tax and/or a decrease in government spending may have negative effects on other parts of an economy, for example, it may lead to an increase in the level of unemployment.

Monetary policy

If a country is experiencing a deficit on the current account of its balance of payments, it may use monetary policy instruments to try to reduce this deficit. For example, to reduce the demand for imports, a government could increase interest rates and/or reduce the money supply. Either of these policies is likely to reduce aggregate demand in an economy and make it less likely that consumers will buy imported goods.

The effectiveness of monetary policy to correct a balance of payments disequilibrium will depend on a number of factors. For example, the effect of an increase in interest rates on demand in an economy will depend on the extent to which the demand is interest-elastic. If demand is relatively interest-inelastic, an increase in interest rates will be unlikely to have much of an impact on the demand for imports. Also, the effect of a change in interest rates in an economy can take a while because of a time lag between a change in interest rates and the full consequences of such an action being seen.

Supply-side policies

If a country is experiencing a deficit on the current account of its balance of payments, it may use supply-side policy instruments to try to reduce this deficit. For example, if a domestic market was made more efficient and more flexible, such as through a policy of privatisation or deregulation, this would be likely to make a country's exports more competitive in international markets, encouraging the demand for them to increase. This would be as a result of increased quality and/or a more competitive price.

The effectiveness of supply-side policy to correct a balance of payments disequilibrium will depend on a number of factors. For example, increased spending on education and training is only likely to have a significant effect over a relatively long period of time. Privatisation may not necessarily lead to greater efficiency if a public sector monopoly is replaced by a private sector monopoly that does not take into account external costs.

Protectionist policies

Protectionist policies have been covered earlier in section 6.2. If a country is experiencing a deficit on the current account, protectionist policies can include:

- tariffs
- import quotas
- export subsidies

- embargoes
- excessive administrative burdens ('red tape').

The main problem associated with such protectionist policies is that they involve restraints on free trade and are therefore generally opposed by the World Trade Organisation.

 ★ Link

See Unit 11, section 11.1, for further details on the balance of payments.

 Raise your grade

Assess to what extent the depreciation of a currency is likely to be effective in reducing a balance of trade deficit. [12]

The depreciation of a currency refers to the fact that its value has been reduced (1). This is often done to reduce a balance of trade deficit (2) because the effect of a depreciation is to make a country's exports cheaper and the imports into the country more expensive.

This is likely to be effective as long as price elasticity of demand is elastic (3) because the lower price of the exports will be likely to increase the demand for them and the higher price of the imports is likely to decrease the demand for them (4). However, although the depreciation is likely to be effective over a period of time, it could lead to a worsening of the situation immediately after the depreciation (5).

In conclusion, the depreciation of a currency is very likely (6) to be effective in reducing a balance of trade deficit (7).

How to improve this answer

1. The candidate has referred to the fact that a depreciation means a reduction in the value of an exchange rate, but this could have been developed more fully by making it clear that a depreciation has to be seen in the context of a floating exchange rate system, in contrast to a devaluation which would only occur in a fixed exchange rate system.

2. The concept of a balance of trade deficit could have been explained more fully in terms of the value of the outflows being greater than the value of the inflows, with the result that the net effect is negative.

3. The candidate has referred to the fact that the depreciation will only be effective if the price elasticity of demand is elastic, but this point needed to be developed more fully in relation to the need for both the price elasticity of demand for exports and the price elasticity of demand for imports to be elastic.

4. The candidate could have referred to the Marshall-Lerner condition which states that a depreciation will only be effective in reducing a balance of trade deficit if the sum of the price elasticity of demand for exports and the price elasticity of demand for imports is greater than one.

5. The candidate recognises that although a depreciation may be effective in time, there may be a worsening of the balance of trade immediately after the depreciation, but it would have been helpful if there had been an explicit reference to the J curve effect. It would also have been helpful if the candidate had included a diagram to show the J curve effect over time.

6. The candidate has made an attempt to address the 'to what extent' aspect of the question by stating that the depreciation is 'very likely' to be effective in reducing a balance of trade deficit.

7. The candidate's conclusion would have been improved if the likely effectiveness of the depreciation had been linked to the Marshall-Lerner condition and the J curve effect.

Knowledge and understanding and analysis:　　Level 2　　3/8

Evaluation:　　　　　　　　　　　　　　　　Level 1　　2/4

Total:　　　　　　　　　　　　　　　　　　　　　　　　5/12

Worked Example

Assess whether export subsidies are a useful tool of protectionism in international trade. [12]

A subsidy is a payment by a government to a firm or industry to help cover the costs of production. The aim is to enable a price to be charged that is lower than would otherwise be the case. This would give exporting firms an advantage over their competitors.

This would be advantageous to a firm as long as the demand for the products being sold was price elastic. It can be regarded as a form of protectionism because it gives such firms an advantage in the context of international trade.

However, it will not be advantageous if demand is relatively price inelastic or if price is not the main factor determining demand for the product. It is also possible that the subsidy may encourage the firm to become complacent. A final factor to consider is that there would be alternative uses for the money used to provide for the subsidy, that is, the subsidy will have an opportunity cost.

Therefore, in conclusion, the extent to which an export subsidy can be considered a useful protectionist tool will depend on whether it can be justified in terms of increased sales, taking into account the alternative uses that could have been made of the money used to finance the subsidy.

Exam-style questions

1 When the money inflows into a country are greater than the money outflows out of a country, as shown in the balance of payments accounts, this is known as:

   (a) a balancing item

   (b) a deficit

   (c) a surplus

   (d) an equilibrium. [1]

2 When an exchange rate is determined by the forces of demand and supply, it is known as a:

   (a) fixed exchange rate system

   (b) floating exchange rate system

   (c) managed float exchange rate system

   (d) weighted exchange rate system. [1]

3 The terms of trade shows the relationship between changes in the:

   (a) prices of exports and imports

   (b) quality of exports and imports

   (c) quantity of exports and imports

   (d) value of exports and imports. [1]

4 A ban on imports from a particular country is known as:

   (a) a duty

   (b) a quota

   (c) a tariff

   (d) an embargo. [1]

5 Which of the following methods is a country likely to use to avoid having import controls imposed against it?

   (a) A tariff

   (b) A voluntary export restraint

   (c) An export subsidy

   (d) An import duty [1]

6 Red tape refers to:

   (a) embargoes

   (b) excessive administrative burdens

   (c) import quotas

   (d) tariffs. [1]

7 Contributions to international organisations are shown in the current account of the balance of payments of a country in the:

   (a) primary income

   (b) secondary income

   (c) trade in goods

   (d) trade in services. [1]

8 Selling a product in another country below the cost of production is known as:

   (a) balancing

   (b) depreciation

   (c) dumping

   (d) strategic. [1]

9 Inflows and outflows of money between countries to take advantage of differences in interest rates are known as:

   (a) comparative money

   (b) differential money

   (c) disequilibrium money

   (d) hot money. [1]

10 Which of the following is an argument for protectionism?

   (a) Consumers are more likely to buy inferior products.

   (b) Industries are encouraged to become inefficient.

   (c) Infant industries can be protected.

   (d) World production is reduced. [1]

11 (a) Explain the difference between a tariff and a quota as a method of protection, and consider which is likely to be more effective. [8]

   (b) Assess whether the arguments in favour of protectionism are always stronger than the arguments against. [12]

12 (a) Explain what can determine the value of a floating exchange rate, and consider by how much an exchange rate should be allowed to float. [8]

   (b) Assess whether fiscal policy or monetary policy is more likely to correct a balance of payments deficit. [12]

The price system and the microeconomy

Key topics

- Utility
- Indifference curves and budget lines
- Efficiency and market failure
- Private costs and benefits, externalities and social costs and benefits
- Types of cost, revenue and profit, short-run and long-run production
- Different market structures
- The growth and survival of firms
- The differing objectives and policies of firms

7.1 Utility

7.1.1 The definition and calculation of total utility and marginal utility

Utility refers to the benefit or satisfaction that is derived from the consumption of a product. **Total utility** is the total satisfaction obtained from consuming a particular number of units of a product. **Marginal utility** is the extra satisfaction that can be gained from consuming one additional unit of a product.

> ★ **Exam tip**
>
> Make sure that you are able to differentiate clearly between the concepts of total utility and marginal utility.

> **Key terms**
>
> **Utility:** the satisfaction gained from the consumption of a product.
>
> **Total utility:** the satisfaction gained from the consumption of all units of a product over a particular time period.
>
> **Marginal utility:** the satisfaction gained from the last unit of a product consumed over a particular time period.

> ★ **Exam tip**
>
> Be careful not to confuse the concepts of total utility and marginal utility. Total utility refers to the satisfaction gained from the consumption of all of the units of a product, whereas marginal utility refers to the satisfaction gained from the consumption of just one more additional unit of a product.

> 💡 **Remember**
>
> The fact that marginal utility diminishes with the consumption of additional units of a product means that consumers are only willing to pay a lower price for these additional units. This explains why a demand curve is downward sloping from left to right, that is, as quantity increases, price falls. It is assumed that the marginal utility of a product can be measured by the price an individual is prepared to pay for it. This is why an individual's demand curve for a product will be the same as their marginal utility curve and an individual will purchase a product up to the point where P=MU.

> 💡 **Remember**
>
> Total utility increases up to a certain quantity of units of a product consumed, but at a decreasing rate. This is because the marginal utility of consuming additional units of a product is decreasing. At the point where total utility is at the maximum, marginal utility is equal to zero. When total utility begins to decline, marginal utility becomes negative. This can be seen in Figure 7.1.

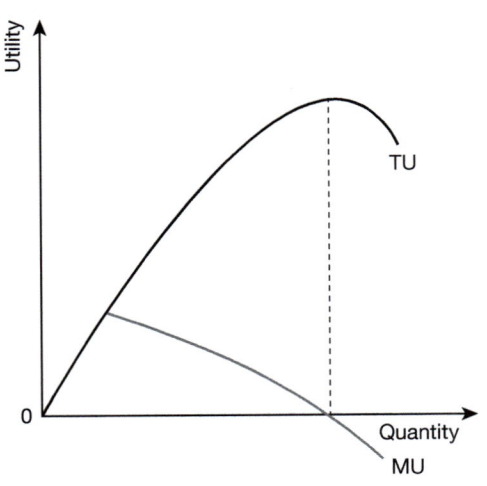

◀ **Figure 7.1** Total utility and marginal utility

7.1.2 Diminishing marginal utility

The **law of diminishing marginal utility** refers to the situation in which the consumption of successive units of a product will eventually lead to a fall in marginal utility. That is, as someone consumes more units of a product, the satisfaction provided by each units will be progressively less.

There is an important relationship between the law of diminishing marginal utility and the derivation of an individual demand schedule. This is covered in section 7.1.4.

> **Key term**
>
> **Law of diminishing marginal utility:** a situation in which as the quantity consumed of a product by an individual increases, the additional or extra satisfaction gained from each unit (the marginal utility) will eventually decline.

7.1.3 The equi-marginal principle

The **equi-marginal principle** shows the relationship between the marginal utility obtained from the consumption of different products and the prices paid for those products. It can be represented as follows:

$$\frac{MUa}{Pa} = \frac{MUb}{Pb} = \frac{MUc}{Pc}$$

To maximise their utility or satisfaction, a consumer will be at the situation shown above for the three products a, b and c. The extra satisfaction produced by the last unit of 'a' consumed, in relation to the money spent to buy this last unit, will be equal to the extra satisfaction produced by the last unit of 'b' consumed, in relation to the money spent to buy this last unit. This will also be equal to the extra satisfaction produced by the last unit of 'c' consumed, in relation to the money spent to buy this last unit.

> **Key term**
>
> **Equi-marginal principle:** the principle that a rational individual, wishing to maximise total utility, will allocate their expenditure amongst different products so as to ensure that the satisfaction or utility gained from the last unit of money spent on each product is the same.

> ★ **Exam tip**
>
> It is often assumed that the equi-marginal principle is a static principle. The reality, however, is that the consumption of the different products will change if there is a change in the price of any of them.

💡 **Remember**

If the price of a product falls, the extra satisfaction gained from the last unit of money spent on the product will give greater satisfaction than that spent on another product that has not fallen in price.

💡 **Remember**

If the price of a product falls, and the prices of other products remain unchanged, the quantity of that product will increase until the equality shown by the equi-marginal principle is restored.

★ **Exam tip**

Make sure that you are able to show not only the equi-marginal principle, but also how that equality can be affected by a change in the price of a product and how the situation of equality shown by the principle can be restored.

7.1.4 The derivation of an individual demand curve

There is an important relationship between the law of diminishing marginal utility and the derivation of an individual demand schedule. If the marginal utility of consuming extra units of a product continually diminishes, a consumer will be unwilling to pay as much for each successive unit consumed; that is, as the utility falls, so will the price that a consumer is willing to pay. This can be shown in an individual demand schedule and explains why a demand curve for a product is downward sloping from left to right.

★ **Link**

See Unit 2, section 2.1, for more information on demand curves.

7.1.5 The limitations of marginal utility theory and its assumptions of rational behaviour

The law of diminishing marginal utility is based on a number of assumptions, but if these assumptions do not actually apply, there will be limitations to the theory. These assumptions include the following:

- the idea that the utility or satisfaction that an individual gains from the consumption of a product can be easily measured, but this may not necessarily be the case

- the idea that consumers behave in a rational way, but this may not always be the case

- the idea that consumers have limited incomes, but it is possible that incomes may rise over a period of time

- the idea that consumers can be expected to maximise their total utility, but this may not always be the case

- the idea that prices are constant, but the prices of products are likely to be continually changing

- the idea that consumer tastes and preferences remain constant, but these may change over time, perhaps as a result of advertising campaigns

- the idea that the consideration of marginal utility is vitally important, but this may not always be the case, especially where consumption is habit-forming or made on impulse

- the idea that all units of a product available for consumption are identical, but if quality control in the production process is not very efficient, this may not always be the case.

Rational behaviour versus behavioural economic models

The **rational behaviour** of consumers is based on the idea that they will maximise their utility, given the following constraints: limited income, a given set of prices and constant tastes and preferences.

★ **Exam tip**

Make sure that you are able to demonstrate an understanding of the limitations of marginal utility theory.

Key term

Rational behaviour: the assumption that individuals take into account the marginal costs and marginal benefits in making decisions in order to achieve an optimal outcome, that is, the maximisation of utility.

Rational behaviour essentially means that:

- individual consumers will take decisions to maximise their utility and satisfaction

- individual consumers will have access to all the information that they require to make a decision at zero cost

- individuals take decisions that are based on a very careful comparison of the benefits and costs to achieve the optimal outcome

- these decisions will be taken by individuals based on changes at the margin, stressing the importance of the margin as a key economic concept

- the tastes and preferences of individuals and their attitudes to risk are assumed to be fixed.

However, **behavioural economic** models have been developed to offer a contrast to the idea of rational behaviour. Behavioural economics attempts to explain the decisions taken by individuals in practice, particularly when they are opposed to those predicted by traditional economic theory, that is, it attempts to explain what might appear apparently 'irrational' behaviour.

The key elements of behavioural economic models include the following:

- Instead of attempting to achieve optimal outcomes as a result of taking decisions, individuals take decisions based on the potential gains and losses that might arise.

- Individuals may not always possess all the relevant information that they require, possibly because of reasons of time and/or cost, giving rise to the existence of an opportunity cost in terms of possible alternative uses of this time and/or money.

- There may be just too much information available, making decision taking more difficult; an individual's ability to act rationally is therefore restricted or 'bounded' and so they may engage in satisficing rather than optimising behaviour (this is known as **bounded rationality**).

- Individuals may take decisions based on rules of thumb (known as **heuristics**), simplifying what is involved in the decision-making process, or on the first piece of information received (known as **anchoring**).

- Decisions can be based on assumptions, even though this could lead to irrational decisions.

- The way that information is presented can influence behaviour (this is known as **framing**).

- Individuals can be 'nudged' to take particular decisions, such as through government advertising.

> **Key terms**
>
> **Behavioural economics:** the branch of Economics that attempts to explain the decisions and choices that individuals make in practice, particularly when they are opposed to those predicted by traditional economic theory.
>
> **Bounded rationality:** the idea that individuals' ability to make rational decisions is limited by the quantity of information available and their ability to absorb and interpret it within the timescale available.
>
> **Heuristics:** rules of thumb or mental shortcuts made by individuals to speed up the decision-making process.
>
> **Anchoring:** the tendency to rely on the first piece of information obtained (the anchor) when making a decision.
>
> **Framing:** the way in which an issue or choice is presented (framed) which may affect the decision made by an individual.

> 💡 **Remember**
>
> Although the idea of rational behaviour has played a key role in traditional economic theory, it is now being increasingly challenged by behavioural economic models.

7.2 Indifference curves and budget lines

7.2.1 The meaning of an indifference curve and a budget line

Indifference curve

An **indifference curve** shows the possible combinations of two products between which a consumer is indifferent. It slopes downwards from left to right and is convex to the origin. The slope of an indifference curve shows the **marginal rate of substitution** between two products, that is, the number of units of one product that an individual is prepared to give up in order to obtain additional units of the other product.

An indifference curve is shown in Figure 7.2. This indicates the possible combinations of apples and pears between which a consumer is indifferent.

A series of indifference curves can be shown in an indifference map, as in Figure 7.3. These indifference curves indicate higher levels of total utility as there is movement away from the origin, that is, I_3 permits an individual to increase consumption of at least one of the two products.

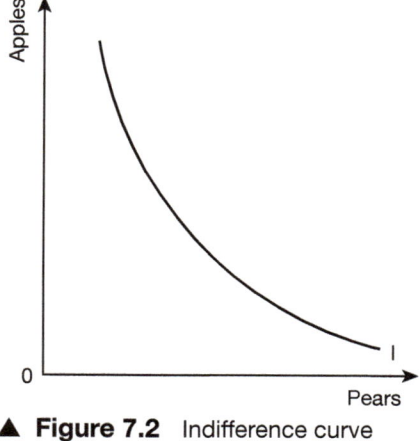

▲ **Figure 7.2** Indifference curve

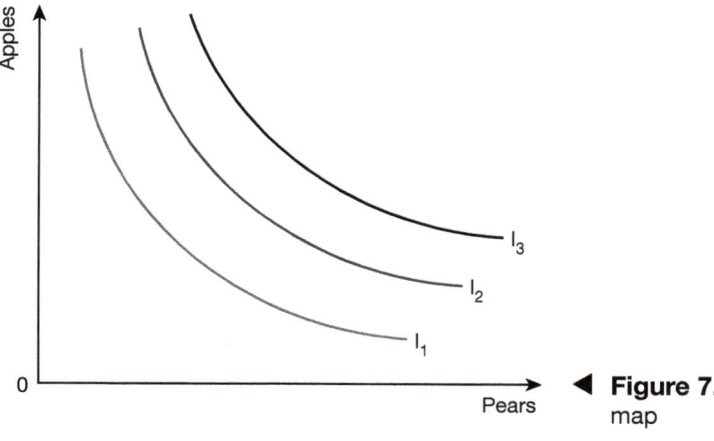

◀ **Figure 7.3** Indifference map

Key terms

Indifference curve: a curve showing all possible combinations of two products between which an individual consumer is indifferent.

Marginal rate of substitution: the quantity of one product that an individual is prepared to give up in order to obtain an additional unit of another product while leaving the individual at the same level of utility.

Remember

It is important that you understand the properties of indifference curves:

- they identify different combinations of two products between which an individual has no preference; that is, the individual is indifferent as to which combination of products they consume

- all points on an indifference curve represent combinations of two products which give an individual equal satisfaction

- there is an infinite number of indifference curves for each consumer, each one associated with a particular level of total utility

- they slope downwards from left to right

- they are convex to the origin

- the slope of an indifference curve indicates the marginal rate of substitution between two products

- an indifference curve becomes shallower as there is movement down the curve, reflecting an individual consumer's **diminishing marginal rate of substitution** of one product for another; that is, as an individual obtains more and more of one product, they are prepared to sacrifice fewer and fewer units of the other product

- indifference curves can never intersect each other.

Budget line

A **budget line** shows the possible combinations of two products that an individual consumer is able to purchase with a given income and fixed prices. Each of the combinations of two products along a budget line would cost the consumer the same total amount of money. Any point along a budget line will indicate the maximisation of consumption at a given level of income.

A budget line is shown in Figure 7.4. This shows an individual's budget line for two products, apples and pears. If all income is spent on apples, it is possible to buy 0B apples and no pears. If all income is spent on pears, it is possible to buy 0A pears and no apples. The budget line is AB. Any combination of apples or pears inside the budget line, or on the budget line, can be consumed by the individual. However, the individual cannot consume beyond the budget line.

7.2.2 The causes of a shift in the budget line

If there is a change in an individual's income, they will be able to consume more apples and more pears. This can be seen in Figure 7.5. The effect of an increase in an individual's income will be to shift the budget line upwards to the right, parallel to the original budget line. This can be seen in the diagram, where the new budget line is CD. If an individual's income was reduced, this would have the effect of shifting the budget line inwards towards the origin, parallel to the original budget line.

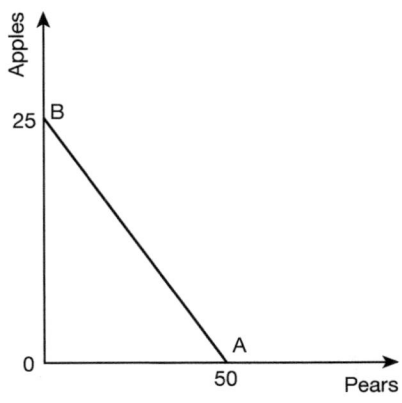

▲ **Figure 7.4** Budget line

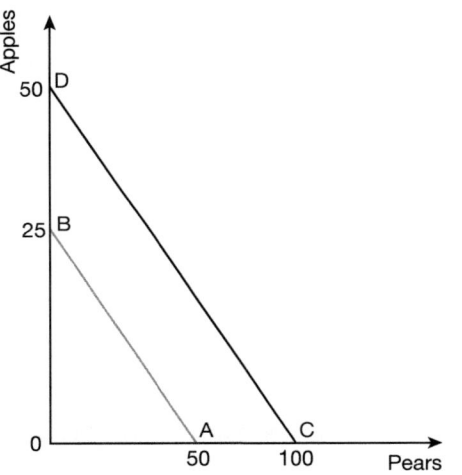

◀ **Figure 7.5** The effect of a change in income on a budget line

A budget line will be affected not only by a change in an individual's income, but also by changes in the prices of the different products. If the price of one of the two products changes, then the slope of the budget line will also change. Figure 7.6 shows the effect of a fall in the prices of apples with the price of pears remaining the same. The budget line will now pivot outwards and is now AC.

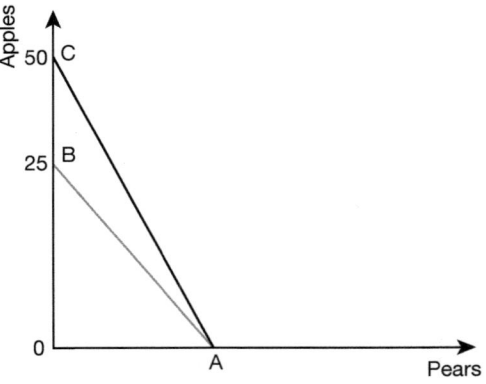

▲ **Figure 7.6** The effect of a change in price on a budget line

The **optimum consumption point** for a rational consumer can be shown by combining indifference curves and a budget line in one diagram. A rational consumer will wish to maximise their total utility by achieving the highest indifference curve that their income permits. This is shown by X in Figure 7.7. At this point, an individual consumer's budget line, VZ, is tangential to the highest attainable indifference curve, I_3. At this point, the individual will consume $0A_1$ apples and $0P_1$ pears.

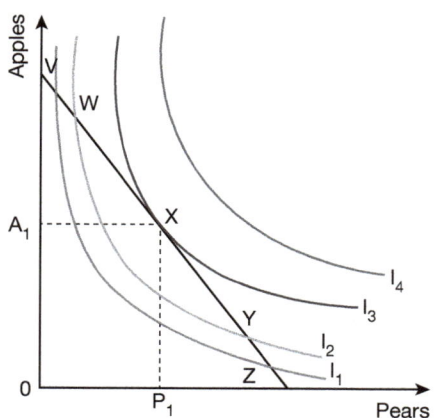

◀ **Figure 7.7** The optimum consumption point for an individual

💡 **Remember**

It is important that you understand the properties of budget lines:

- they show the combinations of two products that an individual is able to consume

- these combinations are limited by an individual consumer's level of income

- these combinations are limited by fixed prices for the two products

- a budget line can also be known as a consumption possibility line

- any combination of two products inside a budget line, or on a budget line, can be consumed

- an individual cannot consume beyond a budget line

- if there is a change in the income of an individual, there will be a parallel shift of a budget line; if income rises, there will be a parallel shift to the right and if income falls, there will be a parallel shift to the left

- if the price of one of the products changes, the slope of the budget line will change, pivoting outwards if there is a fall in price of one of the products and pivoting inwards if there is a rise in price of one of the products.

7.2.3 Income, substitution and price effects for normal, inferior and Giffen goods

A **price effect** includes both an income effect and a substitution effect.

If the price of a product falls, it means that it is now cheaper relative to other products. This means that a consumer is likely to purchase more of the product. The consumer is therefore likely to substitute purchases of products whose price has fallen for other more expensive products. This is known as the **substitution effect**.

The fall in the price of a product will also mean that a consumer's real income has effectively risen so that more of all products, including the one whose price has fallen, can now be purchased. This is known as the **income effect**.

Normal good

If the product is a normal good, the income effect will operate so that consumption of the product whose price has fallen will increase.

Inferior good

If the product is an inferior good, the income effect will operate so that consumption of the product whose price has fallen will decrease, but with an inferior good the substitution effect will be greater than the income effect and so overall there will be an increase in the quantity consumed of the good whose price has fallen.

Key terms

Price effect: the sum of the substitution effect and the income effect of the change in the price of a product on the quantity demanded of that product.

Substitution effect: the change in the quantity demanded of a product as a result of a change in its relative price.

Income effect: the change in the quantity demanded of a product as a result of the fact that a change in its price has brought about a change in a consumer's real income.

Giffen good

If the product is a Giffen good, the income effect will be greater than the substitution effect and so a fall in the price of a good will lead to a decrease in the quantity consumed.

The income and substitution effects of a fall in the price of a good

Indifference curves and budget lines can be used to show the effects of a fall in the price of a product.

Normal good

Figure 7.8 shows the income and substitution effects of a fall in the price of a normal good.

When there is a fall in the price of good B, the movement from X to Z, along the original indifference curve I_1, shows the substitution effect and the movement from Z to Y, on a new indifference curve I_2, shows the income effect. On the horizontal axis, the substitution effect is shown by the movement from $0B_1$ to $0B_3$ and the income effect is shown by the movement from $0B_3$ to $0B_2$. It is clear that with a normal good, the substitution and the income effects of the price fall have worked in the same direction causing an increase in the quantity of B demanded.

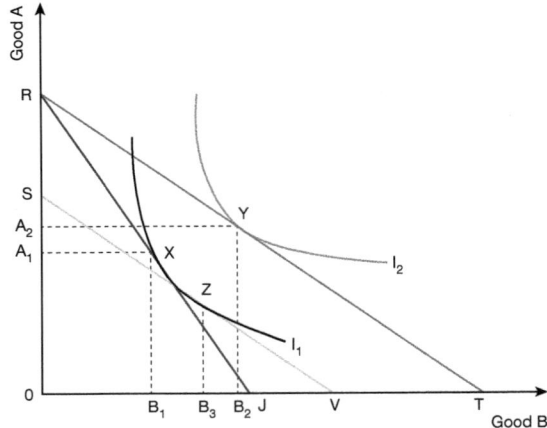

▲ **Figure 7.8** The income and substitution effects of a fall in the price of a normal good

Inferior good

Figure 7.9 shows the income and substitution effects of a fall in the price of an inferior good.

When there is fall in the price of good B, the movement from X to Z, along the original indifference curve I_1, shows the substitution effect and the movement from Z to Y, on a new indifference curve I_2, shows the income effect. On the horizontal axis, the substitution effect is shown by the movement from $0B_1$ to $0B_3$ and the income effect is shown by the movement from $0B_3$ to $0B_2$. It is clear that with an inferior good, the substitution and income effects of the price fall have worked in opposite directions, but the positive substitution effect is greater than the negative income effect so that there is still an increase in the quantity of B demanded.

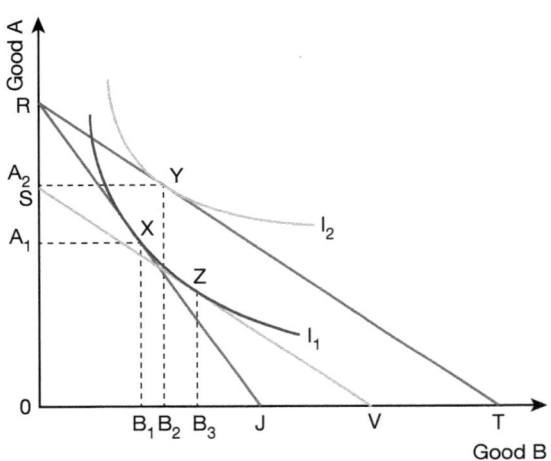

▲ **Figure 7.9** The income and substitution effects of a fall in the price of an inferior good

Giffen good

Figure 7.10 shows the income and substitution effects of a fall in the price of a Giffen good. When there is a fall in the price of good B, the movement from X to Z, along the original indifference curve I_1, shows the substitution effect and the movement from Z to Y, on a new indifference curve I_2, shows the income effect. On the horizontal axis, the substitution effect is shown by the movement from $0B_1$ to $0B_3$ and the income effect is shown by the movement from $0B_3$ to $0B_2$. It is clear that with a Giffen good, the substitution and income effects of the price fall have worked in opposite directions, but the negative income effect is greater than the positive substitution effect so that there is now a decrease in the quantity of B demanded.

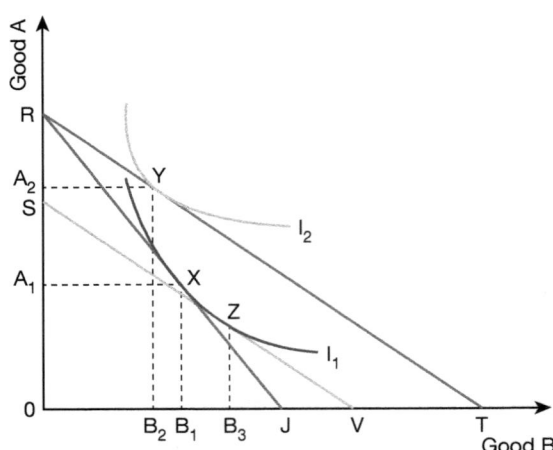

▲ **Figure 7.10** The income and substitution effects of a fall in the price of a Giffen good

💡 **Remember**

It is important that you understand the key features of using indifference curves and budget lines to show the effects in the price of various types of good:

- A price effect includes both an income effect and a substitution effect.

- A substitution effect always leads to an increase in the consumption of the good whose relative price has fallen, that is, the substitution effect will always be positive.

- The income effect will depend on the type of good: if it is a normal good, the income effect will be positive, but if it is an inferior good or a Giffen good, the income effect will be negative.

- With a normal good, both the substitution effect and the income effect are positive and so both effects move in the same direction, meaning that a fall in the price of a good will lead to an increase in its demand.

- With an inferior good, the positive substitution effect and the negative income effect move in opposite directions, but the substitution effect will be greater than the income effect, meaning that a fall in the price of a good will lead to an increase in its demand.

- With a Giffen good, the positive substitution effect and negative income effect move in opposite directions, but the income effect will be greater than the substitution effect, meaning that a fall in the price of a good will lead to a decrease in its demand.

💡 **Remember**

The substitution effect of a fall in the price of a good will always be positive, but the income effect can be either positive or negative depending on what type of good it is.

⭐ **Exam tip**

Make sure that you clearly understand the different effects of a fall in the price of a product, depending on what type of product it is. With a normal good, both the income and substitution effects are positive and so there will be an increase in the demand for such a product. With an inferior good, the positive substitution effect will be greater than the negative income effect and so there will be an increase in the demand for such a product. With a Giffen good, the negative income effect will be greater than the positive substitution effect and so there will be a decrease in the demand for such a product.

⭐ **Exam tip**

Make sure you do not confuse the income and substitution effects of a price change. If there is a fall in the price of a product, the substitution effect will always be positive, but the income effect can either be positive, in the case of a normal good, or negative, in the case of an inferior good or a Giffen good.

7.2.4 The limitations of the model of indifference curves

There are a number of limitations of the model of indifference curves, including that:

- it oversimplifies the situation, as indifference curve analysis is based on a two product model

- it makes unrealistic assumptions about human behaviour, assuming that consumer behaviour is always rational

- it is incompatible with the reality of economic action which demonstrates preference, not indifference

- consumer preferences may change in time, making specific indifference curves less relevant.

7.3 Efficiency and market failure

7.3.1 and 7.3.2 The definitions of, and conditions for, productive efficiency and allocative efficiency

Economic efficiency can be divided into types: productive efficiency and allocative efficiency.

Productive efficiency

One way of measuring **productive efficiency** is at the micro level in terms of the minimum average cost at which a given output can be produced. In this sense, productive efficiency involves two elements. **Technical efficiency** is where the best possible combination of factors of production is used in the production process; that is, the greatest amount of output is produced that is possible from a given set of inputs. **Cost efficiency** is where the production is influenced by the relative costs of different inputs. Figure 7.11 shows productive efficiency in a firm.

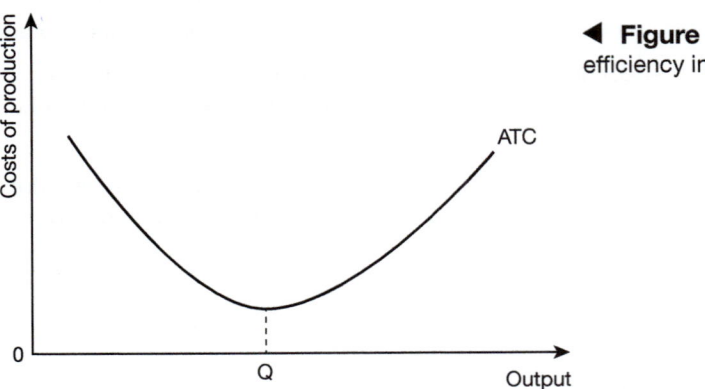

◀ **Figure 7.11** Productive efficiency in a firm

Another way of measuring productive efficiency is at the macro level in terms of the production possibility curve of an economy. The PPC in Figure 7.12 shows the possible combinations of production of two products. Point X, inside the PPC, indicates productive inefficiency because there are unused resources that could be used to produce more of both products. Any point on the PPC, however, such as point Y, shows that all of the available resources in an economy are being fully used in the production of the two products, that is, productive efficiency is being maximised.

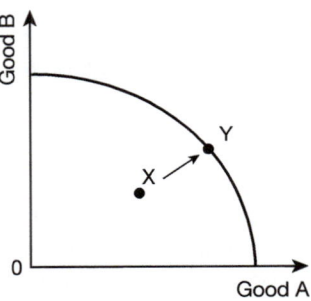

▲ **Figure 7.12** Productive efficiency in an economy

Allocative efficiency

Another element in economic efficiency is **allocative efficiency**. This allocation of resources is the one which fits the wishes of the consumers and producers most closely. It occurs where price is equal to marginal cost. This is because the value that is put on a product by a consumer, that is, the price, is equal to the value put on a product by a producer, that is, the marginal cost of producing one more unit of the product.

★ **Exam tip**

Productive efficiency can occur at the lowest point on any average cost curve and not only at the lowest point on the average total cost curve.

7.3.3 Pareto optimality

Pareto optimality

An optimal resource allocation refers to a situation in which there is the best possible allocation of scarce resources. The Italian economist, Vilfredo Pareto (1848–1923), stated that such a situation existed when it was impossible to make one person better off without making another person worse off. This situation is therefore known as **Pareto optimality**. In this situation, there needs to be both productive efficiency and allocative efficiency.

7.3.4 The definition of dynamic efficiency

Whereas productive and allocative efficiency are examples of static efficiency, that is, they are concerned with the allocation of resources at a given moment in time, **dynamic efficiency** is concerned with changes in the allocation of resources over time. For example, new products may appear as a result of invention and innovation. There may be new methods of production that can be used as a result of technological progress. There could also be changes in the management of resources.

> **Key term**
>
> **Dynamic efficiency:** the greater efficiency that can occur as a result of improvements over a period of time.

> 💡 **Remember**
>
> Productive and allocative efficiency are both examples of static efficiency, that is, they refer to the most efficient allocation of resources in a given period of time. Dynamic efficiency, however, is the result of changes over time, such as in relation to the products that are produced or the way that they are produced.

> 💡 **Remember**
>
> Efficient resource allocation refers to both productive and allocative efficiency, but each of these is a static concept, that is, that level of efficiency is the best that can be achieved at a given moment in time. Over a period of time, however, dynamic efficiency can occur, leading to changes in the allocation of resources.

7.3.5 The definition of market failure

Market failure refers to a market imperfection which gives rise to an allocation of resources which is not as efficient as might otherwise have been the case.

7.3.6 The reasons for market failure

There are many possible reasons for market failure, including:

- the under-production and under-consumption of merit goods
- the over-production and over-consumption of demerit goods
- the non-provision of public goods
- the existence of externalities which are costs or benefits which affect **third parties**, sometimes referred to as **spillover effects**
- information failure leading to a sub-optimal allocation of resources
- government failure where a government intervenes to try to overcome a failure in a market, only to create further distortions
- imperfect competition, such as the existence of a monopoly

- an inequality in the distribution of income and wealth in an economy, giving some individuals more influence in a market than others
- the existence of geographical and/or occupational immobility of factors of production, making it difficult to reallocate them to alternative uses
- price instability in markets, especially in agricultural markets
- asymmetric information, when decision takers do not all have the same information
- moral hazard, where some people are likely to take greater risks if they know that they are covered for such actions.

> **Key term**
>
> **Market failure:** a market imperfection which gives rise to an allocation of resources which is not as efficient as might otherwise have been the case.
>
> **Third party:** individuals or groups that are in some way affected by a decision, even though they are not the main parties in such a decision.
>
> **Spillover effect:** a situation in which a certain decision has an impact on third parties, that is, those who are neither the producers nor the consumers of a certain product.

> ★ **Exam tip**
>
> Do not get confused by what is meant by a third party. Make sure you understand that although a third party can be affected by a decision in some way, the third party is not directly involved in the taking of the decision.

7.4 Private costs and benefits, externalities and social costs and benefits

7.4.1 The definition and calculation of social costs (SC) as the sum of private costs (PC) and external costs (EC)

It is important to understand that **social costs** (SC) represent the true cost of something to society, that is, they include not only private costs (PC), but also the external costs (EC) imposed on a society as the result of an economic action.

Social costs include:

- marginal social costs (MSC)
- marginal private costs (MPC)
- marginal external costs (MEC)

> **Key term**
>
> **Social cost:** the sum of private costs and external costs.

> ★ **Exam tip**
>
> It is easy to confuse social costs and external costs. An external cost is a cost that arises from any activity which is not paid for by the firm or the consumer carrying out the activity, but a social cost includes **both** external costs and private costs.

7.4.2 The definition and calculation of social benefits (SB) as the sum of private benefits (PB) and external benefits (EB)

Just as social costs represent the true cost of something to society, **social benefits** (SB) represent the true benefit of something to society, that is, they include not only private benefits (PB), but also the external benefits (EB) that are of benefit to the whole society as the result of an economic action.

Social benefits include:

- marginal social benefits (MSB)
- marginal private benefits (MPB)
- marginal external benefits (MEB)

> **Key term**
>
> **Social benefit:** the sum of private benefits and external benefits.

> ★ **Exam tip**
>
> It is easy to confuse social benefits and external benefits. An external benefit is a benefit to a third party which arises from an activity carried out by a firm or a consumer, but a social benefit includes **both** external benefits and private benefits.

7.4.3 The definition of positive externality and negative externality

An **externality** refers to an action that results in either **external costs** or **external benefits** in relation to either production or consumption.

Positive externality

A positive externality is where social benefits are greater than private benefits.

Negative externality

A negative externality is where social costs are greater than private costs.

> **Key terms**
>
> **Externality:** an action that results in either external benefits or external costs in relation to either production or consumption.
>
> **External cost:** a cost which arises from any activity which is not paid for by the firm or the consumer carrying out the activity.
>
> **External benefit:** a benefit to a third party which arises from an activity carried out by a firm or a consumer.

7.4.4 Positive and negative externalities of both consumption and production

Positive externalities

Figure 7.13 shows a situation in which there is a **positive externality**; that is, social benefits are greater than private benefits. The original equilibrium position is where the supply curve, S, representing **marginal social cost** (MSC), intersects with the demand curve, D_1, representing marginal private benefit (MPB). However, if all of the benefits are taken into account, this will be shown by the demand curve D_2, representing **marginal social benefit** (MSB) which is made up of both marginal private benefit (MPB) and marginal external benefit (MEB). The effect of taking all benefits and costs into account is that the equilibrium price rises from $0P_1$ to CP_2 and the equilibrium quantity rises from $0Q_1$ to $0Q_2$.

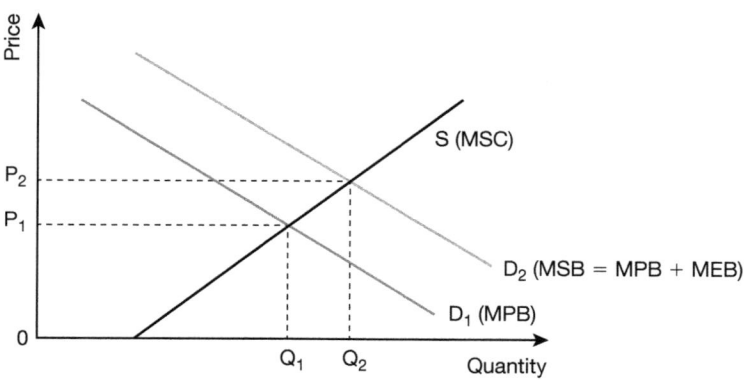

▲ **Figure 7.13** A positive externality

Negative externalities

Figure 7.14 shows a situation in which there is a **negative externality**; that is, social costs are greater than private costs. The original equilibrium position is where the supply curve, S_1, representing marginal private cost (MPC), intersects with the demand curve, D, representing marginal social benefit (MSB). However, if all of the costs are taken into account, this will be shown by the supply curve S_2, representing marginal social cost (MSC) which is made up of both marginal private cost (MPC) and marginal external cost (MEC). The effect of taking all costs and benefits into account is that the equilibrium price rises from $0P_1$ to $0P_2$ and the equilibrium quantity falls from $0Q_1$ to $0Q_2$.

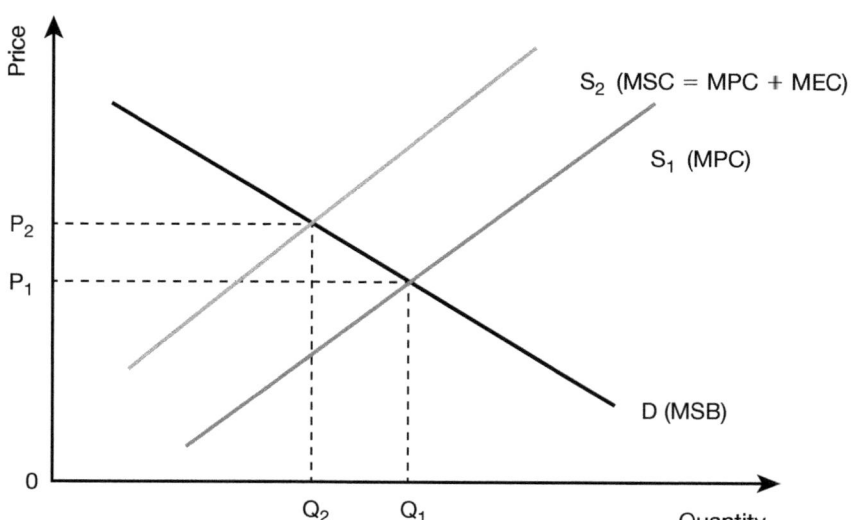

▲ **Figure 7.14** A negative externality

Key terms

Positive externality: a third party effect resulting from production or consumption that creates a benefit to a society.

Marginal social cost: the addition of marginal private cost and marginal external cost.

Marginal social benefit: the addition of marginal private benefit and marginal external benefit.

Key term

Negative externality: a third party effect resulting from either production or consumption that imposes a cost on a society which is not paid for by either the producer or the consumer.

> ★ **Exam tip**
>
> You need to remember that an externality can be either positive or negative and can refer to either consumption or production benefits or costs or to both.

> 💡 **Remember**
>
> Marginal social benefit includes both marginal private benefit and marginal external benefit. Marginal social cost includes both marginal private cost and marginal external cost.

7.4.5 Deadweight welfare losses arising from positive and negative externalities

Deadweight loss is a measure of lost economic efficiency when the socially optimal quantity of a product is not produced. Non-optimal production can be caused by a positive or a negative externality. Externalities bring about a deadweight loss as a result of the differences between marginal social cost or benefit and marginal private cost or benefit.

The deadweight loss, or welfare loss as it can also be called, is the decreased economic well-being caused by the existence of negative externalities, either in the case of a negative consumption externality or a negative production externality.

There can also be a welfare gain in relation to positive externalities, either in the case of a positive consumption externality or a positive production externality.

> **Key term**
>
> **Deadweight loss:** the loss of economic efficiency that occurs when the socially optimal quantity of a product is not produced.

7.4.6 Asymmetric information and moral hazard

Asymmetric information

Asymmetric information is a form of market failure that exists when one individual or party has much more information than another individual or party and uses that information advantage to exploit the other party. Information asymmetry therefore creates an imbalance of power, for example, when the seller of a product knows more about the good or service than the buyer.

Moral hazard

Moral hazard occurs when someone increases their exposure to risk when insured, especially when a person takes more risks because someone else bears the cost of those risks. It therefore refers to a situation in which an individual has an incentive to alter their behaviour when the potential risk is borne by others. For example, if a government promises to support businesses that are losing money, it can encourage those businesses to take greater risks.

> **Key terms**
>
> **Asymmetric information:** a situation in which there is unequal knowledge between the parties of a transaction resulting in an advantage to the party with additional knowledge.
>
> **Moral hazard:** a situation in which a person takes a decision about how much risk to take in the knowledge that someone else bears the cost of that risk.

7.4.7 The use of costs and benefits in analysing decisions

Cost-benefit analysis refers to a process that includes all the costs and benefits that relate to an investment project and which need to be considered before a decision is taken on whether or not to go ahead with the project.

> **Key term**
>
> **Cost-benefit analysis:** a method used to evaluate large-scale investment projects which takes into account all relevant costs and benefits, including both private and external costs and benefits.

There are a number of advantages associated with cost-benefit analysis, including the following:

- It takes into account all of the various costs and benefits resulting from a proposed investment project.

- Many of the various costs and benefits will have market prices attached to them, making it relatively easy to calculate monetary values.

- It can analyse not only costs and benefits today, but also future costs and benefits, enabling the long-term consequences of an investment project to be considered and not only the short-term ones.

- It helps to make it more likely that the correct decision will be taken.

However, cost-benefit analysis does have a number of potential drawbacks and limitations, including the following:

- It may be difficult to identify all of the relevant external costs and benefits to include in the analysis.

- Not all of the costs and benefits will have market prices and this will make it more difficult to calculate their monetary value.

- Shadow prices can be used where market prices do not apply, but these can be very difficult to estimate.

- The estimation of costs and benefits in the future can be a problem and this gives rise to the issue of the time value of money.

- Future values can be discounted to give present values but this may not always be easy to calculate accurately.

- Cost-benefit analysis usually relates to investment projects in the public sector, but even if the analysis suggests that there will be a net benefit to a community, there may be political reasons why the project does not go ahead.

> ★ **Exam tip**
>
> Make sure that you are able to support answers on cost-benefit analysis with appropriate examples of investment projects, such as the building of an airport, a motorway or a railway line.

> ★ **Exam tip**
>
> Knowledge of net present value is not required in relation to the use of costs and benefits in analysing decisions.

> 💡 **Remember**
>
> Remember that although cost-benefit analysis has many potential advantages, there are also a number of limitations in the use of such an analysis.

> 💡 **Remember**
>
> Cost-benefit analysis can be extremely useful in decision-making, but you need to understand that there are some important limitations to its use.

7.5 Types of cost, revenue and profit, short-run and long-run production

7.5.1 The short-run production function

The short-run production function is concerned with:

- fixed and variable factors of production

- the definition and calculation of total product, average product and marginal product

- the law of diminishing returns (the law of variable proportions).

Production function

The **production function** indicates the relationship between inputs and output over a particular time period. It shows how a given output is produced as a result of using the different factors of production involved in the production process.

Fixed and variable factors of production

In the short-run, there will be at least one **fixed factor of production**, for example, machinery. However, it will be possible to change the quantity of a **variable factor of production**, for example, raw materials , in the **short run**.

The definition and calculation of total product, average product and marginal product

It is important to be able to distinguish between these three different concepts. **Total product** is the total output that is produced from using the factors of production. **Average product** is the output per unit of the variable factor, for example, the output per worker per period of time (also known as productivity). **Marginal product** is the additional output that is produced as a result of employing one more variable factor, for example, an extra worker.

> **Key terms**
>
> **Total product:** the total output produced from a combination of factors of production (also known as total physical product).
>
> **Average product:** total product divided by the quantity of the variable factor of production, for example, labour (also known as average physical product).
>
> **Marginal product:** the addition to total product resulting from the employment of an additional unit of the variable factor of production (also known as marginal physical product).

The law of diminishing returns (or law of variable proportions)

In the short run, the process of production involves a combination of fixed and variable factors of production. Extra units of a variable factor, such as labour, can be combined with a fixed factor, such as capital equipment. As more and more units of the variable factor are employed, total output or total physical product (TPP) will continue to increase, but at a diminishing rate. This is because the marginal output or marginal physical product (MPP) and the average output or average physical product (APP), resulting from the employment of one more worker, will eventually diminish. This is known as the **law of diminishing returns** or the law of variable proportions. The relationship between APP and MPP can be seen in Figure 7.15.

> **Key term**
>
> **Production function:** the relationship between quantity of inputs of factors of production and the resulting output.

> **Key terms**
>
> **Fixed factor of production:** a resource input that exists in the short run when the quantity of factors used in the production process cannot be changed, for example, capital equipment.
>
> **Variable factor of production:** a resource input that can be varied in the short run, for example, raw materials.
>
> **Short run:** a period of time in the production process when at least one factor of production is fixed.

> **Key term**
>
> **Law of diminishing returns:** a situation in which as increasing quantities of a variable factor of production are added to fixed quantities of other factors of production, the return to the variable factor will eventually diminish (also known as the law of variable proportions).

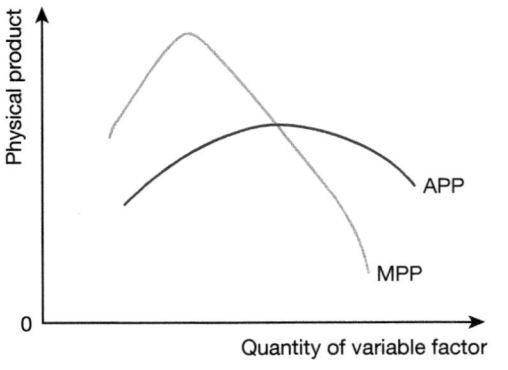

◀ **Figure 7.15** Average and marginal physical product

7.5.2 The short-run cost function

The short-run cost function is concerned with:

- the definition and calculation of fixed costs (FC) and variable costs (VC)

- the definition and calculation of total, average and marginal costs (TC, AC, MC), including average total cost (ATC), total and average fixed costs (TFC, AFC) and total and average variable costs (TVC, AVC)

- explanation of the shape of short-run average cost and marginal cost curves.

The definition and calculation of fixed costs (FC) and variable costs (VC)

It has already been pointed out that it is important to be able to distinguish between fixed and variable factors of production. It is also important to be able to distinguish between **fixed costs** (FC) and **variable costs** (VC) of production. Variable costs are costs that vary with changes in output. If output is zero, there will be no need to pay for any variable costs, such as raw materials, but as output is expanded, the variable costs of production will increase. However, even if output is zero, there are still likely to be some costs of production, such as rent or interest, and these are known as fixed costs of production. They will stay constant at all levels of output.

> **Key term**
>
> **Fixed costs:** costs that do not vary with output.
>
> **Variable costs:** costs that do vary with output

The definition and calculation of total, average and marginal costs (TC, AC, MC)

Total cost (TC) is the full cost of production and is calculated by adding together all of the costs resulting from the use of factors in the production process. Average cost (AC) refers to the cost per unit of production and is calculated by dividing the total cost of production by the number of units that are being produced. Marginal cost (MC) refers to the increase in total cost when output is increased by one additional unit and is calculated by dividing the change in total cost by the change in output.

The definition and calculation of total costs (TC), average costs (AC) and marginal costs (MC) will include:

- average total costs (ATC)
- total fixed costs (TFC)
- average fixed costs (AFC)

- total variable costs (TVC)
- average variable costs (AVC).

Explanation of the shape of short-run average cost and marginal cost curves

Figure 7.16 shows the relationship between **marginal cost, average total cost, average variable cost** and **average fixed cost.**

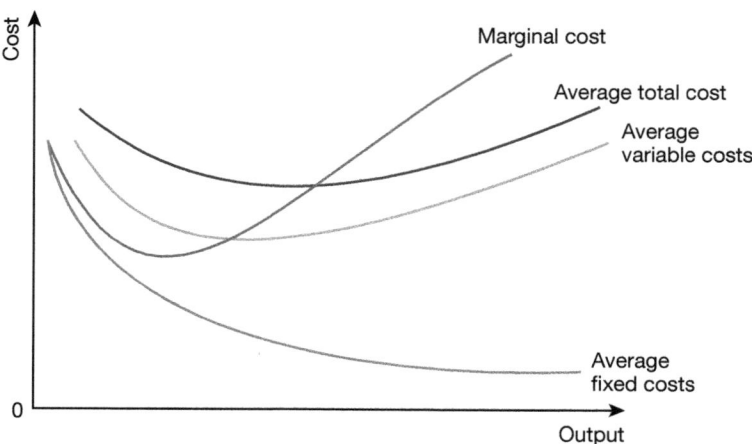

▲ **Figure 7.16** A firm's cost curves

> **Key terms**
>
> **Marginal cost:** the additional cost of producing an extra unit of a product.
>
> **Average cost:** the total cost of employing all the factor inputs divided by the number of units produced (also known as average total cost).
>
> **Average variable costs:** the variable costs of production divided by the output produced.
>
> **Average fixed costs:** the fixed costs of production divided by the output produced.

Explanation of the shape of the short-run average cost (SRAC) curve

In Figure 7.16, you can see that the shape of a firm's **short-run average cost (SRAC) curve** is U-shaped. At lower levels of output, both average variable costs and average fixed costs are falling and so average total cost falls. However, although average fixed costs are continually falling, average variable costs, beyond a certain level of output, will stop falling and start rising. This will cause average total cost to also rise as output is increased.

Key term

Short-run average cost (SRAC) curve: a curve that shows how average costs change as output changes in the period when at least one factor of production is fixed in supply.

> 💡 **Remember**
>
> - In the short run, at least one factor of production is fixed.
> - The production function shows the relationship between the factor inputs required to produce a product and the final output.
> - The law of diminishing returns shows that as increasing quantities of a variable factor are added to fixed quantities of other factors, the return to the variable factor will eventually diminish.
> - The average total cost curve, the average variable cost curve and the marginal cost curve all fall to begin with and then rise.
> - The average fixed cost curve continually falls.

> ⭐ **Exam tip**
>
> It is important to be able to draw the diagrams accurately, avoiding common errors:
> - When drawing APP and MPP curves, make sure that the two curves intersect at the maximum point of the APP curve.
> - When drawing the marginal cost curve, make sure that it crosses the average total cost curve at the minimum point; this is because when marginal cost is less than average cost, average cost will be falling, whereas when marginal cost is more than average cost, average cost will be rising.
> - The marginal cost curve will also cross the average variable cost curve at its minimum point.

7.5.3 The long-run production function

Returns to scale

The short-run production function, and the corresponding short-run costs of production, is based on the fact that there is at least one fixed factor of production. In the **long run**, however, there are no fixed factors of production; all factors of production are variable. This means that it is possible for a firm to increase output by increasing the factors of produced used in the production process.

Returns to scale refer to the relationship between a firm's level of output and the quantity of inputs needed to produce that output.

Increasing returns to scale are where output is increased by a greater increase than the increase in the factors of production, for example, factor inputs are increased by 10% and output is increased by 20%.

Constant returns to scale are where the output is increased by the same percentage as the increase in the factors of production, for example, factor inputs are increased by 10% and output is increased by 10%.

Decreasing returns to scale are where the output is increased by a smaller increase than the increase in the factors of production, for example, factor inputs are increased by 10% and output is increased by 5%.

7.5.4 The long-run cost function

In the long run, all factors of production are variable and so as a firm expands, it is able to increase the quantity of factors that were previously fixed in supply. This means that as it expands its output in the long run, it will move to a new SRAC curve. In the long run, there are potentially an infinite number of SRAC curves.

Key terms

Long run: a period of time in the production process when all factors of production are variable.

Returns to scale: the relationship between a firm's level of output and the quantity of inputs needed to produce that output.

Increasing returns to scale: a situation in which a given increase in the quantity of factor inputs leads to a greater proportionate increase in output.

Constant returns to scale: a situation in which a given increase in the quantity of factor inputs leads to an equal proportionate increase in output.

Decreasing returns to scale: a situation in which a given increase in the quantity of factor inputs leads to a smaller proportionate increase in output.

Explanation of the shape of the long-run average cost (LRAC) curve

The **long-run average cost (LRAC) curve** will actually be a combination of a series of short-run average cost curves, as can be seen in Figure 7.17. The LRAC curve joins all the points where the cost of producing a given output is at its lowest and so it is drawn as a smooth envelope curve.

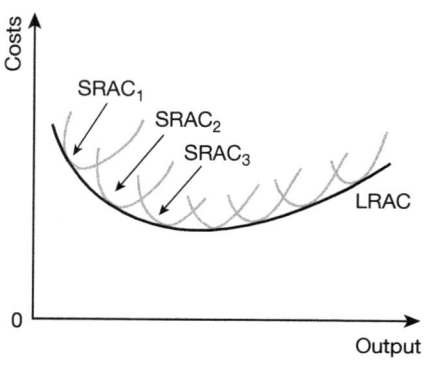

▲ **Figure 7.17** The LRAC envelope curve

The concept of minimum efficient scale

The level of output where the LRAC is first at its lowest point is known as the **minimum efficient scale** (MES); that is, achieving MES minimises long-run average total cost. It is the minimum quantity of output at which internal economies of scale are fully exploited; no further economies of scale can be achieved beyond this scale of operation.

7.5.5 The relationship between economies of scale and decreasing average costs

Declining long-run average costs are the result of **economies of scale**; that is, as the level of output increases, the long-run average cost of production decreases. This can be seen in Figure 7.18.

> **Key term**
>
> **Minimum efficient scale:** the level of output at which the lowest average cost curve begins.
>
> **Economies of scale:** reductions in long-run average cost (LRAC) as the scale of production increases. There can be both internal and external economies of scale.

> **Key term**
>
> **Long-run average cost (LRAC) curve:** a curve that shows how average costs change as output changes in the period when the supply of all factors of production can be increased.

7.5.6 Internal and external economies of scale

It is possible to distinguish between internal and external economies of scale.

Internal economies of scale

Internal economies of scale include:

- **financial**
- purchasing/bulk buying
- managerial
- **technical economies** of **increased or large dimensions**/division of labour/large capital equipment
- research and development
- marketing
- **risk-bearing**/diversification
- economies of scope.

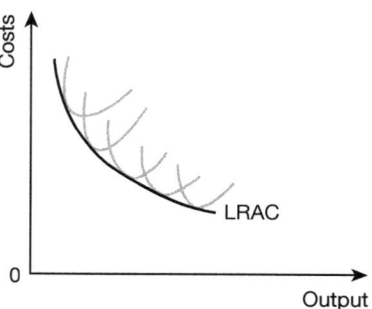

▲ **Figure 7.18** The relationship between economies of scale and decreasing costs

> **Key terms**
>
> **Internal economies of scale:** reductions in LRAC as a result of a firm itself increasing the scale of production.
>
> **Financial economies of scale:** reductions in LRAC resulting from large firms having access to a wider range of sources of finance and on more preferential terms than small firms because they are seen by the financial service providers as a lower risk.
>
> **Technical economies:** reductions in LRAC as a result of the improvements and innovations in the production process as a firm increases the scale of production.
>
> **Economies of increased dimensions:** reductions in LRAC that arise as the result of increasing the size of a container. Increasing the surface area will lead to a greater increase in volume, leading to a reduction in unit costs.
>
> **Risk-bearing economies of scale:** as a firm grows in size, it is able to move into other product areas and markets which reduces the risks associated with a decline in any one of them.

External economies of scale

Whereas internal economies of scale refer to the potential advantages of a firm growing in size, **external economies of scale** refer to the potential advantages to all firms in an industry, including:

- concentration/development of support or ancillary firms in a particular area

- transport and infrastructure

- specialised labour/specialist skills

- knowledge/specialist research and marketing agencies/specific courses in colleges and universities.

Key term

External economies of scale: reductions in LRAC as a result of the industry increasing in size.

7.5.7 Internal and external diseconomies of scale

Figure 7.18 showed the relationship between economies of scale and decreasing costs of production. However, if a firm increases output beyond a certain level, costs may stop decreasing and may even to start to rise. Such a situation is known as **diseconomies of scale** and can be seen in Figure 7.19 where the U-shaped LRAC curve can be seen as first decreasing and then, beyond a certain level of output, increasing.

Key term

Diseconomies of scale: increases in LRAC as the scale of production increases. There can be both internal and external diseconomies of scale.

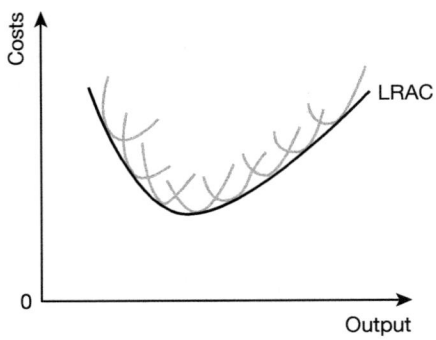

◀ **Figure 7.19** The U-shaped LRAC curve showing decreasing and increasing costs

As with economies of scale, it is possible to distinguish between internal and external diseconomies of scale.

Internal diseconomies of scale

Internal diseconomies of scale include:

- poor communication/slower communication

- lower levels of efficiency/productivity

- lower levels of motivation/alienation/boredom/workers distanced from management

- greater frequency of industrial disputes

- poor management/greater complexity of organisation/difficulties of co-ordination and monitoring of performance

- less flexibility/slow response to changing market conditions.

External diseconomies of scale

External diseconomies of scale refer to situations in which all firms in an industry may be negatively affected, including:

- greater competition for limited inputs/higher cost of inputs

- greater congestion/increase in costs/reduced efficiency.

Key terms

Internal diseconomies of scale: increases in LRAC as a result of a firm itself increasing the scale of production.

External diseconomies of scale: increases in LRAC as a result of the industry increasing in size.

> ★ **Exam tip**
>
> Make sure you do not think that only large firms are able to gain economies of scale; all firms, whatever their size, are able to benefit from economies of scale.

> ★ **Exam tip**
>
> It is important to understand that in the short run, the way in which average costs vary with output is determined by the law of diminishing returns, but in the long run it is determined by the existence of economies of scale and diseconomies of scale.

> 💡 **Remember**
>
> Both economies of scale and diseconomies of scale can be separated into internal and external economies and diseconomies.

7.5.8 The definition and calculation of revenue: total, average and marginal revenue

It is important to be able to distinguish between the three different forms of revenue. **Total revenue** refers to all the money received from the sales of a product. **Average revenue** refers to the total revenue obtained from selling a product divided by the number of units sold. **Marginal revenue** refers to the extra or additional revenue received when one more unit of a product is sold.

> **Key terms**
>
> **Total revenue:** the total amount of income received from the sales of a product.
>
> **Average revenue:** the revenue per unit of a product sold.
>
> **Marginal revenue:** the addition to total revenue when sales of a product are increased by one additional unit.

7.5.9 The definition of normal, subnormal and supernormal profit

Profit is defined as the difference between the total revenue (TR) received by a firm and the total costs (TC) involved in producing what is sold; that is, it is equal to total revenue minus total costs.

It is possible to distinguish between normal profit, subnormal and supernormal profit.

Normal profit refers to the amount of profit that needs to be made by a firm to stay in a particular market and to carry on doing what it is already doing. It represents the opportunity cost of a particular line of business, that is, the profit that can be earned in the next most profitable enterprise. It is included in the average cost curve of a firm.

Subnormal profit is any profit less than normal profit. It is where average cost is greater than price. In the short run, a firm will continue producing while making subnormal profit, as long as the average variable cost (AVC) is covered. However, in the long run, the firm will close down.

Supernormal profit (also known as abnormal profit) is where a firm makes a profit that is over and above normal profit. Whereas normal profit is included in the average cost curve of a firm, supernormal/abnormal profit can be explicitly shown in diagrams as a particular area.

> **Key terms**
>
> **Profit:** the difference between total revenue (TR) and total cost (TC).
>
> **Normal profit:** the amount of profit that can be made by a firm in the next most profitable enterprise.
>
> **Subnormal profit:** any profit that is less than normal profit.
>
> **Supernormal profit:** the amount of profit made by a firm in excess of normal profit; it is also known as abnormal profit.

> 💡 **Remember**
>
> Normal profit is included in the average cost of a firm and so cannot be shown in a diagram. Subnormal or supernormal profit, on the other hand, can be explicitly shown in a diagram.

7.5.10 The calculation of supernormal and subnormal profit

Supernormal profit

Supernormal profit occurs when total revenue is greater than total cost and is calculated by total revenue minus total costs (including both the fixed and the variable costs). The total costs include a reward to all the factors, including normal profit.

Subnormal profit

Subnormal profit occurs when total cost is greater than total revenue and is calculated by total revenue minus total cost. As total cost is greater than total revenue, this will give a negative figure.

7.6 Different market structures

7.6.1 Perfect competition and imperfect competition

Perfect competition

The characteristics of **perfect competition** include the following:

- There are many buyers and sellers.

- The buyers and sellers are price takers, that is, they have to accept the price prevailing in a market (the price is determined through the interaction of demand for, and supply of, the product) and cannot influence it in any way.

- There is perfect knowledge among the producers and consumers, so that they know what is for sale and at what price.

- The product is homogeneous, that is, all products are identical and there is no **product differentiation**.

- There are no **barriers to entry or exit**, so that firms can enter or leave the industry in the long run.

- There is perfect mobility of factors of production in the long run; that is, there is a perfectly elastic supply of all factors of production.

- There are no transport costs.

- All producers have access to the same technology.

- Each firm in the industry faces a perfectly elastic demand curve for its product, although the demand curve for the industry is downward sloping from left to right.

- It is assumed that firms in the industry aim to maximise their profits.

- Only normal profit can be earned in the long run, although supernormal/abnormal profit can be earned in the short run.

- Consumers are indifferent as to which firm they buy a product from; that is, there is no brand loyalty.

- Both consumer surplus and producer surplus are at a maximum.

- The industry is allocatively efficient.

Key terms

Perfect competition: a market or industry that consists of many virtually identical firms which all accept the market price in the industry.

Product differentiation: the process of creating real or perceived differences between products.

Barriers to entry and exit: the various obstacles and restrictions that can make it very difficult, or even impossible, for firms to enter or exit an industry.

Although a firm can make normal profit in a perfectly competitive industry in the short run, it is also possible that it could make supernormal/abnormal profit or subnormal profit, which is profit that is less than normal profit, in the short run.

Figure 7.20 shows a firm in perfect competition that has made supernormal/abnormal profit in the short run.

The supernormal/abnormal profit is shown by the area CPAB. This will attract new firms into the industry, reducing the market price from $0P_1$ to $0P$, and the supernormal/abnormal profit will be eliminated so that only normal profit will exist.

Figure 7.21 shows a firm in perfect competition that has made subnormal profit in the short run.

The subnormal profit is shown by the area PABC. This will cause firms to exit the industry, increasing the price from $0P$ to $0P_1$, and the subnormal profit will be eliminated so that only normal profit will exist.

Figure 7.22 shows a firm in perfect competition that is making normal profit.

Figure 7.22 also shows the long-run equilibrium for the firm and the industry in perfect competition where all firms in the industry are making normal profit.

> ### Remember
>
> - The long-run equilibrium for the firm in perfect competition is:
>
> $MC = MR = AC = AR$
>
>   The firms in the industry are both productively efficient
>
>   (P = minimum AC) and allocatively efficient (P = MC).
>
> - The long-run equilibrium for the industry in perfect competition is that there is no tendency for the number of firms in the industry to change.

Imperfect competition

Imperfect competition includes a number of different types of market structure, including:

- monopoly
- monopolistic competition
- oligopoly
- natural monopoly.

Monopoly

The characteristics of **monopoly** include the following:

- There is one firm in an industry, that is, one single seller.
- Legally, a monopoly can also be defined in terms of a particular percentage of market share, for example, 25%.
- A monopoly is a price maker, not a price taker.
- There are no substitutes for the product being sold by the monopolist.
- Strong barriers to entry make it very difficult, if not impossible, for new firms to enter the industry.
- Supernormal/abnormal profits can be made in both the short run and long run.
- The demand for the firm's product is also the market or industry demand, so the demand curve for both the firm and the industry is down sloping from left to right.
- Marginal revenue is always less than average revenue.
- It is assumed that the firm aims to maximise its profits.

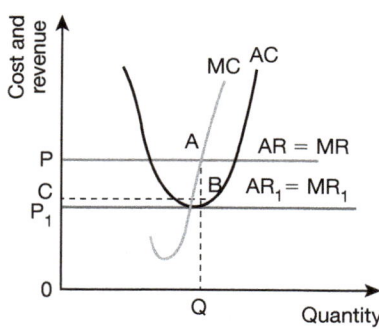

▲ **Figure 7.20** A firm making supernormal/abnormal profit in the short run

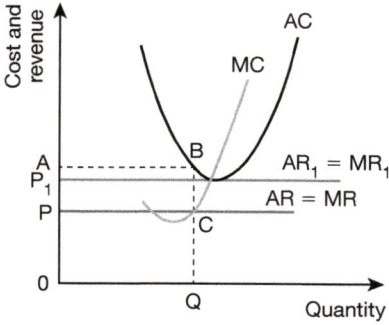

▲ **Figure 7.21** A firm making subnormal profit in the short run

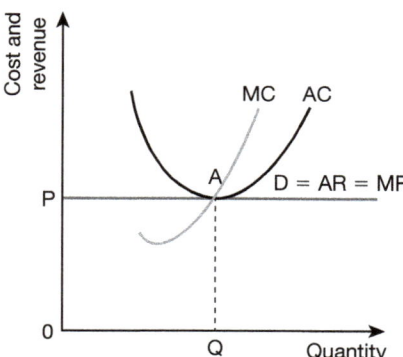

▲ **Figure 7.22** A firm making normal profit in a perfectly competitive industry

> ### Remember
>
> Although perfect competition does not exist in the real world, it provides a very useful 'ideal type' model which can be used to compare firms and industries that do exist in the real world.

> ### Key terms
>
> **Imperfect competition:** a type of market that lacks some, or all, of the features of perfect competition.
>
> **Monopoly:** a market in which there is only one supplier.

Figure 7.23 shows the equilibrium price and equilibrium quantity for a profit-maximising monopoly firm. The monopolist is a price maker and so faces downward sloping demand (AR) and marginal revenue (MR) curves. The profit maximising output is at 0Q where marginal cost (MC) is equal to marginal revenue (MR). The price is 0P, but the cost is 0C, so the firm is able to make supernormal/abnormal profits of CPAB. These can exist in the long run as well as the short run due to the very strong barriers that make it difficult for new firms to enter the industry.

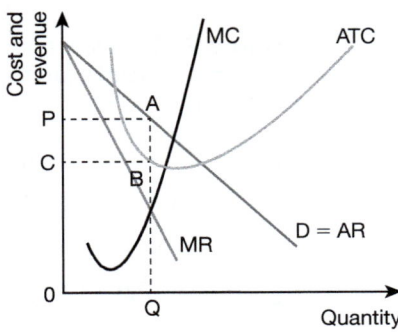

◀ **Figure 7.23** Equilibrium price and equilibrium quantity for a profit-maximising monopoly firm

> 💡 **Remember**
>
> Barriers to entry into a market can include:
>
> - high start-up costs
> - control of sources of supply
> - copyrights and patents
> - legal protection
> - economies of scale
> - brand loyalty
> - mergers and takeovers
> - location.

> ★ **Exam tip**
>
> The monopoly diagram is often drawn incorrectly. Make sure you realise that the equilibrium price and equilibrium quantity positions are determined by where MC and MR intersect. This is the profit maximisation position. The MC curve crosses the ATC curve at its minimum point. The cost of production is determined where the ATC curve is directly below where the horizontal price line meets the AR curve.

Monopolistic competition

The characteristics of **monopolistic competition** include the following:

- There are a large number of firms in the industry.
- There are a large number of consumers.
- Products are differentiated and not homogeneous or identical.
- Each firm in the industry faces a downward sloping demand curve.
- Demand for a product is relatively, but not perfectly, price elastic (much more elastic than is the case in monopoly).
- There is a great deal of advertising of products in the industry to develop brand loyalty.
- There are no barriers to entry or exit, so firms can enter or leave the industry in the long run.
- Only normal profits can be earned in the industry in the long run.
- It is assumed that firms in the industry aim to maximise their profits.

In the short run, a firm in monopolistic competition can make supernormal/abnormal profit, but as there are no barriers to entry, this will attract new firms into the industry so the supernormal/abnormal profits are competed away. In the long run, only normal profits will be earned as can be seen in Figure 7.24.

> **Key term**
>
> **Monopolistic competition:** a market with many firms producing similar, but differentiated, products.

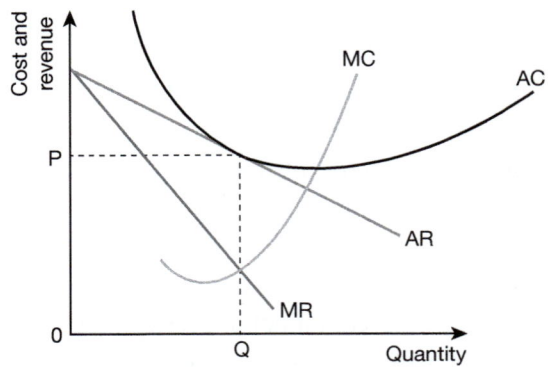

▲ **Figure 7.24** Long-run equilibrium for a firm in monopolistic competition

★ **Exam tip**

The demand or AR curves in monopoly and in monopolistic competition are often drawn the same, but the D or AR curve in monopolistic competition should show that the demand curve is significantly more elastic in monopolistic competition than in monopoly.

★ **Exam tip**

Make sure you do not use the term 'monopolistic' in a confusing way that makes it difficult to understand whether a firm in monopoly or a firm in monopolistic competition is being referred to. Make sure that you make it very clear which firm you are referring to in the exam.

Oligopoly

The characteristics of **oligopoly** include the following:

- There are only a small number of firms in the market (sometimes there might be only two firms, in which case it is called a duopoly).

- There are differentiated, not homogeneous, products.

- Great use is made of advertising to create and maintain brand loyalty.

- Barriers to entry make it very difficult for new firms to enter the industry.

- Firms can make supernormal/abnormal profits in both the short run and the long run.

- There could be a mixture of price makers and price takers.

- The firms are mutually interdependent.

- There could be a degree of **collusion** between firms operating in a cartel.

- There is a kinked demand curve.

- There is a great deal of price stability/rigidity.

One characteristic of a firm in oligopoly is that it faces a kinked demand curve. This occurs because in oligopoly, firms try to anticipate the reactions of rival firms to their actions. It is assumed that if an oligopolistic firm increases its price, other firms in the market will not follow and so demand above the kink is elastic. However, it can also be assumed that if an oligopolistic firm reduces its price, other firms in the market will follow and so demand below the kink is inelastic.

The **kinked demand curve** can be seen in Figure 7.25. It is a characteristic of a **non-collusive oligopoly**. One key feature of the diagram is that there is a discontinuity in the marginal revenue (MR) curve. Changes in marginal cost (MC) between MC_1 and MC_3 do not change the profit maximising price and output; that is, prices are likely to be relatively fixed despite changes in cost.

Key terms

Oligopoly: a market that is dominated by a few firms which are mutually interdependent.

Collusion: a situation in which firms come together to fix prices and output in a market; collusion can be either formal or informal.

Kinked demand curve: a feature of a non-collusive oligopoly where an individual firm believes that other firms will not follow a price increase, but will follow a price decrease so that the demand curve will be elastic for any price increase and inelastic for any price decrease so that it will therefore be kinked at the current price.

Non-collusive oligopoly: one model of monopoly in which firms do not collude.

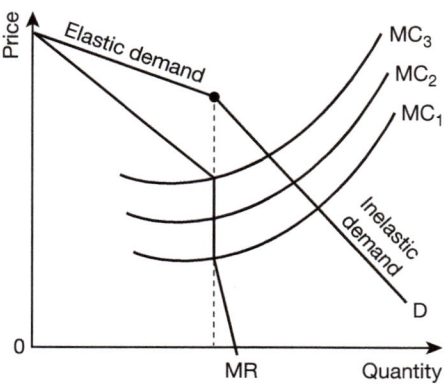

◀ **Figure 7.25** The kinked demand curve

In addition to the non-collusive oligopoly, there is also a collusive oligopoly. Collusion between such oligopolistic firms can be formal or informal, and if it is formal, it can involve the creation of a cartel which is an agreement between firms to fix price and output in a market. This situation can be seen in Figure 7.26 where the profit maximising position is where MC = MR.

There are a number of conditions necessary for a cartel to operate successfully as a **collusive oligopoly** and these include the following:

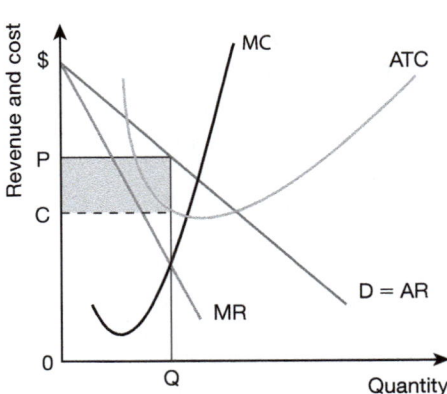
▲ **Figure 7.26**   Collusive oligopoly

- A limited number of firms in the industry, all of whom are members of the cartel, making it easier to share information and to keep a check on each other

- A similar cost structure for all firms

- Relatively high barriers to entry to prevent new firms entering the industry

- All firms are expected to obey the rules of the cartel

- A relatively stable market

- The firms in the cartel produce identical, or very similar, products which will make price agreements easier to establish

> **Key term**
>
> **Collusive oligopoly:** one model of oligopoly in which firms do collude, often through the existence of a cartel.

> ★ **Exam tip**
>
> Be careful not to confuse a non-collusive and a collusive oligopoly, stating incorrectly that the kinked demand curve is a feature of a collusive oligopoly, rather than a feature of a non-collusive oligopoly. Another common error is to describe the demand curve in a non-collusive oligopoly as kinky, rather than kinked.

> ★ **Exam tips**
>
> - Make sure you understand that with a kinked demand curve, demand is price elastic above the kink and price inelastic below the kink.
>
> - Also, ensure you understand that the marginal revenue curve in a non-collusive oligopoly is discontinuous; that is, there can be a change in cost but this will not necessarily bring about a change in price or output.

Natural monopoly

A **natural monopoly** exists when a single supplier has a very significant cost advantage as a result of being in a monopoly situation. If competition existed, there would be an increase in the costs of production. It is therefore advantageous for a natural monopoly to continue in existence because it will avoid the extra costs that will come about as the result of a duplication of resources. In a natural monopoly, it may well be that one firm will be able to benefit from sufficient economies of scale to satisfy the level of demand more efficiently than two or more firms. A natural monopoly will usually have relatively high start-up costs and because they experience economies of scale over most of their production, the minimum efficient scale of production is only achieved at an extremely high level of output.

> **Key term**
>
> **Natural monopoly:** an industry or service that is most efficient when run as a monopoly because the average costs would be higher if the market was shared by more than one supplier.

Figure 7.27 shows the situation for a natural monopoly. The long-run average total cost (LRATC) curve is downward sloping throughout its length and the long-run marginal cost (LRMC) curve is always below it. The profit maximising output is at 0Q, but this output will not enable the full benefits of the economies of scale to be achieved. It would therefore be better if output was $0Q_1$, which is allocatively efficient, but this would mean that the firm operated at a loss and so either the government would need to take the natural monopoly into state ownership or it would need to provide it with a subsidy.

> 💡 **Remember**
>
> A situation of natural monopoly is where the advantages of a monopoly outweigh the disadvantages.

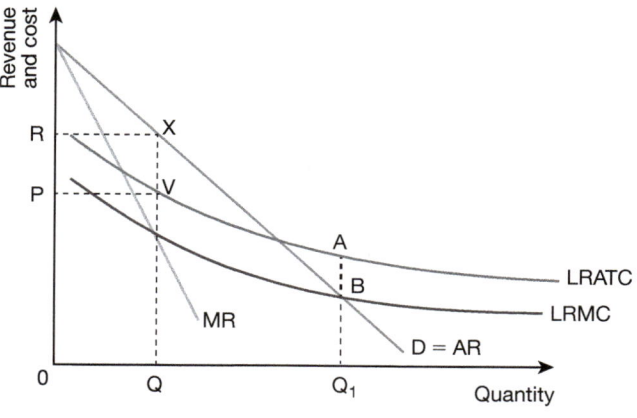

▲ **Figure 7.27** Natural monopoly

7.6.2 The structure of the markets as explained by the number of buyers and sellers, product differentiation, the degree of freedom of entry and the availability of information

It is possible to distinguish between the structure of different markets according to:

- the number of buyers and sellers
- product differentiation
- the degree of freedom of entry
- the availability of information.

	Perfect competition	Monopoly	Monopolistic competition	Oligopoly
Number of sellers	Many	One	Varied, but not too many	Few
Product differentiation	Homogeneous	No close substitutes	Differentiated	Varied
Freedom of entry	Not restricted	High barriers to entry	Not restricted	Some barriers to entry
Availability of information	Perfect knowledge	Incomplete	Incomplete	Incomplete

7.6.3 Barriers to entry and exit

Barriers to entry into, and exit from, markets are the various factors that can prevent firms, or make it difficult for them, to enter or leave a market. The existence of barriers to entry and exit make a market less competitive; the greater the barriers that exist, the less competitive a market will be.

There are a number of barriers to entry and exit, including the following:

- **Legal barriers:** a patent can act as a legal barrier to entry into a market because other firms will not have permission to produce and sell a particular product.
- **Market barriers:** in some markets, a great deal of money is spent on establishing a strong brand image and the expense of such advertising could act as a barrier to entry.
- **Cost barriers:** economies of scale occur when increased output leads to lower average costs and so new firms, with relatively low output, will experience relatively higher costs and this can act as a barrier to entry.

- **Physical barriers:** some countries will have supplies of a particular product, but other countries will not, for example, oil reserves are only found in certain countries and the absence of such resources will act as a barrier to entry into this market.

In terms of comparing the structure of different markets, there are no barriers to entry or exit for firms in perfect competition, monopolistic competition or contestable markets, but there are some barriers to entry and exit in oligopoly and many barriers to entry and exit in monopoly.

7.6.4 The performance of firms in different market structures

The performance of firms can be compared in a number of different ways.

Revenues and revenue curves

The AR and MR curves will be horizontal in perfect competition, but will be downward sloping in monopolistic competition, oligopoly, monopoly and natural monopoly, with the MR curve below the AR curve (in oligopoly, the AR curve will be kinked and the MR curve will be discontinuous).

Output in the short run and the long run

The profit maximising output in all of the market structures will be determined where MC = MR.

Profits in the short run and the long run

Firms can make supernormal/abnormal profit, normal profit and subnormal profit, but in perfect competition, monopolistic competition and contestable markets only normal profit can be made in the long run, whereas in oligopoly and monopoly supernormal/abnormal profit can continue to be made in the long run.

The shutdown price in the short run and the long run

A firm can make subnormal profits in the short run and continue in production as long as average variable costs are being covered, otherwise it will be forced to shut down; in the long run, a firm will need to make at least a normal profit, that is, price will need to equal average cost.

The derivation of a firm's supply curve in a perfectly competitive market

In the short run, a firm's supply curve in perfect competition is its marginal cost curve above the point where it intersects the AVC curve; in the long run, a firm's supply curve in perfect competition is its marginal cost curve above the point where it intersects the ATC curve, that is, equal to or above its break-even point.

Efficiency and X-inefficiency in the short run and the long run: firms in perfect competition are **efficient** in the long run in terms of both productive efficiency and allocative efficiency; this is not the case in the other market structures where there is **X-inefficiency**; that is, production is not at the minimum average cost and price is not equal to marginal cost because of a lack of competition in an industry and a situation of organisational slack in a firm.

> **Key terms**
>
> **Efficiency:** the use of resources in the most economical or optimal way possible.
>
> **X-inefficiency:** the inefficiency that can occur in a monopoly when production is not at the lowest point on the average total cost curve; it is where production takes place at a cost above the average cost curve and the marginal cost curve due to a lack of strong competition in an industry and because of organisational slack in a firm.

Contestable markets: features and implications

The characteristics and implications of **contestable markets** include the following:

- There are no barriers to entry or exit; entry into a contestable market is relatively easy (in a perfectly contestable market, the costs of entry and exit are zero).

- The product being produced in the market is relatively standardised and any new firms entering the market will have access to the same technology as firms already established in the market.

- The low entry and exit barriers mean that the market may suffer from **hit and run competition** where firms enter the market when profits are relatively high and leave when profits are relatively low.

- Firms already in a contestable market continually face the threat of competition, making them behave as if these potential firms were already operating in the market; this means that although there may only be a few firms in a contestable market, they act in a competitive way (therefore, it is not the number of firms in the market that is important, but the threat of potential competition from new firms possibly entering the market).

- This puts pressure on the firms to be efficient.

- Supernormal/abnormal profits can be made in the short run, but only normal profits in the long run, as new firms are attracted by the abnormal profits to enter the market.

- There will be no, or relatively low, **sunk costs**, that is, costs that are already invested in a market and cannot be recovered.

- There is no collusion between existing firms in the market.

 Remember

The lower the entry and exit costs, the more contestable the market will be.

Key terms

Contestable market: a market in which there is the threat of potential competition in the future, in which case even though an existing firm may currently have a monopoly position, it may decide to act more like a perfectly competitive firm in order to deter such competition.

Hit and run competition: a situation in which firms enter a contestable market when profits are relatively high and leave it when profits are relatively low.

Sunk costs: costs which were paid when a firm entered a market and are non-recoverable when it leaves, for example, the costs of research and development.

 Remember

The key feature of a contestable market is not the number of firms that are operating in the market, but the threat of competition from new firms entering the market. This makes the firms behave in a competitive manner, even if there is very little competition in the market.

Price competition and non-price competition

Price competition: there is price competition in perfect competition where buyers and sellers are price takers, but there is a greater degree of price rigidity in oligopoly and monopoly firms are price makers, subject to the demand curve; that is, a monopoly firm can determine price, but not how much will be demanded at that price.

Non-price competition: firms in monopolistic competition and oligopoly compete through various forms of non-price competition a great deal, including:

- the use of advertising and product promotion
- the creation and maintenance of brand loyalty
- sales promotions, such as BOGOF ('buy one, get one free')
- the control of the distribution of products to particular retail outlets
- distinctive packaging
- differences in quality or design.

Key term

Non-price competition: alternatives to price reductions as methods used by firms to increase sales and market share, for example, advertising, after-sales service.

Collusion and the Prisoner's Dilemma in oligopolistic markets, including a two-player Pay-off Matrix

Collusion

Collusion between firms is a particular characteristic of an oligopoly market structure and it can either be of a formal or an informal nature

The behavioural analysis approach to the decision-making of a firm has introduced **game theory** to economic analysis, such as in relation to the **Prisoner's Dilemma** and the **two-player Pay-off Matrix**.

The Prisoner's Dilemma

This is an example of game theory where there is a competitive situation in which attempts by two or more individuals or firms to find the best strategy for themselves by acting independently results in a final outcome that is worse than if they had colluded or worked co-operatively. The dilemma is that the best outcome would be to co-operate or collude, but if it is not possible to communicate, collusion becomes impossible. Even if collusion had been possible, two individuals would need to trust the other person to stick to any deal that had been agreed.

The two-player Pay-off Matrix

In game theory, the possible strategies for each individual, or player in the game, can be shown in a matrix that shows the possible outcomes (or pay-offs) for the two players of their respective strategies or decisions.

> **★ Exam tip**
>
> Game theory is an interesting aspect of the increasing importance given to the behavioural analysis approach to the decision-making of a firm and you should be prepared to include examples of it in any answers to questions on a firm's decision-making.

> **★ Exam tip**
>
> You need to be able to make comparisons of the performance of firms using a number of criteria.

7.6.5 The definition and calculation of the concentration ratio

The **concentration ratio** in a market shows the percentage in a particular industry that is accounted for by a certain number of firms. For example, six firms in a particular market might have a 90% share of the market between them. The concentration ratio can be used in any market, but it is particularly associated with an oligopoly market structure.

> **💡 Remember**
>
> A concentration ratio does not have to relate to a specific number of firms in a market. It can apply, for example, to four, five or six firms in a market. What it shows is that if it is related to a four-firm concentration ratio, it measures the proportion of the output produced by the four largest firms in the market.

Key terms

Game theory: the analysis of strategies and decision-making by rational players in any activity or situation in which those involved know that their decision will have an impact on other players and the way that these other players are expected to react will affect the original decision made.

Prisoner's Dilemma: in game theory, a competitive situation in which attempts by two or more individuals or firms to find the best strategy for themselves by acting independently results in a final outcome that is worse than if they had colluded or worked co-operatively.

Two-player Pay-off matrix: in game theory, a table or matrix that shows the outcomes (pay-offs) for the players of their respective strategies or decisions.

Key term

Small firm: a designation for firms of a certain size which fall below certain criteria such as annual turnover, the number of employees or the total value of assets.

7.7 The growth and survival of firms

7.7.1 The reasons for different sizes of firms

Economies usually contain a mixture of different sized firms. There are many reasons for the growth of firms, including the following:

- **To decrease costs:** to take advantage of possible economies of scale, leading to a decrease in the costs of production of a firm.

- **To reduce risk:** to be stronger and therefore safer from a hostile takeover or merger proposal (in the case of a firm becoming larger through external growth).

- **To increase profits:** a larger firm may be able to gain greater profitability.

- **To fulfil management objectives:** a possible desire of owners and/or managers to expand.

- **To dominate a market:** to take advantage of opportunities to gain increased sales from a larger market share.

Despite the potential advantages of large firms, however, a number of **small firms** continue to exist in many economies. The reasons for the continued existence of small firms include the following:

- The size of the market served by the firms is small.

- The market may be highly localised.

- The firm may operate in a very specific niche market, for example, producing customised products.

- The firm is providing customers with a service that requires personal attention.

- The firm may only have recently started and so is relatively small at the moment, for example, many large firms today started off relatively small before expanding.

- The owners of the firm may have made a deliberate decision to keep it small, for example, an individual's desire to be their own boss.

- Small firms may receive specific financial support from governments in some countries.

- Small firms may be relatively more flexible in responding to changes in demand and in changes in consumer tastes and preferences.

- Small firms may be more innovative and pioneering.

- A small firm may be unable to grow because of the difficulties involved in raising the necessary funds to finance any expansion.

- In some industries, the process of 'contracting out' may lead to an increase in the demand for small firms.

- Small ancillary firms may have a key role to play in some industries in supplying specialised component parts to larger firms.

- A small firm may be more efficient than a large firm, for example, labour relations may be better and so there is less likelihood of industrial disputes in a small firm.

- The start-up costs for a small firm are likely to be significantly less than for a large firm, making them easier to start economic activity.

> **Key term**
>
> **Small firm:** a designation for firms of a certain size which fall below certain criteria such as annual turnover, the number of employees or the total value of assets.

7.7.2 The internal growth of firms

It is important to be able to distinguish between the internal and external growth of firms. The internal, or organic, growth of a firm comes about as a result of a firm increasing in size through producing and selling more products. This can come about as the result of diversification where a firm widens its production in order to be able to sell its products in a range of different markets.

> **Remember**
>
> The criteria that determines whether a particular firm should be described as small or not will vary from country to country.

The extent of the growth of a firm can be measured through a number of ways, including:

- the volume of sales

- sales revenue (also known as sales turnover)

- the number of employees

- market share

- the amount of profit.

7.7.3 The external growth of firms

Mergers and takeovers

The external growth of a firm comes about as a result of integration where two or more firms combine together. This process can take the form of a **merger**, **takeover** or **acquisition**. A merger is where two or more firms combine as a result of mutual agreement. This is in contrast to a takeover or acquisition which usually involves some form of hostile bid by one firm for another.

The methods of integration

There are different methods of integration, including the following:

- **Horizontal integration**: this is when two or more firms at the same stage of the production process join together; an example would be where two or more financial services providers integrate.

- **Vertical integration**: this is when two or more firms at different stages of the production process join together; there are two types of vertical integration.

- **Backward vertical integration**: this is where the integration involves going back to an earlier stage in the production process, such as when it is necessary to secure sufficient supplies of raw materials; an example would be a tyre manufacturer taking over a rubber plantation.

- **Forward vertical integration**: this is where the integration involves going forward to a later stage in the production process, such as when it is necessary to secure sufficient distribution of the finished product; an example would be a car manufacturer taking over a garage.

- **Conglomerate integration**: whereas horizontal and vertical integration involve firms joining together that are operating in the same industry, conglomerate integration is where two or more firms that are operating in entirely different industries join together. The reason for this form of integration is to spread risk by operating in more than one industry, a process known as **diversification**. It has already been pointed out that conglomerate integration is different from horizontal and vertical integration in that it brings together firms that are operating in different industries and not simply at different stages of the production process in the same industry. A strategy of diversification by a firm is designed to reduce risk by becoming involved in a number of industries which are unlikely to all change in the same direction. The aim of diversification is to reduce the risk that a firm is exposed to and this should produce a more consistent performance under a wide range of different economic conditions.

> **Key terms**
>
> **Merger:** a process whereby two or more firms come together under one management.
>
> **Takeover:** a process whereby a firm makes a bid to assume control of another firm, often by purchasing a majority stake in the firm. It is possible to distinguish between a welcome takeover and a hostile takeover.
>
> **Acquisition:** a process whereby a firm buys most, if not all, of another firm to assume control of it. It occurs when a firm buys more than 50% ownership in another firm.
>
> **M and A activity:** merger and acquisition activity that involves transactions in which the ownership of firms is transferred or combined.

> **Key terms**
>
> **Internal growth:** an increase in the size of a particular firm without involving any other firm; this process is also referred to as organic growth.
>
> **External growth:** an increase in the size of a particular firm through a process of integration with other firms.
>
> **Integration:** the joining together of two or more firms through a merger, a takeover or an acquisition; the integration can take a number of different forms.
>
> **Horizontal integration:** the integration of two or more firms at the same stage of production.
>
> **Vertical integration:** the integration of two or more firms at different stages of production. It can involve either backward vertical integration or forward vertical integration.
>
> **Backward vertical integration:** this is where a firm joins with another firm at an earlier stage of the production process.
>
> **Forward vertical integration:** this is where a firm joins with another firm at a later stage of the production process.
>
> **Conglomerate integration:** the integration of two or more firms which are operating in completely different markets rather than at different stages of the same market.
>
> **Diversification:** a situation in which a firm decides to operate in a number of different markets to spread risk.

★ Exam tip

★ Exam tip

If there is a question in the exam about integration, make sure that you write about all three types of integration, that is, horizontal integration, vertical integration (including both backward vertical integration and forward vertical integration) and conglomerate integration. It is also helpful to be able to include relevant examples of each type of integration to show that you clearly understand the differences between the various types of integration.

★ Exam tip

Make sure you do not describe conglomerate integration as a form of integration that is very similar to horizontal or vertical integration. It is very different. Conglomerate integration brings together firms that are operating in different industries and not firms that are operating in the same industry, as is the case with horizontal and vertical integration.

The reasons for integration

There are a number of possible reasons for the growth of firms through integration, including:

- to benefit from possible economies of scale, leading to a decrease in the average costs of production of a firm

- to be a stronger economic entity and therefore safer from a hostile takeover proposal

- to take advantage of opportunities to benefit from a larger market share, such as increased profitability

- the possible desire of the owners and/or managers to expand.

The consequences of integration

There are a number of possible consequences of integration, including the following:

- **Economies of scale:** integration enables firms to take advantage of different economies of scale, such as the cost savings associated with marketing and technology; this will enable them to keep costs and prices down.

- **Rationalisation:** the process of eliminating those parts of the operation of a business that are inefficient and unprofitable and integration could help to bring this about.

- **Sharing of knowledge:** integration enables knowledge to be shared and this could reduce or remove elements of asymmetric information.

- **Strength:** integration could send out a signal to other firms not to attempt a takeover bid.

- **Research and development:** integration may enable more funds to be allocated to research and development so that new innovative products can be produced, increasing the competitiveness and profitability of the business in the long run.

7.7.4 Cartels

Cartels have already been referred to in the context of a collusive oligopoly market structure when it was pointed out that there could be a degree of collusion between firms in an oligopoly market, operating together through a cartel.

> **Key term**
>
> **Cartel:** a formal agreement between firms to collude to fix prices and output in a market.

The conditions for an effective cartel

A cartel is a grouping of producers that work together to defend their shared interests. Cartels are created when a few large producers decide to collude, for example, to fix prices for members so that competition on price is avoided. They can also restrict output released onto the market. An example of such a cartel is OPEC, the Organisation of the Petroleum Exporting Countries. It was established in 1960 and consists of 13 countries. It controls about 50% of global oil production and about 80% of the world's oil reserves.

There are a number of conditions for an effective cartel, including the following:

- **Barriers to entry:** a cartel is more likely to be effective when there are high barriers to entry into a market or an industry.

- **Control over both price and output:** a cartel is also more likely to be effective if it can not only fix prices for members, but also restrict output.

- **Setting rules:** a cartel will need to set rules governing the behaviour of members; if members follow these rules, risks that would exist without a cartel are reduced.

- **Policing rules:** a cartel is also more likely to be effective when all members can be 'policed' in some way to ensure that the rules are being obeyed.

The consequences of a cartel

There are a number of positive consequences of a cartel for producers, including the following:

- **Protection of shared interests:** members of a cartel work together to defend their shared interests.

- **Avoidance of price competition:** cartels fix prices for their members, so that competition on the basis of price is avoided.

- **Effect on revenue:** where a cartel is able to control both price and output, revenue will be substantially increased.

- **Control of market:** the existence of a cartel will give members a dominant position in a market; for example, OPEC controls 80% of the oil producing market.

However, there are also a number of negative consequences of a cartel for consumers, including the following:

- **Higher prices:** the members of a cartel can all raise prices together, which reduces the price elasticity of demand for any particular member and makes products more expensive for consumers.

- **Restricted output:** members of a cartel may agree to limit output onto a market, such as through a quota system, reducing competition.

- **Lack of transparency:** members of a cartel may agree to hide prices or withhold information, such as in relation to hidden charges to consumers involved in certain transactions.

- **Carving up a market:** members of a cartel may collectively agree to break up a market into regions or territories and not compete in each other's area, reducing choice for consumers.

7.7.5 The principal-agent problem arising from differing objectives of shareholders/owners and managers

It is important to understand that there may be a **divorce of ownership and control** of a firm. For example, the shareholders own a firm, but they will not be able to exercise full day-to-day control of it.

This gives rise to the **principal-agent problem**. The principal is the owner of a firm and the owners will employ an agent, or manager, to run the firm and take the everyday decisions affecting the firm. The problem that arises from this divorce is that the agent may not run the firm in exactly the way that the principal would like.

> **Key terms**
>
> **Divorce of ownership and control:** the situation that arises when a firm is owned by one group of people (the shareholders) and controlled and run by another group of people (the managers).
>
> **Principal-agent problem:** the problem that can arise from the divorce of ownership from control in a firm, so that the principals (the shareholders) may have different aims and objectives from the agents (the managers).

> 💡 **Remember**
>
> The divorce of ownership from control in a firm, giving rise to the principal-agent problem, means that the principals of a firm (the shareholders) are not able to guarantee that their agents (the managers) will operate the firm in the principals' best interests.

> ★ **Exam tip**
>
> The existence of the principal-agent problem means that the principal and the agent may have different objectives and it would be helpful if you could give possible examples of such a problem. For example, the principal may have the objective of profit maximisation, but the agent may have the objective of salary maximisation.

7.8 The differing objectives and policies of firms

This topic is concerned with:

- the traditional profit-maximising objectives of firms

- an understanding of other objectives of firms

- price discrimination

- other pricing policies

- the relationship between price elasticity of demand and a firm's revenue.

7.8.1 The traditional profit-maximising objective of firms

Profit maximisation has traditionally been regarded as the main objective of a firm. This will be at the output where marginal cost (MC) = marginal revenue (MR).

> **Key term**
>
> **Profit maximisation:** the situation in which marginal cost (MC) is equal to marginal revenue (MR).

> 💡 **Remember**
>
> Although profit maximisation has traditionally been assumed to be the main objective of a firm, this assumption has been increasingly called into question for a number of reasons:
>
> - The growth of modern public limited companies, particularly multinational companies, has shown that it may be difficult for them to maximise profits, even if they wanted to.
>
> - These companies have a large number of stakeholders who may pursue other goals instead of, or in addition to, profit maximisation.
>
> - The traditional aim of profit maximisation assumes that a firm can actually calculate its MC and MR, but this is not without difficulties.
>
> - In terms of MR, a firm needs to be able to accurately estimate the position and elasticity of its demand (AR) curve, which can be extremely difficult.
>
> - In terms of MC, this may also be difficult to calculate accurately; there is also the issue of whether a firm should use short-run or long-run marginal costs.
>
> - There is evidence to suggest that instead of using MC and MR to determine the price and output, a firm may adopt a different strategy, such as applying a percentage mark up to average costs; this is known as cost plus pricing.

7.8.2 Other objectives of firms

It is now increasingly recognised that a firm may have other possible objectives, apart from profit maximisation, and these could include the following:

- Survival: one objective of a firm, especially in the first years of its existence, might be to survive; this would be particularly the case in markets in which firms do not tend to survive for a long period of time.

- Strategic: a firm may decide to establish its aims and objectives within a broad strategic approach, such as in relation to 'corporate social responsibility' and the strategic objective of not causing any significant environmental problems. Game theory offers scope for firms to behave in a strategic way.

- Profit **satisficing**: where there is a divorce of ownership from control, the managers of a firm may wish to deal with all the stakeholders of a firm in such a way that all stakeholders are satisfied; in this situation, satisfactory, rather than maximum, profits may be the objective of a firm.

- Sales maximisation: in this situation, managers aim to maximise the volume of sales of a firm.

> ⭐ **Exam tip**
>
> In the exam, be willing to be critical of the idea that the objective of all firms is to maximise profits.

> **Key terms**
>
> **Satisficing:** a situation in which a firm aims for a minimum level of attainment of a number of objectives.
>
> **Revenue maximisation:** an alternative theory of the objectives of a firm which assumes that managers aim to maximise revenue as opposed to profit.

- **Revenue maximisation**: in some firms, the objective may be to maximise the revenue of a firm rather than the profits; in this situation, the output would be higher and the price lower than the profit maximising position.

7.8.3 Price discrimination

Price discrimination occurs when different prices are charged to different customers and when the different prices are not a reflection of differences in the costs of production. The differences in price occur because of differences in the price elasticity of demand for different products. Price discrimination occurs in monopoly where the firm is able to keep different markets separate. This separation of markets could involve different geographical regions, different times of the day or different ages.

The conditions for effective price discrimination

Certain conditions must apply for price discrimination to exist and these include the following:

- The firm practising price discrimination must be able to exercise some monopoly power in the market.

- It must be possible to separate the market.

- It must not be possible to buy in one market and sell in another (this is known as **arbitrage**).

- The price elasticities of demand for a product must be different in the separate markets.

It is possible to distinguish between three degrees of price discrimination:

- **First degree price discrimination**: this occurs when the monopoly firm is able to charge each individual consumer the maximum amount that they are prepared to pay for a product.

- **Second degree price discrimination**: this occurs

where different prices are charged for successive blocks of consumption.

- **Third degree price discrimination**: this refers to the selling of the same product in different markets to different consumers at different prices.

> **Remember**
>
> Although profit maximisation is traditionally assumed to be the main objective of a firm, it is now increasingly recognised that firms may have other possible objectives.

> **Key terms**
>
> **Price discrimination:** the practice of selling the same product in different markets at different prices for reasons that have nothing to do with the costs of production.
>
> **Arbitrage:** the ability to buy in one market and sell in another.
>
> **First degree price discrimination:** the practice of charging each consumer the maximum they are prepared to pay for a product.
>
> **Second degree price discrimination:** the practice of charging consumers different prices for successive blocks of consumption of a product.
>
> **Third degree price discrimination:** the practice of charging different consumers different prices for the same product.

The consequences of price discrimination

There are a number of consequences of price discrimination for both the producer and the consumer.

Consequences for the producer include the following:

- **Increase in revenue and profit:** a monopoly firm is able to increase its revenue and profit by practising price discrimination; it is able to extract consumer surplus and turn it into supernormal profit.

- **Cross-subsidisation:** a firm practising price discrimination will be able to use the supernormal profit to cross-subsidise loss-making activities in other operations that could have important social benefits.

- **Economies of scale:** an increase in total output resulting from selling extra units of a product at a lower price might help a monopoly firm to exploit economies of scale, resulting in lower long-run average costs.

Consequences for the consumer include the following:

- **Consumer payments:** each customer pays the price that he or she is willing to pay rather than forgo the product (the actual price paid will depend on the whether the price discrimination being practised is first degree, second degree or third degree).

- **Consumer surplus:** the consumer surplus is reduced in most cases, representing a loss of welfare; however, some consumers, who can now buy a product at a lower price, may benefit.

- **Contestable markets:** price discrimination might make a market more contestable, allowing cheap prices to be charged to certain customers.

7.8.4 Other pricing policies

Other possible pricing policies that could be used by firms include:

- limit pricing
- predatory pricing
- price leadership.

Limit pricing

Limit pricing refers to a situation in which price is below the profit-maximising price. For example, a firm may decide to limit price in an attempt to discourage new firms from entering an industry and so protecting the position of the firm that adopts this pricing policy.

Predatory pricing

Oligopoly can sometimes give rise to **predatory pricing**. This is where a firm charges a price that is lower than those of competitors in a deliberate attempt to force other firms out of the industry.

Price leadership

Price leadership is most likely to exist in an oligopoly market structure where there is some degree of collusion between the firms in the market. In this situation, firms in the market will follow the price leadership of one firm. The objective is to maximise the profits of all the firms by behaving as if they were one monopolistic firm. This agreement on price could be informal and there are three models of such price leadership: the dominant firm model, barometric price leadership and parallel pricing.

However, price leadership, although usually part of an informal agreement, could be part of a formal cartel arrangement.

7.8.5 The relationship between price elasticity of demand and a firm's revenue

The relationship in a normal downward sloping demand curve

If there is a downward sloping demand curve, it means that marginal revenue is less than price. This is because price has to be reduced for all products to sell just one more product. Average revenue is in fact the downward-sloping demand curve. A firm's total revenue is rising when demand is elastic, at its maximum when there is unitary elastic demand, and falling when demand is inelastic.

The relationship in a kinked demand curve

It has already been pointed out that the demand curve in oligopoly is kinked. This occurs because firms in an oligopolistic market structure try to anticipate the reactions of rival firms to their actions. The kinked demand curve is an example of how the behaviour of firms can be analysed when there is no collusion between them and it shows the **mutual interdependence** of firms in an oligopoly market.

It is assumed that if an oligopolistic firm increases its price, other firms in the market will not follow and so demand above the kink is price elastic. In

---

Key terms

Limit pricing: a policy adopted by a firm in monopoly or oligopoly of setting price below that which would maximise profits in order to deter new entrants from entering the market.

Predatory pricing: a situation in which a market leader reduces prices in a deliberate attempt to force other firms out of a market.

Price leadership: the practice in an oligopoly where one firm sets or changes price and other firms in the market follow this lead.

★ **Exam tip**

You need to be able to demonstrate an understanding of each of these different pricing policies in the exam.

Key term

Mutual interdependence: a characteristic of an oligopolistic market in which each firm is aware that any action it takes will have an impact on other firms in the industry and as a consequence will have to take this into account when taking any decisions.

this situation, a fall in price will lead to a rise in total revenue. It is also assumed that if an oligopolistic firm reduces its price, other firms in the market will follow and so demand below the kink is price inelastic. In this situation, a rise in price will lead to a rise in total revenue.

 Raise your grade

Assess why the idea of rational behaviour is being increasingly challenged by behavioural economic models. [20]

The rational behaviour of consumers is based on the idea that they will maximise their utility (1). Rational behaviour assumes that individual consumers will have access to all the information that they require to make a decision (2) and that individuals take decisions that are based on a very careful comparison of the benefits and costs to achieve the optimal outcome (3).

However, it has often been pointed out that many economic decisions are not rational and so behavioural economic models have been developed to offer a contrast to the idea of rational behaviour.

Behavioural economics explains the decisions taken by individuals in practice, particularly when they are opposed to those predicted by traditional economic theory.

There are a number of key elements of behavioural economic models. It is argued, for example, that individuals may not always possess all the relevant information that they require to take decisions (4). Alternatively, it could be that there is too much information available, making decision making more difficult (5). It is possible that individuals may take decisions based on rules of thumb (known as 'heuristics'), simplifying what is involved in the decision-making process (6). The way that information is presented can influence behaviour (7). Individuals can be persuaded to take particular decisions, such as through government advertising (8).

This increasing challenge to the idea of rational behaviour by behavioural economists has attempted to address the criticisms made about rational behaviour and it has succeeded in offering an alternative, and perhaps more realistic, analysis and explanation of consumer behaviour.

How to improve this answer

1. There is no mention here of the constraints that are assumed to exist, such as a limited income and constant tastes and preferences.

2. There could have been reference to the assumption that this information can be obtained at zero cost.

3. The candidate could have stressed that these decisions are taken at the margin.

4. The concept of opportunity cost could have been brought in, for example, alternative uses of the time taken to obtain the information.

5. The candidate could have brought in the idea of 'bounded rationality' here.

6. There could have been reference here to 'anchoring', where the first information obtained is regarded as the most important.

7. This point could have been developed more fully in relation to the idea of 'framing'.

8. This point could have been developed more fully, in terms of 'nudging' people to behave in certain ways.

AO1 and AO2: Level 2   8/14

AO3:   Level 1   2/6

Total: 10/20

Worked Example

Assess whether firms always benefit from an increase in the level of output that they produce. [20]

It is likely to be the case that firms will sometimes benefit from an increase in the level of output that they produce because as output increases, the long-run average cost curve falls, giving rise to economies of scale.

There are a number of internal economies of scale that a firm can benefit from. For example, financial economies could lead to a reduction in the rate of interest paid on a loan by a firm. Purchasing economies could be made by negotiating discounts as a result of bulk buying. Managerial economies may be in the form of a larger firm employing specialist managers who can operate more efficiently, leading to a reduction in the average cost of production. There are a number of potential technical economies of scale, such as through the use of large capital equipment. Economies of scale could be in the form of benefits gained from research and development. Risk-bearing economies could exist through diversification where a firm is able to be involved in different markets.

There are also a number of external economies of scale that could affect all firms in an industry, such as the availability of support or the existence of ancillary forms in a particular area, various potential benefits of transport and infrastructure, the availability of specialised labour possessing specialist skills or the availability of specific courses in colleges and universities.

However, it must be remembered that beyond a certain level of output, the long-run average cost curve can begin to rise, giving rise to the existence of diseconomies of scale. Internal diseconomies of scale could include slower communication, lower levels of efficiency and productivity, lower levels of motivation leading to employees becoming alienated, bored, demotivated and distanced from management, the possibility of a greater frequency of industrial disputes, poor management and difficulties of co-ordination and a slow response to changing market conditions.

There could also be possible external diseconomies of scale, including greater competition for limited inputs leading to higher costs of inputs and the possibility of greater congestion leading to reduced efficiency and an increase in costs.

Therefore, it is not true to assert that firms will always benefit from an increase in the level of output that they produce. They could do, due to the existence of internal and/or external economies of scale, but this will not necessarily always be the case due to the existence of internal and/or external diseconomies of scale.

Exam-style questions

1   Marginal utility refers to the satisfaction gained:

   (a) from all of the units of a product consumed

   (b) from the first unit of a product consumed

   (c) from the last unit of a product consumed

   (d) on average from all of the units of a product consumed.   [1]

2   The substitution effect will:

   (a) always be negative

   (b) always be positive

   (c) depend on whether the good is a Giffen good

   (d) depend on whether the good is an inferior good.   [1]

3   A third party interrupted by loud music from a neighbour is an example of a:

   (a) negative externality in relation to consumption

   (b) negative externality in relation to production

   (c) positive externality in relation to consumption

   (d) positive externality in relation to production.   [1]

4   An example of a market failure is the:

   (a) non-provision of a public good

   (b) optimal allocation of resources

   (c) over-production of a merit good

   (d) under-production of a demerit good.   [1]

5   Marginal social benefit is the addition of:

   (a) marginal external benefit and marginal cost

   (b) marginal private benefit and marginal cost

   (c) marginal private benefit and marginal external benefit

   (d) marginal private benefit and marginal social benefit.   [1]

6   What does cost-benefit analysis use when it is not possible to use market prices?

   (a) Discounted prices

   (b) Shadow prices

   (c) Transitional prices

   (d) Underground prices   [1]

7   Which of the following is an example of an external economy of scale?

   (a) Bulk buying to obtain a discount

   (b) Managerial specialisation

   (c) Research and development by a firm

   (d) The provision of specific courses at colleges   [1]

8   Profit is defined as the difference between:

   (a) average revenue and average cost

   (b) marginal revenue and marginal cost

   (c) total revenue and average cost

   (d) total revenue and total cost.   [1]

9   A kinked demand curve occurs in oligopoly because:

   (a) demand is elastic above the kink and inelastic below it

   (b) demand is inelastic above the kink and elastic below it

   (c) the marginal revenue curve is below the average revenue curve

   (d) the marginal revenue curve is discontinuous.   [1]

10   Which of the following is an example of a principal of a firm?

   (a) A consumer

   (b) A manager

   (c) A shareholder

   (d) An employee   [1]

11   Assess whether cost-benefit analysis will guarantee that a decision about whether to build a new airport is the correct one.   [20]

12   Assess whether a monopoly will always operate against the interests of consumers.   [20]

Government microeconomic intervention

Key topics

- Government policies to achieve efficient resource allocation and correct market failure

- Equity and redistribution of income and wealth

- Labour market forces and government intervention

8.1 Government policies to achieve efficient resource allocation and correct market failure

8.1.1 The application and effectiveness of measures to tackle different forms of market failure

These measures include specific and *ad valorem* **taxes**, subsidies, price controls, production quotas, prohibitions and licences, regulation and deregulation, the direct provision of products, pollution permits, property rights, nationalisation and privatisation, the provision of information and behavioural insights and nudge theory.

Specific and *ad valorem* indirect taxes

Indirect taxes can be used to achieve the efficient allocation of resources and to correct market failure. An indirect tax can be used to discourage the consumption of demerit goods, such as alcohol and tobacco, by making them more expensive, and as long as the demand for such products is relatively elastic, the consumption of them will fall in response to the higher price being charged.

It is important to be able to distinguish between specific and *ad valorem* indirect taxes.

The impact and incidence of specific indirect taxes were covered in section 3.2.1 of Unit 3. A specific tax, such as an excise duty, is where a fixed amount has to be paid. This is shown by a parallel shift to the left of the supply curve so that the vertical distance between the two supply curves remains constant, as in Figure 3.1.

An *ad valorem* **tax**, such as VAT (value added tax), is where a particular percentage has to be paid, for example, 20% on the price of a product. This is shown by a shift to the left of the supply curve, but as the tax is in the form of a percentage, rather than a specific amount, the gap between the two supply curves will widen (Figure 8.1).

> **Key term**
>
> **Ad valorem tax:** this is where the tax on the consumption of a product is a percentage of the value of the product rather than a fixed amount.

> ★ **Link**
>
> See Unit 3, section 3.2.1, and Unit 5, section 5.2.4, for further information on taxation.

> 💡 **Remember**
>
> When a specific tax is imposed, the supply curve shifts to the left parallel to the original supply curve. When an *ad valorem* tax is imposed, the supply curve shifts to the left, but the vertical distance between the two supply curves widens.

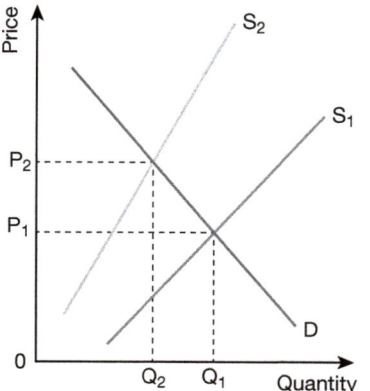

◀ **Figure 8.1** The imposition of an *ad valorem* tax

Subsidies

The impact and incidence of subsidies were covered in section 3.2.2 of Unit 3. A subsidy can be used to encourage the consumption of merit goods, such as education and health care, by making them less expensive and as long as the demand for such products is relatively elastic, the consumption of them will rise in response to the lower price being charged.

> ★ **Exam tip**
>
> It is easy to confuse the application of indirect taxes and subsidies in a market. An indirect tax will be shown by a shift of the supply curve to the left, leading to an increase in price, and a subsidy will be shown by a shift of the supply curve to the right, leading to a decrease in price.

> ★ **Exam tip**
>
> Make sure that you are able to both explain the effect of the introduction of indirect taxes and subsidies in a market and to illustrate the effect through the use of appropriate diagrams.

Price controls

Another policy that can be used to correct market failure is the use of price controls. These are of two types:

- **maximum price control:** if the equilibrium price of a product, such as an essential food item, in a market is too high for many people to afford, a maximum price control can be established by a government to prevent the price rising above a certain level
- **minimum price control:** if the equilibrium price of a product, such as a demerit good (for example, tobacco), in a market is too low, encouraging overconsumption, a minimum price control can be established by a government to prevent the price falling below a certain level.

> ★ **Link**
>
> See Unit 3, sections 3.1.3–3.2.5, in relation to controlling prices in markets and especially maximum prices, minimum prices and buffer stock schemes.

Production quotas

A government could decide to set a limit to the quantity of a product that may be produced in a specified time period. A quota is often used as an import control, but it could be used in a domestic economy to limit production. For example, if the production of a certain product is too high, lowering the market price, a **quota** can be used as a 'cap' on a certain level of production. If a producer exceeds this quota, a levy could be imposed on them which they would be required to pay.

> **Key term**
>
> **Production quota:** a limit to the quantity of a product produced over a certain period of time.

> ★ **Exam tip**
>
> A production quota and an import quota can be confused. A production quota involves a restriction on the domestic production of a product, whereas an import quota involves a restriction on a product entering a country from another country.

Prohibitions and licences

Another policy to achieve efficient resource allocation and to correct market failure in an economy is through the use of **prohibitions** and **licences**.

A prohibition refers to a ban on certain products being supplied in an economy. For example, a government could decide to make a product illegal and this would have the effect of prohibiting its consumption.

An alternative to a prohibition is the use of a licence to correct market failure. A licence involves a government giving permission to producers to sell a product. The impact of using licences is usually not as effective as prohibition, but it does give a government some control in a market, and it can decide to make the policy more effective by reducing the number of licences issued.

> **Key terms**
>
> **Prohibition:** a situation in which a certain product is banned in a country.
>
> **Licence:** a situation in which permission is given, often by a government, but where the permission is limited or restricted in some way.

★ **Exam tip**

It is easy to confuse the impact of a prohibition and a licence. A prohibition is more effective in that it involves a complete ban on the production and/or consumption of certain products. A licence, on the other hand, is a way of giving a government greater power to influence production and/or consumption in a market by limiting the extent of such production and/or consumption.

★ **Exam tip**

It would be useful, in answering a question on the correction of market failure in an economy, if you were able to include relevant examples of prohibitions and licences to support your answer.

Regulation and deregulation

Regulation

A government could try to correct the existence of market failure in an economy through the use of **regulations**. A regulation refers to a rule or law that can be used to reduce the extent of market failure.

There are many examples of such regulations in different countries, such as in relation to:

- the control of monopolies

- consumer protection

- protection of the environment

- control of the transportation system.

In each of these situations, there will usually be a **regulatory body** set up to enforce the regulations.

In the case of the control of monopolies, for example, a government may establish regulations to control monopolies. If a firm has too much monopoly power in a market, it can be referred to a commission (a regulatory body which can look into a monopoly situation), which can then investigate whether the monopoly is acting against the public interest. Proposed mergers or acquisitions could also be referred to such a regulatory body whenever it is thought that they might be against the public interest, limiting the degree of choice for consumers.

> **Key terms**
>
> **Regulations:** a variety of laws and rules which apply to firms in different circumstances.
>
> **Regulatory bodies:** organisations that impose requirements, restrictions and conditions, set standards and secure compliance or enforcement.

💡 **Remember**

Regulatory bodies perform the function of ensuring that regulations are adhered to. For example, regulations may exist to control monopolies and to ensure that any proposed merger is not against the public interest. If it is thought that a proposed merger would be against the public interest, it can be referred to a regulatory body.

Deregulation

Although regulations can be used as part of a policy to correct market failure, it is also possible that there are too many regulations in existence in an economy and that these regulations are making it impossible for efficient resource allocation to be achieved. In such situations, a government could decide to reduce the number of regulations that exist in an economy so that a greater degree of competition is allowed to exist in a market than would otherwise be the case. This process is known as **deregulation**. If greater competition did take place in a market, it is likely to lead to an increase in the level of efficiency of resource allocation and to a reduction in the extent of market failure.

> **Key term**
>
> **Deregulation:** a reduction in the number of regulations, laws and rules that operate in an industry or an economy, usually to allow a greater degree of competition in a market.

Direct provision

Another policy that can be used to correct market failure in an economy is through the **direct provision of certain goods and services**.

In many countries, the government has decided to directly provide particular goods and services through the public sector which can exist alongside the private sector.

> 💡 **Remember**
>
> A government may decide to directly provide certain goods and services if it was thought that the consumption of such products would be relatively low if only provided through the private sector. For example, a government could decide to directly provide certain merit goods, such as education and health care.

⭐ **Link**

See Unit 3, section 3.2.3, for information on the direct provision of goods and services.

Pollution permits

A **pollution permit**, or tradable permit as it is also called, is a particular example of a licence that can be issued by a government. The permit allows a firm to pollute the environment in some way, but only up to a certain extent. This level of pollution will be less than when the permit was first issued. Each successive permit will allow a lower and lower level of pollution to exist.

> 💡 **Remember**
>
> It may not be possible to eliminate pollution completely, but the use of pollution permits should bring down the level of pollution that exists in an economy over a period of time.

> ⭐ **Exam tip**
>
> Try not to argue that pollution permits will entirely eradicate pollution in an economy. Instead, focus on the fact that a policy of using pollution permits is designed to reduce the extent of pollution that exists in an economy over a period of time.

Property rights

Property rights refer to the right of the owner of an economic good to decide how such a good should be used. Market failure can occur because of the absence of clear property rights, so one way to correct market failure is to bring about greater clarity in relation to property rights. A government could decide to extend property rights, such as through the establishment of voluntary agreements. An example might be in relation to the dumping of rubbish, creating an environmental problem. If such a voluntary agreement was unsuccessful, a government could decide to introduce a system of pollution permits.

> 💡 **Remember**
>
> In most situations, property rights are private and so it is relatively easy to establish the rights of a person in relation to their property, that is, the assets that they own. If there is a dispute about these private property rights, redress can be obtained through legal action. However, in some cases, property rights are not private but relate to open spaces and to air and water. In these situations, there are common, rather than private, property rights. The existence of common property rights can give rise to market failure, such as in relation to pollution, and so a government might decide to extend property rights so that they cover open spaces, air and water.

Nationalisation and privatisation

Nationalisation

Nationalisation refers to the process of transferring firms and/or industries from the private sector to the public sector. Ownership thus becomes public ownership and these nationalised firms and/or industries will be controlled in some way by the government. It involves the creation of a monopoly where there is just one firm in an industry and this firm can control the supply of a product in a market. The effect on the market can be positive, such as avoiding a wasteful duplication of resources, or negative, such as when decisions are taken for political, rather than for economic reasons.

Monopoly can be regarded as an example of market failure. This is because the equilibrium price is likely to be higher and the equilibrium quantity is likely to be lower than would be the case in perfect competition. Unlike the situation in perfect competition, the supernormal/abnormal profits are not competed away in the long run because there are barriers to entry which make it very difficult for new firms to enter the market.

Figure 8.2 shows the price and output decisions that would be taken by a monopoly firm. The profit maximisation position is determined by where MC = MR and this will give an equilibrium price of 0P and an equilibrium quantity of 0Q. This is an example of market failure because there is a lack of both productive and allocative efficiency. The lack of competition in the industry also gives rise to X-inefficiency.

In such a situation, a government could decide to nationalise this monopoly firm, that is, take it under state ownership. A price could be charged that would be lower than in a private sector monopoly and a quantity could be produced that would be higher than in a private sector monopoly, but the government would need to be able and willing to support the nationalised firm with public funds.

Privatisation

An alternative policy to correct market failure, instead of through nationalising the firm, would be through a process of **privatisation**. Whereas nationalisation refers to the process of transferring the ownership of assets from the private sector to the public sector, privatisation refers to the process of transferring ownership in the opposite direction, that is, from the public sector to the private sector. It is also known as denationalisation.

The effect on the market can be positive, such as bringing about an improvement in efficiency; with greater competition in the market, price is likely to be lower and output higher than would otherwise be the case. However, the effect on the market could be negative, such as an increase in negative externalities.

> **Key term**
>
> **Nationalisation:** the process whereby private sector firms and/or industries become part of the public sector of an economy, with the government or state owning and controlling these resources.

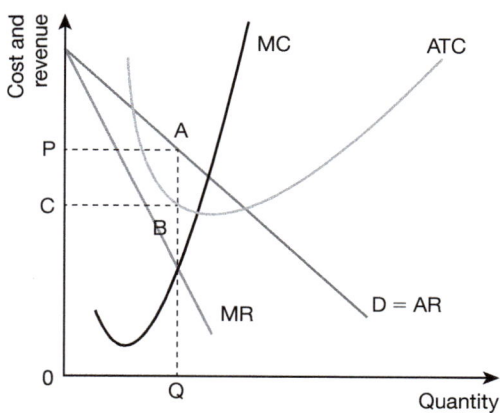

▲ **Figure 8.2** Price and output decisions under monopoly

> ★ **Link**
>
> See Unit 3, section 3.3.4, for information on the state provision of essential goods and services.

> **Key terms**
>
> **Privatisation:** the process whereby public sector firms and/or industries become part of the private sector of an economy, with the government no longer owning or controlling these resources.
>
> **Contracting out:** the transfer of responsibility for providing a particular service from the public to the private sector. This can also be known as outsourcing.

> 💡 **Remember**
>
> You need to understand that the process of privatisation can take different forms, including the creation of a public limited company in the private sector, deregulation in the form of removing legal restrictions and controls, and **contracting out** or outsourcing where the responsibility of providing particular services is transferred from the public to the private sector.

The provision of information

Market failure can be caused by inadequate or inaccurate information. It is assumed that consumers will always aim to maximise their utility or satisfaction, but this aim can only be achieved if they are in possession of the required information. If this information is not readily available, they will be less likely to make rational decisions. This is why **information failure** can be a major cause of market failure.

To correct this type of market failure, a government needs to try to increase the availability, accuracy and reliability of appropriate information to consumers in an attempt to influence their economic behaviour. This will help them to make rational decisions in relation to the consumption of merit goods and demerit goods and ensure that scarce resources are allocated as efficiently as possible. Nudge theory is an example of where a government could try to discourage consumers from consuming demerit goods.

Key term

Information failure: a situation in which people lack the full and accurate information that would enable them to make the best decisions about consumption.

★ **Link**

See Unit 3, section 3.2.6, for information on the provision of information.

💡 **Remember**

A government could try to overcome the problem of information failure by improving the information that is made available to consumers. In the case of merit goods, a government would try to ensure that people were as well informed as possible about the potential advantages of consuming merit goods, such as education and health care. In the case of demerit goods, a government would try to ensure that people were as well informed as possible about the potential disadvantages of consuming demerit goods, such as alcohol and tobacco.

Behavioural insights and 'nudge' theory

Behavioural economics has already been referred to in Unit 7. Behavioural economic models are designed to provide an insight into why consumers do not always act in a rational way. These insights stress the importance of understanding the actual behaviour of people in an economy rather than the traditional approach which stresses the idea that people are assumed to behave rationally.

The behavioural approach emphasises that it is possible to 'nudge' people to act in a particular way, different from how they would act if there was no government intervention. This is why it is also known as **nudge theory**. An example of this would be in relation to a government policy to discourage the consumption of certain demerit goods.

Key terms

Behavioural economics: the branch of Economics that attempts to explain the decisions and choices that individuals make in practice, particularly when they are opposed to those predicted by traditional economic theory.

Nudge theory: an attempt by a government to alter the economic behaviour of people in some particular way.

💡 **Remember**

A government can try to nudge consumers to change their economic behaviour in some way. For example, medical evidence is very clear about the damage that can be caused by the consumption of tobacco and yet millions of people still smoke. It is clear that the medical evidence has had no effect, or a very limited effect, on the consumption pattern of many people. A government could therefore adopt a policy of nudging people away from smoking, stressing how harmful such a product is to the health of people. For example, a government could insist that all packets of cigarettes sold in a country should carry a health warning.

★ **Link**

See Unit 7, section 7.15, on assumptions of rational behaviour and behavioural economic models.

★ **Exam tip**

It would be helpful if you were able to give examples to support an answer on nudge theory. For example, a government could start with a moderate nudge, such as when a packet of cigarettes contains the warning: 'smoking can damage your health'. If this nudge was not sufficient to substantially change the demand for cigarettes, packets of cigarettes could contain a stronger warning, such as: 'smoking can kill'.

8.1.2 Government failure in microeconomic intervention

The definition of government failure

Section 8.1.1 of this unit has indicated a number of different ways in which a government can intervene to achieve efficient resource allocation and correct market failure. However, **government failure** could occur where a government intervenes in order to correct market failure but in doing so, creates other distortions or imperfections in the market. Government intervention in a market can therefore cause economic inefficiency that would not have existed in a free market, and this is referred to as government failure.

Key term

Government failure: the failure of a government to achieve desired objectives as a result of intervention in a market.

The causes of government failure

Government failure occurs when government intervention in an economy causes an inefficient allocation of resources and a decline in economic welfare. Government failure often arises from attempts to solve market failure, but as a result it can lead to the creation of different problems, such as other distortions or imperfections in the market.

The causes of government failure can include the following:

- Lack of incentives: the profit motive is usually lacking in the public sector and public sector workers may be paid less than equivalent workers in the private sector; these factors could lead to inefficiency.

- Poor information: a government's policy will only be effective if it has all the required information on which to base policy decisions, but politicians may not always have all the necessary information required to take appropriate decisions; for example, it is not easy to place a monetary value on a negative externality, such as pollution. Any inaccurate information is likely to undermine the effectiveness of any government microeconomic intervention.

- Political interference: a government decision may be taken for short-term political gain rather than for more long-term economic reasons.

- Moral hazard: a government could take decisions that encourage risk taking, for example, a decision to support financial institutions to avoid any of them failing and going out of business.

- Regulatory capture: a government could become too friendly with those they are trying to regulate.

- Unintended consequences: a government policy to reduce poverty through the provision of benefits could lead to a situation of 'welfare dependency'.

The consequences of government failure

There are a number of possible consequences of government failure, including the following:

- Taxation: a government may decide to use a progressive income tax to bring about a more equitable distribution of income, but if the top rate of tax is very high, there may be a disincentive for the higher paid to work as much; some workers may even decide to leave the country and seek employment elsewhere.

- Employment: a government may be reluctant to take a decision which makes people redundant, for example, if workers are relatively unproductive, because this will lead to an increase in the level of unemployment.

- Net welfare loss to society: when the consequences of government intervention are contrasted with the original problem that necessitated the intervention, it may be that the overall effect is a net welfare loss to society, that is, the consequences of the government failure have actually made the situation worse than before.

- Distortion of price signals: one of the advantages of a free market is that it gives out price signals which lead to an efficient allocation of resources, but government intervention in a market could distort those signals so that the outcome could be an inefficient allocation of resources; for example, a government may decide to support a failing industry through subsidies when a better decision might have been to allow it to fail.

★ **Exam tip**

★ **Exam tip**

Make sure that you are able to support any comments in the exam on government failure with appropriate examples.

8.2 Equity and redistribution of income and wealth

8.2.1 The difference between equity and equality

Equity

One objective of government microeconomic intervention is the achievement of **equity**. This is concerned with the ideas of fairness and justice, such as a government policy to bring about a more equitable distribution of income and wealth.

Equality

Equality refers to a situation in which everyone is at the same level, for example, the idea of equal life chances or of everyone having the same income and wealth. It is where there is the same status, rights and responsibilities for all the members of a group or a society.

Key terms

Equity: the idea of fairness or justice, such as in relation to the distribution of income and wealth in an economy.

Equality: the same rights and responsibilities for all the members of a group or society.

8.2.2 The difference between equity and efficiency

Another objective of government microeconomic intervention is the achievement of **efficiency**. This involves the achievement of both productive and allocative efficiency. The attainment of this objective would ensure that the scarce resources in an economy were allocated in the best possible way.

Key term

Efficiency: the use of resources in the most economical or optimal way possible.

★ **Exam tip**

It is important to be able to distinguish clearly between equity and efficiency. A certain allocation of resources in an economy may be efficient, but this does not necessarily mean that it will be equitable.

8.2.3 The distinction between absolute poverty and relative poverty

It is important to distinguish between absolute poverty and relative poverty.

Absolute poverty

Absolute poverty is a type of poverty that occurs when the resources required for minimum physical health are lacking, defined by limited access to food, clothing and shelter. The World Bank defines the poverty line as US\$1.90 a day (using purchasing power parity). It refers to a particular condition which is the same in every country and which does not change over a period of time.

Key terms

Absolute poverty: a condition where household income is below a necessary level to maintain basic living standards in relation to food, shelter and housing.

Relative poverty: a condition where household income is a certain percentage below the median income of a country.

Relative poverty

Relative poverty is a type of poverty that means low income relative to others in a country. For example, it could be stated as an income that is below 50% or 60% of the median income of people in a particular country.

8.2.4 The poverty trap

A problem with an increase in earned income is that it is possible that as some people receive more money, they may no longer be entitled to as many benefits as before. The effect of this is that they can actually be worse off as a result of an increase in income. This situation is known as a **poverty trap** and creates a disincentive effect. For example, a person may not wish to work longer hours because the extra income received from this work may mean that they are no longer entitled to some benefits that they were originally entitled to before working the extra hours. The existence of the poverty trap means that a person may become worse off as a result of earning more money because they are no longer entitled to certain benefits.

Key term

Poverty trap: a situation in which an increase in income results in a loss of benefits so that a person is no better off or possibly worse off.

💡 **Remember**

The poverty trap comes about as a result of the combined effect of the marginal rate of taxation paid on any additional income earned by a person and the rate at which benefits are no longer payable to that person by the state.

If a government is in favour of a more equitable distribution of income and wealth, the existence of a poverty trap may prevent this from being achieved. This is why many economists favour the introduction of a negative income tax which would prevent the poverty trap from occurring.

💡 **Remember**

A person may be worse off as a result of working more hours and gaining a higher wage if, as a result, they are no longer entitled to receive as much money as before in benefits.

8.2.5 Policies towards equity and equality

Negative income tax

Whereas an income tax involves people paying tax to a government, according to their earned income, a **negative income tax** involves people receiving money from a government. It is also a progressive system where people earning below a certain amount receive money from the government. In this way, people will be able to receive a minimum income. The key feature of a negative income tax is that it combines the payment of income tax and the receipt of benefits in one system. All people earning above a certain income level would pay income tax and receive no benefits, while all people earning below that income level would not pay any income tax, but would receive benefits.

Key term

Negative income tax: a system which brings together the payment of tax and the receipt of benefits.

💡 **Remember**

A negative income tax involves the combination of the payment of income tax and the receipt of benefits in one system.

Universal benefits and means-tested benefits

There are two types of benefit: a universal benefit and a means-tested benefit.

Universal benefits

A **universal benefit** is paid to every person who is entitled to such a benefit, irrespective of their income or wealth.

Means-tested benefits

A **means-tested benefit** is paid to a person depending on their income and wealth. Such a benefit has the advantage of targeting those people who are most in need of the money and so is more effective in bringing about income and wealth redistribution.

Universal basic income

A **universal basic income** is a government guarantee that each person in a country receives a minimum income. The idea is that the basic income will provide enough money to cover the basic cost of living.

8.3 Labour market forces and government intervention

8.3.1 The demand for labour as a derived demand

The factor of production, labour, is not demanded for its own sake, but for what it is able to contribute to the production process. This is known as **derived demand**.

8.3.2 The factors affecting the demand for labour in a firm or an occupation

There are a number of factors that can affect the demand for labour in a firm or an occupation, in addition to the quantity demanded of the product produced by the labour already referred to in section 8.3.1. These include the following:

- The price of labour and the other factors of production: the demand for labour will depend, to some extent, on the price of labour, that is, the wage or salary, compared with the prices of the other factors of production.

- The productivity of labour and the other factors of production: the demand for labour will depend, to some extent, on the productivity of labour relative to the productivity of the other factors of production. The demand for labour is closely linked to the **marginal physical product** of labour; this refers to the additional output produced if a firm increases the labour input by one unit.

> **Key term**
>
> **Marginal physical product:** the amount of extra output that is produced if a firm increases its input of labour by one unit.

8.3.3 The causes of shifts in and movements along the demand curve for labour in a firm or an occupation

A movement along a demand curve for labour

The demand curve for labour is a function of the wage paid. The higher the wage rate, the lower the demand for labour; the lower the wage rate, the higher the demand for labour. The demand curve for labour, therefore, slopes downwards from left to right. Other possible factors affecting the demand for labour are assumed to be constant. Therefore, if the wage rate changes, there will be a movement along the demand curve.

A shift of a demand curve for labour

A shift of a demand curve for labour occurs when there is a change in a determinant of the demand for labour, apart from a change in the wage rate. These changes include:

- changes in the productivity of labour
- changes in the skills of labour
- changes in the prices of the products produced
- changes in the demand for the products
- changes in the prices of substitutes and complements of the products.

The demand curve for labour would shift inwards at a time of recession when the demand for products falls and there will be a decline in the demand for labour at each wage rate. The demand curve for labour would shift outwards in a boom when the demand for products rises and there will be a rise in the demand for labour at each wage rate.

8.3.4 Marginal revenue product (MRP) theory

The definition and calculation of marginal revenue product

Firms are interested not only in the extra output that is produced by employing one more unit of labour, but also in the revenue obtained from selling the additional output that has been produced. The **marginal revenue product (MRP)** of labour is obtained by multiplying the marginal physical product (MPP) of labour by the marginal revenue (MR) received by a firm.

> **Key term**
>
> **Marginal revenue product:** the extra output produced by an additional worker (the marginal physical product or MPP) multiplied by the additional revenue earned by a firm from this output (the marginal revenue or MR), that is, $MRP = MPP \times MR$

> ★ **Exam tip**
>
> Make sure that you do not confuse marginal physical product (MPP) and marginal revenue product (MRP). MPP refers to the extra output resulting from employing one more worker. MRP refers to the extra revenue received by a firm from selling the additional output that results from employing one more worker.

The derivation of an individual firm's demand for labour using marginal revenue product

It has already been pointed out in Unit 7 that a profit maximising firm will produce where marginal cost (MC) is equal to marginal revenue (MR). This situation also applies to a profit maximising employer of labour. This employer will employ labour up to the point where the extra cost of employing an additional worker is equal to the extra revenue earned by the firm from this output. If it is assumed that the product produced is sold in a perfectly competitive market and that all units of a product are sold at the same price, then the employer will employ workers up to the point where the wage rate equals the marginal revenue product of labour. The MRP curve shows the quantity of labour that is employed at each wage. Therefore, the firm's demand curve for labour is the MRP curve.

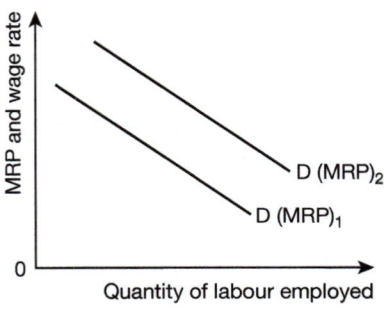

▲ **Figure 8.3** An individual firm's demand for labour

Figure 8.3 shows the individual firm's demand curve for labour, which is also the MRP curve. Any change in the wage rate will bring about a movement along the firm's demand curve. A rise in the wage rate will lead to a fall in the quantity of labour demanded by a firm and a fall in the wage rate will lead to a rise in the quantity of labour demanded by a firm. However, there can also be a shift of the demand curve for labour as a result of a change in the MPP of labour and/or a change in the price of the product. Figure 8.3 shows a shift of the demand curve for labour to the right, from D(MRP)$_1$ to D(MRP)$_2$. This could be the result of an increase in labour productivity, increasing MPP, and/or an increase in the price of the product. Although the diagram shows an individual firm's demand curve for labour, the industry's demand curve for labour will be the sum of each of the individual firm's demand for labour at each wage.

The slope of the individual firm's demand curve for labour will depend on the elasticity of demand for labour, that is, the degree of responsiveness of the demand for labour in response to a change in the wage rate. Figure 8.4 shows differences in the **elasticity of demand for labour**. If the demand for labour is elastic, then a change in the wage rate will bring about a greater percentage change in the quantity of labour demanded. If the demand for labour is inelastic, then a change in the wage rate will bring about a smaller percentage change in the quantity of labour demanded.

> **Key term**
>
> **Elasticity of demand for labour:** a measure of the responsiveness of the demand for labour to a change in the wage rate.

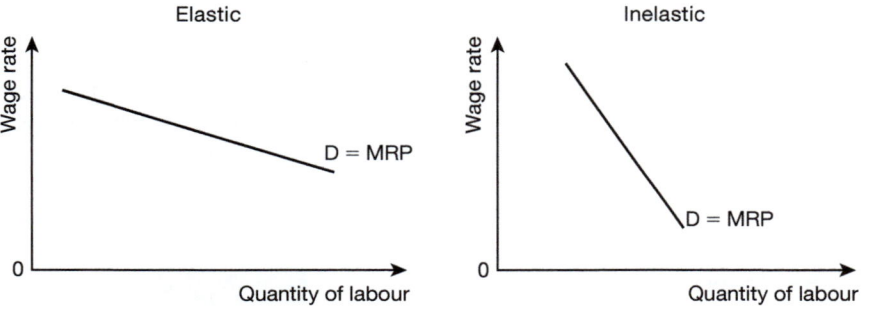

▲ **Figure 8.4** Differences in the elasticity of demand for labour

> **★ Exam tip**
>
> Remember to also label the demand curve for labour as the MRP curve.

> **💡 Remember**
>
> The elasticity of demand for labour can be influenced by a number of possible factors:
>
> - the proportion of labour costs to the total costs of production: if the proportion is relatively high, the elasticity of demand for labour is likely to be high and if the proportion is relatively low, the elasticity of demand for labour is likely to be low
>
> - the ease of factor substitution: if labour can be easily replaced by another factor, for example, capital, the demand for labour is likely to be relatively elastic and if labour cannot be easily replaced by another factor, the demand for labour is likely to be relatively inelastic
>
> - the price elasticity of demand for the final product: if the price elasticity of demand for the final product is relatively high, then the elasticity of demand for labour is likely to be high and if the price elasticity of demand for the final product is relatively low, then the elasticity of demand for labour is likely to be inelastic
>
> - time: the elasticity of demand for labour is likely to increase over time, that is, become more elastic, as firms have longer to find appropriate substitutes for labour.

8.3.5 The factors affecting the supply of labour to a firm or to an occupation

Wage factors

If it is assumed that a firm is in a perfectly competitive market for labour and so cannot influence the price, that is, the wage, of labour, then the firm is a price taker and so the supply of labour is perfectly elastic, shown by a horizontal MC curve.

However, although this is the case for an individual firm, for the industry as a whole the supply curve of labour will be upward sloping from left to right because more people will make themselves available for work when there is an increase in the wage rate paid to labour. This can be seen in Figure 8.5. When the wage rate in an industry increases from $0W$ to $0W_1$, the quantity of labour supplied increases from $0Q$ to $0Q_1$. If there is a further increase in the wage rate to $0W_2$, the quantity of labour supplied increases to $0Q_2$.

It is possible that for an individual worker, an increase in the wage rate may persuade that worker to work fewer hours so as to be able to enjoy more leisure time. This shows the opportunity cost of working more hours in terms of the reduced leisure time. This situation gives rise to a backward-bending supply curve for a particular worker. This can be seen in Figure 8.6. When the wage rate is $0W_1$, the number of hours worked is $0Q_1$. When the wage rate is increased to $0W_2$ or $0W_3$, the number of hours worked by the individual worker increases to $0Q_2$ or $0Q_3$. However, if there is an increase in the wage rate above $0W_3$, there is a decrease in the number of hours worked by the individual worker.

The slope of the labour supply curve will depend on the **elasticity of supply of labour**, that is, the degree of responsiveness of the supply of labour in response to a change in the wage rate. Figure 8.7 shows differences in the elasticity of supply of labour. If the supply of labour is elastic, then a change in the wage rate will bring about a greater percentage change in the quantity of labour supplied. If the supply of labour is inelastic, then a change in the wage rate will bring about a smaller percentage change in the quantity of labour supplied.

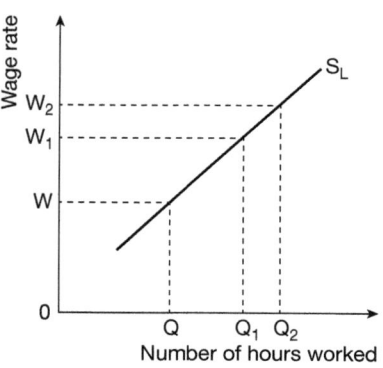

▲ **Figure 8.5** An industry supply curve for labour

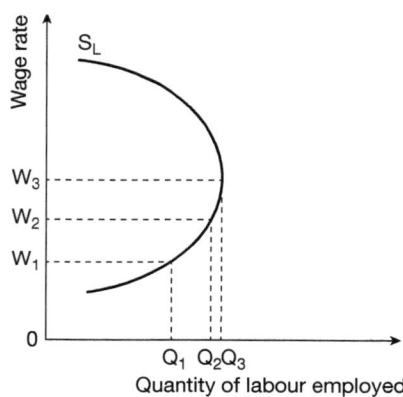

▲ **Figure 8.6** Backward bending supply curve for labour

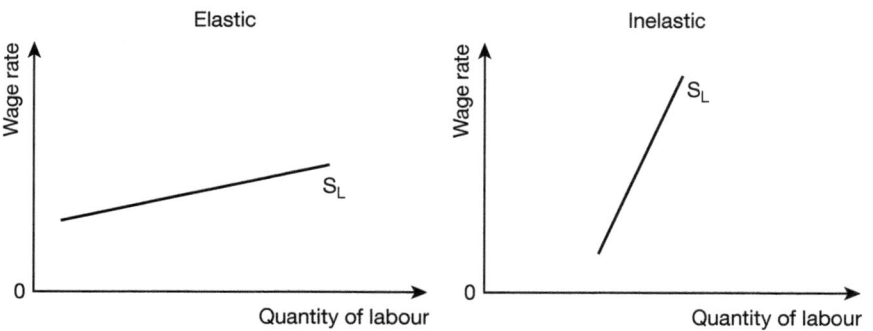

▲ **Figure 8.7** Differences in the elasticity of supply of labour

The supply curve of labour will be influenced by the **occupational mobility of labour** and the **geographical mobility of labour**.

Key terms

Elasticity of supply of labour: a measure of the responsiveness of the supply of labour to a change in the wage rate.

Occupational mobility of labour: the ease or otherwise with which individuals can move between occupations.

Geographical mobility of labour: the ease or otherwise with which individuals can move between geographical areas.

Non-wage factors

In addition to wage factors, there are also non-wage factors that can affect the supply of labour to a firm or to an occupation. These can include:

- the working conditions
- the promotion prospects and career opportunities
- the hours of work
- the pension provision

- the availability of fringe benefits
- the facilities available at work
- the strength of vocation/job satisfaction
- the training/professional development provided.

Net advantages

There are various advantages of being in work. One of these is the reward to workers in the form of wages, salaries and any other kind of financial benefit. These financial advantages are known as **pecuniary advantages**.

However, there may be other advantages of being in work that are non-financial, such as the job satisfaction that a person gains from employment. These non-financial advantages are known as **non-pecuniary advantages**.

The balance between the financial, or pecuniary, advantages and the non-financial, or non-pecuniary, advantages of any employment gives rise to what are termed the **net advantages**.

> **Key terms**
>
> **Pecuniary advantages:** monetary rewards obtained in a particular occupation.
>
> **Non-pecuniary advantages:** non-monetary rewards obtained in a particular occupation.
>
> **Net advantages:** the overall advantages to a worker of choosing one job rather than another; these can consist of both pecuniary and non-pecuniary advantages.

> ★ **Exam tip**
>
> Make sure you do not assume that the only reason why workers stay in one form of employment rather than move to another is because of the wage or salary received; that is, they stress the importance of the financial or pecuniary advantages. However, there are a number of possible non-pecuniary advantages that can influence employment decisions, such as job satisfaction, a sense of vocation, status, working conditions, flexibility, such as in relation to hours worked and the length of holidays.

> 💡 **Remember**
>
> Net advantages of a particular employment can consist of both pecuniary and non-pecuniary benefits.

The long-run supply of labour

There are a number of possible factors that could influence the long-run supply of labour and these include:

- the size of the population of a country
- the extent of immigration into, and emigration out of, a country
- the labour participation rate
- the tax rates that are applied to income earned

- the level of benefits paid by the state
- improvements in the occupational mobility of labour
- improvements in the geographical mobility of labour.

8.3.6 The causes of shifts in and movements along the supply curve of labour to a firm or an occupation

Labour supply is defined as the number of workers willing and able to work, multiplied by the hours they are willing and able to work. The higher the wage rate, the more labour is supplied; the lower the wage rate, the less labour is supplied. The supply curve of labour, therefore, slopes upwards from left to right. Other possible factors affecting the supply of labour are assumed to be constant. Therefore, if the wage rate changes, there will be a movement along the supply curve.

A shift of a labour supply curve

A shift of a labour supply curve occurs when there is a change in a determinant of the supply of labour, apart from a change in the wage rate. These changes include:

- the size of the working population of a country, that is, the number of people of working age who are willing and able to work and this will be affected by such factors as changes in the retirement age and the school leaving age
- the tax and benefit levels
- net migration, that is, the extent of immigration and emigration
- people's preferences for work
- net advantages of work.

8.3.7 Wage determination in perfect markets

Equilibrium wage rate and employment in a labour market

Equilibrium in a labour market is just like equilibrium in any other market and is achieved where demand is equal to supply. This can be seen in Figure 8.8 where the equilibrium wage is 0W and the equilibrium quantity is 0Q. Figure 8.8 shows the situation for both the market and an individual firm; the wage rate is determined in the market where D_L is equal to S_L and all firms in the industry have to accept this wage, that is, the firms are price, or wage, takers.

The characteristics of a perfect factor, for example, labour, market are very similar to those of a perfect product market:

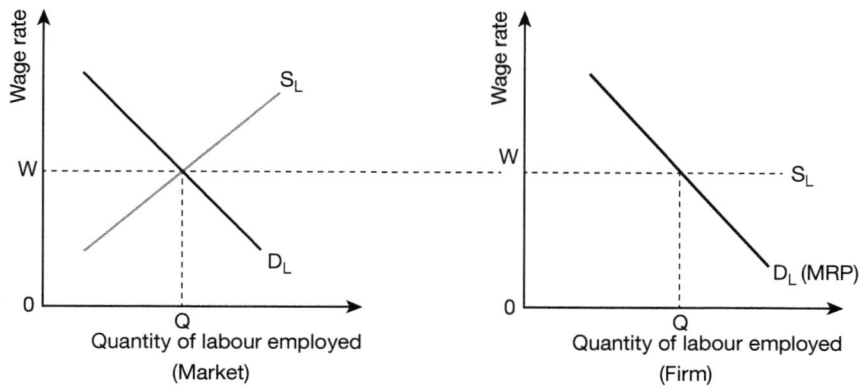

▲ **Figure 8.8** Wage determination in perfect markets

- a large number of firms employing labour
- a large number of homogeneous workers who are perfectly mobile within the industry
- perfect knowledge in the market for both employers and employees.

8.3.8 Wage determination in imperfect markets

Wage determination in imperfect markets applies to three different situations:

- the influence of trade unions on wage determination and employment in a labour market
- the influence of government on wage determination and employment in a labour market using a national minimum wage
- the influence of monopsony employers on wage determination and employment in a labour market.

The influence of trade unions on wage determination and employment in a labour market

Wage determination in perfect markets has already been covered, but it is not necessarily the case that a labour market operates as a perfect market. For example, the workers may be members of a **trade union** and these organisations may be able to influence the process of wage determination in what would therefore be seen as an imperfect market.

Trade unions represent the interests of their members in wage negotiations with the employers through what is called **collective bargaining**. Sometimes a trade union will operate a **closed shop** to increase its bargaining power

> **Key terms**
>
> **Trade union:** an organisation of workers which is active on behalf of its members, such as in relation to the improvement of wages and salaries.
>
> **Collective bargaining:** a process of negotiation over pay and working conditions between a trade union, representing employees, and the employers.
>
> **Closed shop:** a situation in which workers are only able to work in a particular industry if they are members of a trade union.

where the entire workforce employed in an industry belong to the trade union.

One way of doing this is by a reduction in the supply of labour, for example, by forcing the employers to make it more difficult for workers to enter into an industry. The effect of this will be to bring about an increase in the level of wages. This can be seen in Figure 8.9. The trade union brings about a restriction on the entry of labour into a particular industry, such as through raising the minimum level of qualifications or period of training required to work in the industry. This will have the effect of shifting the supply curve of labour to the left, from S_L to S_{L1}. As a result of this, the wage rate will increase from 0W to $0W_1$, although the number of workers employed will fall from 0Q to $0Q_1$.

An alternative approach would be for the trade unions to negotiate wage increases for their members as a result of the increased productivity of the workers. For example, the trade unions could agree to the workers adopting more flexible working practices or to using new technology. This can be seen in Figure 8.10 where there is a shift of the demand curve to the right from D_1 to D_2. This has the effect of increasing the wage rate from $0W_1$ to $0W_2$ and increasing the quantity of labour from $0Q_1$ to $0Q_2$.

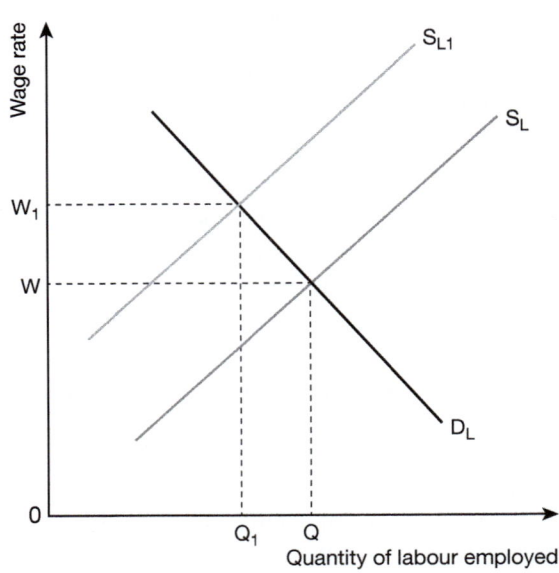

▲ **Figure 8.9** The effect of restricting the supply of labour in an industry

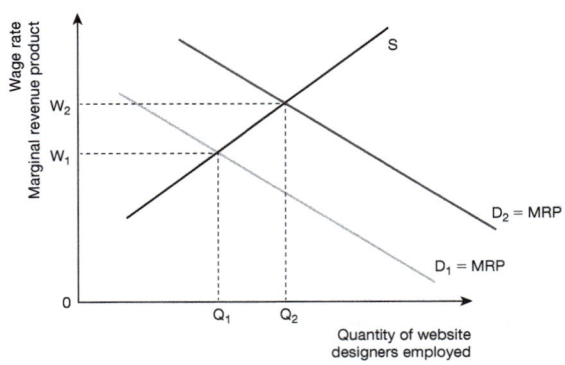

▲ **Figure 8.10** The effect of increasing the demand for labour in an industry

★ **Exam tip**

Trade unions can try to increase the wages of their members either by decreasing the supply of labour or by increasing the demand for labour, but the advantage of increasing the demand for labour is that there is an increase in both the wage rate and the quantity of labour employed, whereas with a decrease in the supply of labour, although there is an increase in the wage rate, there is also a decrease in the quantity of labour employed.

The influence of government on wage determination and employment in a labour market using a national minimum wage

The existence of an imperfect market has already been seen in the context of trade unions intervening in labour markets to try to increase the wage rates of their members. Another example of intervention is where a government intervenes to influence wage rates in a market, such as through the establishment of a **national minimum wage**.

Figure 8.11 shows the effect of a government intervening to establish a national minimum wage. The equilibrium wage rate in the market, without any government intervention, would be 0W, where demand and supply intersect, and the equilibrium quantity would be 0Q. However, a government may decide that the wage rate of 0W is too low and so decides to intervene in the market by passing a law to establish the wage rate at $0W_1$. This has the advantage that all those in employment now receive a wage rate of $0W_1$, rather than 0W, but the drawback of this government intervention is that although $0Q_2$ workers are willing to work at this rate of pay, only $0Q_1$ will be demanded at the higher rate of pay.

Key term

National minimum wage: a wage rate that is set by a government and which is made legally binding on employers, although there may be exemptions in terms of particular occupations and the wage rate may differ for people of various ages.

★ **Link**

See Unit 3, section 3.3.4, for information on a minimum wage.

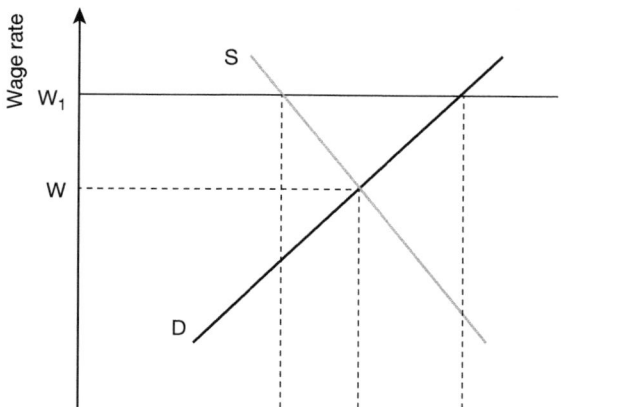

◀ **Figure 8.11** A national minimum wage

The influence of monopsony employers on wage determination and employment in a labour market

Another example of how wage determination can occur in an imperfect market is through the existence of a **monopsony**. It has been assumed, up to now, that there are likely to be a number of firms operating in an industry and so the demand for labour curve will be made up of a number of firms in an industry.

However, in the case of a monopsony, or single buyer, there is only one firm in the market that wishes to employ labour. Unlike the situation in a market in which there are many firms in an industry, where each firm is a price, or wage taker, accepting the prevailing wage rate in the market, if a firm is a monopsonist it would be able to pay a lower wage.

> **Key term**
>
> **Monopsony:** a single buyer of a product or a factor of production, for example, labour.

Labour is employed by a monopsonist, but supplied competitively

Figure 8.12 shows the situation of a single buyer of labour, the monopsonist, and labour supplied competitively. The average cost of labour is shown by AC_L and this is also the supply curve of labour (S_L). The marginal cost of labour curve (MC_L) is above the AC_L curve. The monopsonist will employ workers by equating the marginal cost paid to employ a worker with the marginal revenue product gained from this employment, that is, where $MRP = MC_L$, with 0Q quantity of labour employed. This is the profit maximising position. The wage that the monopsonist pays to employ labour is 0W. However, because the marginal cost of labour is above and diverging from the average cost of labour, to employ more workers the monopsonist must increase the wage rate for the last worker and all the workers before.

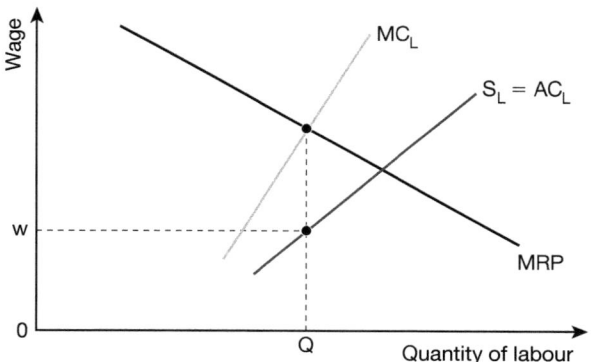

▲ **Figure 8.12** A monopsony labour market

Bilateral monopoly: labour is employed by a monopsonist and supplied by a monopoly

As well as a single buyer of labour, the monopsonist, it is also possible that instead of being supplied competitively, labour is supplied by a monopoly, that is, a trade union. The trade union will want to have a higher wage rate and a higher employment level. However, as already pointed out, the monopsonist will want to have a wage rate of 0W and an employment level of 0Q. The monopsony buyer and the monopoly seller will negotiate these wage and employment positions and the eventual wage and quantity established in the market will depend on the relative bargaining strengths of the monopsony buyer and the monopoly seller. This situation is called a **bilateral monopoly**.

> **Key term**
>
> **Bilateral monopoly:** a situation in which labour is being bought by a single buyer, the monopsonist, and being sold by a single seller, the trade union or monopolist.

151

8.3.9 The determination of wage differentials by labour market forces

If labour markets are very competitive, with identical workers and perfect mobility of labour, wages will move towards the same equilibrium level. However, wages can differ greatly and these wage differentials can be determined by a number of possible factors, including:

- variation in human capital resulting from differences in education and training

- differences in productivity, resulting from variations in the skills and experience of workers

- discrimination in relation to gender, ethnicity, disability and age

- compensation for risk-taking, working in poor conditions or having to work unsocial hours.

These factors will influence the elasticity of supply of workers and wages will tend to be higher the more inelastic the supply.

8.3.10 Transfer earnings and economic rent

Definition of transfer earnings

Transfer earnings refer to those earnings that are the minimum that would be necessary to keep a factor production in a particular use.

Definition of economic rent

Economic rent refers to the additional payment that a worker receives above transfer earnings.

Factors affecting transfer earnings and economic rent in an occupation

Figure 8.13 shows the distinction between transfer earnings and economic rent. The area under the supply curve, 0BAQ, represents the transfer earnings, and the area between the supply curve and the horizontal line across from W, BWA, represents the economic rent.

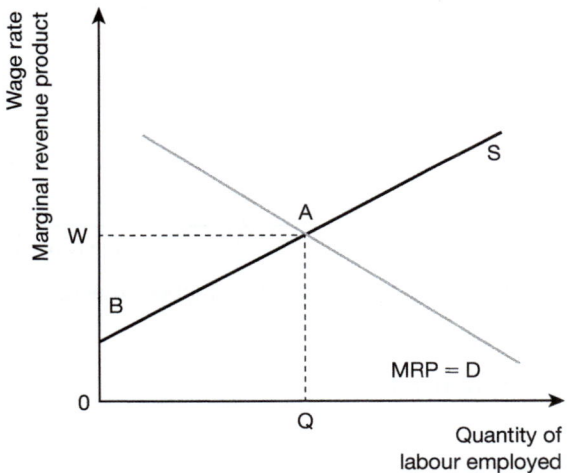

◀ **Figure 8.13** Transfer earnings and economic rent

The elasticity of demand and the elasticity of supply will determine the relative size of economic rent and transfer earnings in an occupation.

For example, a very good professional footballer will be able to gain a relatively large economic rent because both demand and supply are relatively inelastic. A cleaner, on the other hand, will receive a relatively small economic rent because both demand and supply are relatively elastic.

The amount of economic rent that a worker is able to obtain is limited by the fact that in many occupations there is not usually a high level of **mobility of labour**; in fact, in many labour markets, there is a high degree of **immobility of labour**.

There can sometimes be differences in wages in an industry in different parts of a country. This is because although there might be an officially agreed wage rate in an industry that is supposed to apply across a whole country, specific demand and supply circumstances may mean that the actual earnings of some workers in some parts of the country are higher. This situation is known as **wage drift**.

💡 **Remember**

It is possible to divide an individual's earnings into transfer earnings and economic rent. Transfer earnings are the opportunity cost of a certain job. If at least this amount had not been earned, the individual will have moved out of the job and into the next best-paid alternative job. This assumes that the individual is only concerned with the pecuniary, that is, the monetary, rewards of the job. Economic rent refers to the earnings that are above the transfer earnings.

⭐ **Exam tip**

Make sure you understand that the proportion of any given wage that represents transfer earnings and economic rent depends upon the elasticity of supply of labour. The more inelastic the supply of labour, the greater is the proportion of any earnings that represent economic rent relative to transfer earnings. The more elastic the supply of labour, the smaller is the proportion of any earnings that represent economic rent relative to transfer earnings.

⭐ **Exam tip**

It is common to include a diagram in answers to illustrate transfer earnings and economic rent, but these are often labelled the wrong way round. Make sure that you label the area below the supply curve as transfer earnings and the area above the supply curve as economic rent.

Another common error is to confuse transfer earnings with transfer payments, but they are completely different. Transfer earnings refer to the minimum payment required to keep a factor of production, such as labour, in its present use, whereas transfer payments are a form of payment to those in society who are less well off, paid for out of the revenue received from taxation.

 Raise your grade

Assess how 'nudge' theory can be used to inform government policies to correct market failure. [20]

Behavioural economics can offer insights into the economic behaviour of people (1). For example, a government might decide to adopt a policy of nudging people in a particular direction, such as in relation to the consumption of demerit goods (2).

The consumption of alcohol could be an example of where such a government policy might be successful. Medical evidence is very clear about the potential dangers to a person's health of excessive alcohol consumption. A government might therefore decide to intervene in a market to try to reduce the extent of alcohol consumption (3).

The effectiveness of such a policy to change consumer behaviour will depend on a number of factors (4), but it is likely that the behaviour of at least some consumers will be changed.

How to improve this answer

1. The candidate refers to the fact that behavioural economics is able to offer insights into the economic behaviour of people, but this point could have been developed more fully. For example, the candidate could have stressed how behavioural economic models are designed to provide an insight into why consumers do not always act in a rational way. These insights stress the importance of understanding the actual behaviour of people in an economy rather than the traditional approach which stresses the idea that people are assumed to behave rationally.

2. The behavioural approach emphasises that it is possible to 'nudge' people to act in a particular way, different from how they would act if there was no government intervention. It is appropriate that the candidate has referred to a government policy to discourage the consumption of demerit goods, but it would have been useful if they had explained the meaning of the term 'demerit goods' at this point.

3. The candidate has referred to the possibility of a government intervening in a market to try to reduce the extent of alcohol consumption, but has not given any indication of how this could actually be done. It would have been helpful if the candidate had referred to the idea of advertisements for alcohol containing certain warnings, such as 'drink sensibly'.

4. The candidate has referred to the fact that the effectiveness of such a policy to change consumer behaviour will depend on a number of factors, but has not indicated what any of these factors might be. For example, it might depend on the strength of the wording of any health warnings, the extent to which consumers are aware of such warnings or the extent to which the warnings are part of a much wider information campaign, such as the decision of a government to launch a 'Drink Awareness' campaign to make as many people as possible aware of the possible health dangers of excessive alcohol consumption.

AO1 and AO2: Level 2   6/14

AO3:   Level 1   2/6

Total: 8/20

Worked Example

Assess to what extent a country can increase the supply of labour in the long run. [20]

It is possible that the supply of labour could be increased in the long run.

The size of the population of a country could increase over a period of time. One reason could be as a result of a natural increase in population when the birth rate exceeds the death rate. Another reason could be if there was net migration into a country, that is, the number of immigrants coming into a country is greater than the number of emigrants leaving a country.

The supply of labour would also increase if there was an increase in the labour participation rate, for example, if more people could be allowed and encouraged to work. This could come about through an increase in the retirement age in a country. The level of taxation on earned income could also influence supply, especially if tax levels increased substantially, as this could have a disincentive effect in an economy. The level of state benefits could also be a factor.

Improvements in the occupational mobility of labour could increase the supply of labour in particular industries, such as through improvements in the education and training provision in a country. Improvements in the geographical mobility of labour could also have a potential impact on the supply of labour, such as through an improvement in the provision of information about job vacancies in other geographical areas.

It can therefore be seen that an increase in the supply of labour is more likely in the long run than in the short run because many of these factors will take a number of years to have a significant impact. However, it may not necessarily be that easy to increase the supply of labour, even in the long run. For example, there may be net migration out of a country, reducing the size of its population, and the level of benefits may be so high that people are discouraged from working.

Exam-style questions

1 An indirect tax will shift:

  (a) the demand curve to the left

  (b) the demand curve to the right

  (c) the supply curve to the left

  (d) the supply curve to the right. [1]

2 X-inefficiency in monopoly comes about as a result of:

  (a) external economies of scale in an industry

  (b) organisational slack in a firm

  (c) strong competition in an industry

  (d) technical efficiency in a firm. [1]

3 A pollution permit is also known as a:

  (a) capital tax

  (b) property right

  (c) tradable permit

  (d) transfer payment. [1]

4 The transfer of ownership of assets from the private sector to the public sector is known as:

  (a) deregulation

  (b) nationalisation

  (c) outsourcing

  (d) privatisation. [1]

5 A negative income tax involves:

  (a) a regressive system

  (b) benefits and tax payments

  (c) benefits only

  (d) tax payments only. [1]

6 If the demand for labour is elastic, then a change in the wage rate will bring about:

  (a) a greater percentage change in the quantity of labour demanded

  (b) a larger proportion of workers in trade unions

  (c) a smaller percentage change in the quantity of labour demanded

  (d) no change in the quantity of labour demanded. [1]

7 A financial advantage of employment is known as a:

  (a) fringe advantage

  (b) net advantage

  (c) non-pecuniary advantage

  (d) pecuniary advantage. [1]

8 Transfer earnings refer to those earnings that are:

  (a) in excess of the opportunity cost of employment

  (b) paid by a government to those people not in employment

  (c) shown in a wage diagram by the area above the supply curve

  (d) the minimum that would be necessary to keep labour in a particular use. [1]

9 A closed shop is where:

  (a) a firm is unable to employ any additional workers

  (b) all workers in a particular industry are members of a trade union

  (c) all workers in a trade union are ordered to go on strike

  (d) it is impossible to calculate the marginal revenue product of the workers. [1]

10 A monopsony refers to:

  (a) a government establishing a national minimum wage

  (b) a monopoly buyer of labour

  (c) a monopoly seller of labour

  (d) an industry where 100% of workers are in a trade union. [1]

11 Assess whether the introduction of a national minimum wage will always be beneficial. [20]

12 Assess to what extent a trade union will always be able to determine the wage rates that are paid to its members. [20]

The macroeconomy

Key topics

- The circular flow of income
- Economic growth and sustainability
- Employment/unemployment
- Money and banking

9.1 The circular flow of income

9.1.1 The multiplier process

The definition of the multiplier

The **multiplier** measures the extent to which an increase in an injection into the circular flow of income of an economy brings about a multiplied effect on the level of income. However, it is also important to understand that an increase in an injection into the circular flow of income is also likely to have an effect on the withdrawals or leakages out of the circular flow of income. Each successive increase in aggregate demand, as a result of the injection into the circular flow of income, will therefore become progressively less.

Key formulae and calculations

In order to calculate the size of the multiplier, it is necessary to understand what is meant by the marginal propensity to withdraw. It is also necessary to understand the difference between an average propensity and a marginal propensity.

An average propensity measures the total of, say, consumption or saving, as a proportion of total income. The **average propensity to consume (APC)** will therefore show the proportion of total income that is spent. The **average propensity to save (APS)** will show the proportion of total income that is saved. The **average propensity to import (APM)** will show the proportion of total income that is spent on imports. The **average rate of taxation** shows the proportion of total income that is taxed.

However, economists are also interested in marginal propensities. A marginal propensity measures the proportion of any change in income that is, say, spent on consumption or saved. The **marginal propensity to consume (MPC)** will therefore show the proportion of any change in income that is spent on consumption. The **marginal propensity to save (MPS)** will show the proportion of any change in income that is saved.

The size of the multiplier is calculated through marginal propensities. In a two sector economy, involving only households and firms, it is calculated by 1 divided by the marginal propensity to save, that is:

$$\frac{1}{\text{MPS}}$$

In a three sector economy, involving households, firms and the government, it is calculated by 1 divided by the marginal propensity to save + **the marginal rate of taxation**, that is:

$$\frac{1}{MPS + MRT}$$

In a four sector economy, involving households, firms, government and the international economy, it is calculated by 1 divided by the marginal propensity to save + the marginal rate of taxation + the **marginal propensity to import**, that is:

$$\frac{1}{MPS + MRT + MPM}$$

The size of the multiplier is usually simplified by expressing it as 1 divided by the **marginal propensity to withdraw**, that is:

$$\frac{1}{MPW}$$

> **Key terms**
>
> **Marginal rate of taxation:** the proportion of any change in income that is paid in direct tax.
>
> **Marginal propensity to import:** the proportion of any change in income that is spent on imports.
>
> **Marginal propensity to withdraw:** the total of MPC, MRT and MPM.

> ★ **Exam tip**
>
> Even if an exam question does not explicitly refer to the multiplier, this does not mean that it should not be included in an answer. In any question on the determination of the level of income in an economy, you should assume that you will need to include an explanation and analysis of the multiplier and the multiplier process in your answer.

> 💡 **Remember**
>
> It is important that you understand what is involved in the multiplier process. If there is an injection into the circular flow of income, the increase in national income will be greater than the size of the injection. The extra income creates extra expenditure and this creates extra income, as the multiplier process is based on the idea that one person's spending is another person's income. There will be successive rounds of spending, but in each successive round the multiplier effect will be reduced because of the impact of leakages or withdrawals from the circular flow of income.

National income determination using AD and income approach with the multiplier process

There are two ways to determine the level of income in an economy: one way is by using the AD and income approach and the other way is by using the withdrawal (leakage) and injection approach.

The AD and income approach

The level of equilibrium income in an economy is determined where aggregate expenditure is equal to output. This is shown in Figure 9.1. Real GDP is shown on the horizontal axis and aggregate expenditure is shown on the vertical axis. The 45-degree line shows where planned expenditure equals real national income. The economy is in equilibrium at E where AE crosses the 45-degree line at Y.

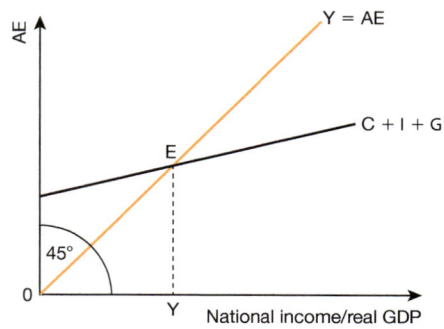

▲ **Figure 9.1** The AD and income approach to national income determination

The withdrawal (leakage) and injection approach

The level of income in an economy is also determined where the injections into the circular flow of income of an economy are equal to the withdrawals or leakages. This is shown in Figure 9.2. Real GDP is shown on the horizontal axis and the injections and withdrawals are shown on the vertical axis. The economy is in equilibrium at E where injections (J) are equal to withdrawals (W).

The calculation of the effect of changing AD on national income using the multiplier

A change in aggregate demand can have a much greater final impact on the level of equilibrium national income than the initial change because of the multiplier effect. This refers to the fact that an initial injection into the circular flow of income stimulates further rounds of spending, that is, one person's spending is another person's income. This will eventually lead to a bigger effect on output and employment than the initial injection.

The effect of an increase in injections into the circular flow of income in an economy will be to increase national income. The size of the multiplier (denoted by the symbol k) can be calculated by dividing the change in national income by the change in the injections.

> **Remember**
>
> The two different methods will produce the same level of equilibrium income.

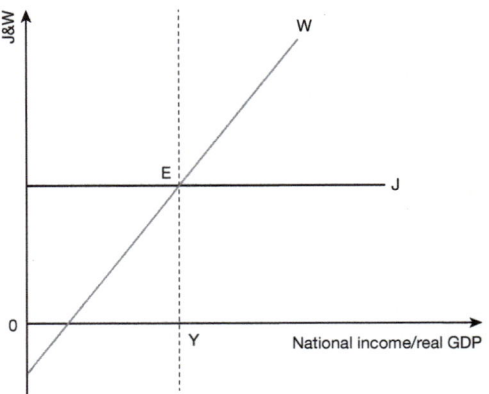

▲ **Figure 9.2** The withdrawal and injection approach to national income determination

> **Remember**
>
> It is possible to distinguish between a positive multiplier and a negative multiplier. A positive multiplier is when an initial increase in an injection, or a decrease in a leakage, leads to a greater final increase in real GDP. A negative multiplier is when an initial decrease in an injection, or an increase in a leakage, leads to a greater final decrease in real GDP.

> **★ Link**
>
> See Unit 4, section 4.2, for an introduction to the circular flow of income.

9.1.2 The components of aggregate demand (AD) and their determinants

The Aggregate Demand (AD) function

The Aggregate Demand (AD) function refers to the total expenditure on, and the total demand for, all that is produced in an economy. It can be represented as follows:

$$AD = C + I + G + (X - M)$$

There are four determinants of Aggregate Demand:

- the consumption function: autonomous and induced consumption
- the investment function: autonomous and induced investment; the accelerator
- government spending
- net imports (exports minus imports).

The consumption function

The first component of AD is consumption. Consumption refers to the expenditure by households in an economy over a period of time. The main influences on consumption include:

- the level of disposable income in an economy; the consumption function indicates the relationship between income and consumption
- the distribution of income and wealth
- the rate of interest on borrowing money to finance consumption
- the availability of credit
- expectations about the future prospects of the economy.

Autonomous and induced consumer expenditure

It is important to be able to distinguish between two different types of consumption: **autonomous consumption** and **induced consumption**.

Autonomous consumption

Autonomous consumption or consumer expenditure refers to consumption that is not related to income, that is, consumption when income is zero.

Induced consumption

Induced consumption or consumer expenditure refers to consumption that is related to income, that is, as extra income is gained, some of this will be spent (the percentage of extra income that is spent is known as the marginal propensity to consume).

> 💡 **Remember**
>
> It is possible that consumption actually exceeds income. In this situation, the difference between consumption and income would need to be financed by the use of past savings. This is known as **dissaving**.
> Saving is generally regarded as good for an individual, enabling a person to be able to buy something in the future. However, it can be viewed as potentially bad for an economy as a whole because it is a leakage or withdrawal from the circular flow of income and so could lead to a fall in national income. This contradiction is known as the **paradox of thrift**.

Key terms

Dissaving: a situation when consumption exceeds income and so this shortfall has to be financed by using savings that have accumulated in the past.

Paradox of thrift: the contradiction between the potential advantages and the potential disadvantages for an economy of people deciding to save.

The savings function

It has already been pointed out that it is possible to distinguish between autonomous and induced consumer expenditure. It is also possible to distinguish between autonomous and induced savings. **Autonomous savings** are not related to changes in the level of national income in an economy, whereas **induced savings** are related to changes in the level of national income.

Autonomous and induced investment

The second component of AD is investment. Investment refers to the expenditure by firms in an economy over a period of time, such as expenditure on factories, machinery and equipment. The main influences on investment include:

- the rate of interest on funds to finance investment expenditure
- changes in technology
- the cost of capital goods
- changes in consumer demand
- government policies, such as in relation to taxes and subsidies
- expectations about the future prospects of the economy.

Autonomous and induced investment

It is important to be able to distinguish between two different types of investment: **autonomous investment** and **induced investment**.

Autonomous investment

This refers to investment that is not the result of any changes in the level of national income in an economy, that is, it is independent of any such changes.

Induced investment

This refers to investment that is the result of any changes in the level of national income in an economy, that is, it is dependent on any such changes.

The accelerator

The concept of the **accelerator** is based on the relationship between changes in the level of national income in an economy and changes in induced investment. It assumes that there is a fixed **capital : output ratio** and states that investment is a function of a change in national income.

> 💡 **Remember**
>
> It is important to understand that the accelerator is concerned with the relationship between investment and the rate of change of output. It is not the level of output that is important, but the rate of change of that output.

> **Key terms**
>
> **Autonomous investment:** capital investment that is not related to changes in the level of national income in an economy.
>
> **Induced investment:** capital investment that is related to changes in the level of national income in an economy.

> **Key terms**
>
> **Accelerator:** a way of calculating the effect of a change in national income on investment, that is, the extent to which the level of investment depends on the rate of growth of aggregate demand.
>
> **Capital : output ratio:** the amount of capital required to produce a particular level of output.

> ★ **Exam tip**
>
> Be careful not to confuse the multiplier and the accelerator. The multiplier shows the effect of an injection on the level of national income in an economy, whereas the accelerator shows the effect of the rate of growth of demand on the level of investment.

Government spending

The third component of AD is government expenditure. Government expenditure refers to the money spent by a government, such as the wages and salaries of those who are employed in the public sector and the money spent on public sector investment projects, such as the building of a new road. The main influences on government spending include:

- government policies on expenditure decisions
- tax revenue
- demographic changes.

Net exports (exports minus imports)

The fourth component of AD is net exports. Net exports refer to the difference between the value of the exports that leave a country and the value of the imports that enter a country. The main influences on net exports include:

- a country's GDP
- the GDP of other countries
- the relative prices of a country's exports
- the quality, reliability and reputation of a country's exports
- exchange rate movements.

> ★ **Link**
>
> See Unit 4, section 4.3, on Aggregate Demand.

9.1.3 The full employment level of national income and the equilibrium level of national income; inflationary and deflationary gaps

It is important to understand that an **equilibrium level of national income** in an economy may not necessarily be at the **full employment level of national income**.

Key terms

Equilibrium level of national income: a situation in which the aggregate demand for goods and services is equal to the aggregate supply of goods and services in an economy.

Full employment level of national income: a situation in which the aggregate demand for goods and services is equal to the aggregate supply of goods and services in an economy in which there is full employment of resources, that is, real GDP = potential GDP.

Inflationary gap and the level of national income

An **inflationary gap** shows a situation where the equilibrium level of income in an economy is greater than the full employment level of income, that is, aggregate demand is greater than aggregate supply.

This can be seen in Figure 9.3. At the equilibrium level of income of 0Y, where the 45-degree line (AD = Y) intersects with AD_0, the level of aggregate demand in the economy is actually AD_1, that is, the level of aggregate demand exceeds the level of output at full employment, causing upward pressure on prices. The inflationary gap is shown by the vertical distance between AD_0 and AD_1.

Key term

Inflationary gap: a situation in which the level of aggregate demand in an economy is greater than the aggregate supply at full employment, causing a rise in the general level of prices in the economy.

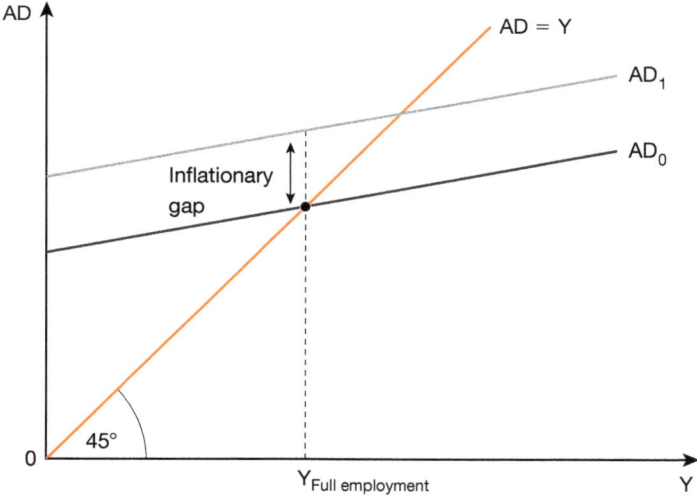

▲ **Figure 9.3** Inflationary gap

Deflationary gap and the level of national income

A **deflationary gap** shows a situation in which the equilibrium level of income in an economy is less than the full employment level of income, that is, aggregate supply is greater than aggregate demand.

This can be seen in Figure 9.4. The full employment level of income is at 0Y, determined by where the 45-degree line intersects with AD_1. However, the level of aggregate demand in the economy is shown by AD_0 and this is

Key term

Deflationary gap: a situation in which the level of aggregate demand in an economy is less than the aggregate supply at full employment, causing unemployment.

less than AD_1. The equilibrium level of income is at $0Y_1$, less than the full employment level of income. A deflationary gap therefore occurs when the level of aggregate demand in an economy is below the level of output at full employment. The deflationary gap is shown by the vertical distance between AD_0 and AD_1.

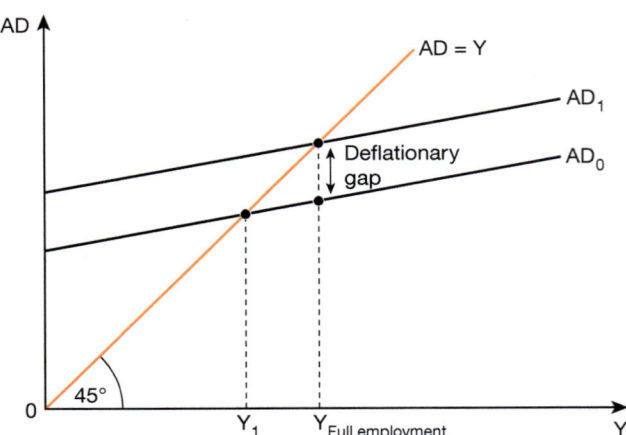

▲ **Figure 9.4** Deflationary gap

★ **Exam tip**

Do not assume that the equilibrium level of income and the full employment level of income in an economy will be the same. This will not necessarily be the case. It is possible that an output gap in the form of either an inflationary gap or a deflationary gap could occur.

9.2 Economic growth and sustainability

9.2.1 Actual growth versus potential growth in national output

Economic growth

Economic growth is defined as the increase in the national output of a country over a period of time. It is usually measured in terms of a change in gross domestic product. It is important to be able to distinguish between actual growth and potential growth in national output.

Actual versus potential growth in national output

Actual economic growth occurs when the existing factors of production in an economy are used more efficiently so as to achieve a higher level of output. For example, a higher level of output could be obtained through a reduction in the number of people unemployed in an economy. This can be seen in Figure 9.5. A movement from X, within the production possibility curve AB, to a position of Y, on the production possibility curve, shows actual economic growth.

Potential economic growth occurs when there is a shift, outwards, of a production possibility curve. In Figure 9.5, this is where the production possibility curve shifts out from AB to CD. This could come about as the result of an increase in the quantity of the factors of production available in an economy and/or an increase in the quality of those factors of production. The position Z was not possible to be reached on the AB production possibility curve, but it can now be reached on the CD production possibility curve. Potential growth therefore comes about as the result of an increase

Key terms

Actual economic growth: the rate of growth in the national output when all the resources in an economy are fully employed, indicated by a movement from inside to a position on a production possibility curve.

Potential economic growth: the rate at which an economy can grow, resulting from a greater quantity and/or quality of factors of production used in the production process, indicated by a shift outwards of a production possibility curve.

in the potential capacity of an economy, shown by an outward shift of the production possibility curve.

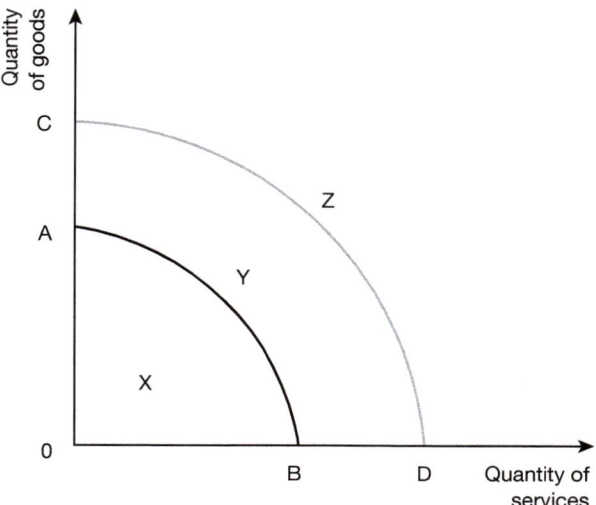

▲ **Figure 9.5** Actual and potential growth

💡 **Remember**

Actual economic growth involves a movement from a position inside a production possibility curve to a position on a production possibility curve, but this will involve an opportunity cost; that is, if there is an increase in the quantity of goods produced, there will be a decrease in the quantity of goods produced. However, potential economic growth involves a shift, outwards, of a production possibility curve and this will not involve an opportunity cost; that is, it will be possible to increase both the quantity of goods and the quantity of services produced.

★ **Exam tip**

Candidates sometimes confuse actual and potential economic growth. It is important to understand that actual economic growth does not involve a shifting, outwards, of a production possibility curve, but potential economic growth does involve such a shift.

9.2.2 Positive and negative output gaps

An **output gap** indicates the difference between the actual output of an economy and the maximum potential output of an economy. It is expressed as a percentage of GDP.

A country's output gap may be either positive or negative:

- Positive output gap: where an economy is outperforming expectations because its actual output is higher than the economy's recognised maximum capacity output.

- Negative output gap: where actual output in an economy is below the economy's full capacity for output.

Key term

Output gap: the difference between the actual output and the potential output of an economy.

💡 **Remember**

An output gap is a general term and can be either in the form of an inflationary gap, when AD is more than AS, or a deflationary gap, when AS is more than AD.

9.2.3 The business (trade) cycle

The phases of the cycle

A **business cycle** or trade cycle refers to fluctuations in output and employment that can occur in an economy over a period of time. The cycle involves four stages:

- slump: a period of low aggregate demand and relatively high unemployment

- recovery: the level of aggregate demand begins to increase

- boom: a period of relatively high economic growth

- recession: a period of economic downturn, defined as two successive quarters of negative GDP growth

Figure 9.6 shows the business cycle. The wavy line shows the four stages of the cycle and the straight line shows the growth of real GDP over time.

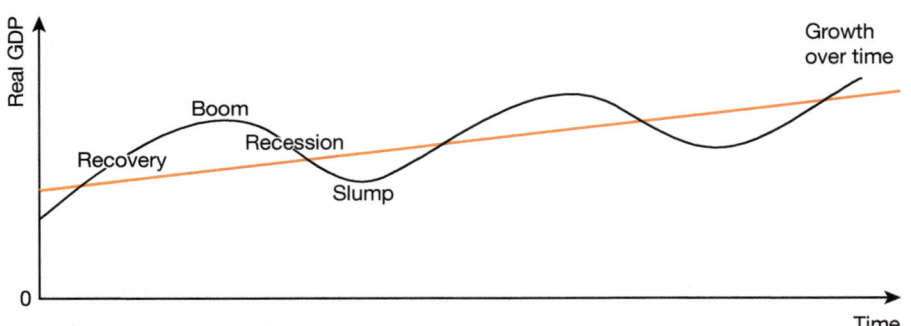

▲ **Figure 9.6** The business (trade) cycle

> 💡 **Remember**
>
> Although the four stages of the business, or trade, cycle are shown by a wavy line in the diagram, the straight line that indicates the change in real GDP over time is upward sloping. This shows that although GDP may rise and fall in cycles, over a period of time the overall trend is upwards. It is important that the upward trend in real GDP is recognised and not just the ups and downs of the trade cycle.

The causes of the cycle

There are a number of factors that can cause different phases of the cycle to occur, including:

- changes in interest rates
- changes in technology
- changes in global trade
- changes in levels of economic confidence
- changes in exchange rates
- changes in house prices

- the multiplier effect
- the accelerator effect
- changes in the level of liquidity in the financial sector
- volatility in stock market indices
- changes in fiscal policy.

The role of automatic stabilisers

Automatic stabilisers have already been referred to in Unit 5, section 5.2. They are fiscal policy instruments that influence the rate of GDP growth and help counter swings in the business cycle.

When there is a boom and a high rate of economic growth, automatic stabilisers will help to reduce it, for example, a government will receive more tax revenue.

When there is a slump and a low rate of economic growth, automatic stabilisers will help to increase it, for example, a government will increase spending on unemployment benefits.

9.2.4 Policies to promote economic growth and their effectiveness

Economic growth can be brought about in an economy by a number of policies, including:

- encouragement of immigration in order to increase the number of workers

- education and training initiatives to improve the quality of labour, for example, the acquisition of new or improved skills, leading to a higher level of productivity

- government financial support for research and development, in terms of both invention and innovation

- government policies to support and encourage an improvement in the state of technology

- government financial incentives to encourage an increase in investment in capital stock, for example, machinery and equipment; this can also be called an increase in gross fixed capital formation

- a reduction in taxes on the profits of businesses to allow firms to keep more funds that can be used to finance investment

- government encouragement to saving, that is, to bring about an increase in the savings ratio, because a high level of savings will provide the necessary funds to finance investment

- government support for a move towards more capital-intensive, and away from labour-intensive, production

- government initiatives to improve information so as to lead to an increased mobility and flexibility of factors of production

- government support for the development of new markets, for example, for exports

- a lowering of interest rates to encourage an upturn or recovery in the business, or trade, cycle.

9.2.5 Inclusive economic growth

The definition of inclusive economic growth

Inclusive economic growth refers to growth that is distributed fairly across society and creates opportunities for all. It is growth that benefits everyone, offering a more prosperous and equitable economy.

> **Key term**
>
> **Inclusive economic growth:** growth that combines increased prosperity with greater equality, creates opportunities for all and distributes the benefits of increased prosperity fairly.

The impact of economic growth on equity and equality

Inclusive economic growth is a concept that advances equitable opportunities for economic participants with benefits incurred by every section of society. It aims to ensure that economic growth benefits everyone and it will therefore have a positive impact on equity and equality in an economy.

Policies to promote inclusive growth

Policies to promote inclusive economic growth need to be concentrated in a number of specific areas, emphasising that it:

- takes place in the sectors in which the poor work, for example, agriculture

- occurs in places where the poor live, for example, undeveloped areas with few resources

- uses the factors of production that the poor possess, for example, unskilled labour

- reduces the prices of consumption items that the poor consume, for example, food, fuel and clothing.

Policies to promote inclusive economic growth therefore need to focus on poverty reduction and eradication. They need to address inequality and enhance growth and economic inclusion by:

- expanding access to quality education
- expanding access to quality healthcare
- investing in infrastructure
- deepening financial inclusion to reach the most vulnerable
- incentivising increased female labour force participation.

There are various ways to bring inclusive economic growth about, including the following:

- Progressive incomes and wealth taxes can contribute to reducing inequality without sacrificing growth.
- A universal basic income has the potential to reduce poverty and inequality where a government provides a guaranteed minimum income for all; it indicates the state's responsibility to support incomes in a universal way.

9.2.6 Sustainable economic growth

The definition of sustainable economic growth

Sustainability refers to the ability to use existing resources to satisfy the needs of the present generation without compromising the ability of future generations to satisfy their needs. Sustainable economic growth can therefore be defined as economic growth that takes into account the needs of future generations as well as those of the present generation.

Key terms

Sustainability: a situation in which the needs of the present generation can be met without imposing costs on future generations.

Conservation: the use of resources in a wise manner, ensuring the highest possible benefits on a continuing and long-term basis.

Using and conserving resources

Economic growth clearly has benefits for a country, but it is also important to recognise that there can also be costs of growth.

This contrast between the potential benefits and costs of economic growth can be seen in relation to the use or **conservation** of resources. The use of resources can contribute significantly to economic growth, but it should not be forgotten that many natural resources are finite in supply, that is, they will eventually run out at some time in the future. This is why there is a strong argument in favour of the conservation of resources, stressing that this is a more sustainable approach that takes into account not only the needs of the present generation, but also the needs of future generations.

★ Exam tip

It is sometimes argued that a country should aim for as high a rate of economic growth as possible, but it needs to be recognised that it is possible for a country to have too high a rate of economic growth, for example, if this leads to significant pollution and to the rapid depletion of scarce resources. It is important that reference is made to the concept of sustainable economic growth.

Remember

There are good arguments for both the use of resources and the conservation of resources. Sustainable economic growth requires that resources are both used and conserved for future use.

The impact of economic growth on the environment and climate change

Rapid economic growth today may create environmental problems for future generations, including the depletion of oil and fish stocks, and global warming. There are clear environmental costs to economic growth; economic growth leads to higher levels of resource consumption, the depletion or loss of non-renewable resources, and greater pollution. The increase in pollution can cause health problems and these will reduce the quality of life.

Some of the key facts of climate change during the last 30 years include the following:

- Global temperatures have increased by 0.5°C.
- Sea levels have risen by 10 cm.
- Carbon dioxide in the atmosphere has increased by 17%.

Policies to mitigate the impact of economic growth on the environment and climate change

Policies to promote sustainable economic growth include the following:

- Technology: a government can provide financial incentives for private firms to invest in new technology, for example, alternative sources of energy such as wind power and solar power.

- Human capital development: government can invest in human capital by allocating more resources, and widening access to, education and training.

- Deregulation: a reduction of red tape could encourage foreign direct investment in economies.

- Incentivisation: government can provide incentives to encourage people to start up their own small and medium-sized businesses.

- Pollution permits: these can be reduced to lower the extent of pollution in an economy over a period of time; fines can be imposed on those firms that do not respond appropriately to these permits.

- Alternative transport to cars: government promotion of cycling and walking and of investment in public transport, including buses, trams and trains.

- Taxation: government could impose taxes on airline tickets to discourage consumption and reduce the carbon footprint and impose carbon taxes on energy suppliers to reduce the level of carbon emissions; such initiatives would be drivers of decarbonisation.

- Legislation: government could ban sales of new conventional petrol and diesel cars to encourage the purchase of greener alternatives, such as electric cars or use of bio-fuel as a source of energy, although this would require money to be spent on developing the necessary infrastructure to provide for the charging of electric vehicles.

- Financial support: government could offer interest-free home and business renovation loans to drive energy efficiency; it could also offer such loans for environmentally-efficient new buildings.

- Recycling: a government could use financial incentives to encourage recycling schemes and initiatives that will reduce demand for scarce raw materials.

- Commitment to action on climate change: the United Nations is encouraging countries to raise their emissions targets to include net zero emissions by 2050 (so far, 121 UN member countries have agreed to this target of achieving carbon neutrality) to protect people from the dangerous impact of climate change; this will require appropriate actions to be implemented to achieve this target.

- Reforestation: a government could encourage firms to commit to a policy that requires them to plant a new tree for every tree that they cut down.

9.3 Employment/unemployment

9.3.1 The definition of full employment

Unemployment refers to a situation in which people are able and willing to work, but are unable to find employment.

Full employment generally refers to a situation in which everyone in an economy who wants a job has a job, with the exception of those who are frictionally unemployed. This is usually about 4–5% of the working population.

> ★ **Link**
>
> See Unit 4, section 4.4, for more information on economic growth.

> **Key term**
>
> **Full employment:** the level of employment in an economy where everyone who is able and willing to work has a job, with the exception of those who are frictionally unemployed.

> ★ **Exam tip**
>
> Full employment does not mean that the unemployment rate in an economy is 0.0% because there will always be an element of frictional unemployment where people are in the process of leaving one job and searching for another.

9.3.2 Equilibrium and disequilibrium unemployment

Different types of unemployment have been covered in Unit 4, section 4.5.3. It is possible to distinguish between the following two broad types of unemployment:

- **Equilibrium unemployment:** this type of unemployment exists when the labour market is at equilibrium, meaning jobs exist but people are either unable or unwilling to take the jobs that exist. Examples of equilibrium unemployment include frictional unemployment, seasonal unemployment and structural unemployment.

- **Disequilibrium unemployment:** this type of unemployment exists when the wage rate rises above equilibrium and the labour market is prevented from clearing. Examples of disequilibrium unemployment include cyclical/demand-deficient unemployment and real wage or classical unemployment.

Hysteresis effect

If unemployment in an economy is persistent, the unemployed could find that their skills become outdated, leading to a low level of confidence and motivation as employment becomes increasingly difficult to find. This is known as the **hysteresis effect**.

9.3.3 Voluntary and involuntary unemployment

It is possible to distinguish between voluntary and involuntary unemployment:

- **Voluntary unemployment:** a situation in which a worker deliberately chooses not to work because of a low wage rate.

- **Involuntary unemployment:** a situation in which a worker is willing to work at the market wage, but is prevented from doing so by factors beyond their control, such as a deficiency of aggregate demand or inflexibility in the labour market, especially wage rigidity. Geographical and occupational immobility of labour can be a major cause of involuntary unemployment. In an economy with involuntary unemployment, there is a surplus of labour at the current real wage.

9.3.4 The natural rate of unemployment

The definition of the natural rate of unemployment

The natural rate of unemployment stresses the link between the level of unemployment and the level of inflation in an economy. It is that level of unemployment associated with a non-accelerating level of inflation, often referred to as **NAIRU:** the non-accelerating inflation rate of unemployment.

> **Key terms**
>
> **Equilibrium unemployment:** a situation in which jobs exist but people are unable or unwilling to take them.
>
> **Disequilibrium unemployment:** a situation in which the labour market is prevented from clearing.
>
> **Hysteresis effect:** the tendency for unemployment to lead to longer-term unemployment as workers find that their skills and knowledge become increasingly outdated.

> **Key terms**
>
> **Voluntary unemployment:** a situation in which a worker chooses to be unemployed.
>
> **Involuntary unemployment:** a situation in which a worker is willing to work at the prevailing wage but cannot find a job.

> **Key terms**
>
> **The natural rate of unemployment:** the level of unemployment in an economy that is associated with a non-accelerating level of inflation.
>
> **NAIRU:** the non-accelerating inflation rate of unemployment.

> 💡 **Remember**
>
> The natural rate of unemployment, or NAIRU, is an equilibrium position where the aggregate demand for labour is equal to the aggregate supply of labour at the current real wage rate. As a result of this situation of equilibrium, there is no upward pressure on the level of prices in an economy, that is, it is non-accelerating.
>
> It is often associated with monetarist economists, such as Milton Friedman, who argued that the natural rate of unemployment could not be reduced as any increase in aggregate demand would lead to higher inflation and higher unemployment.

The determinants of the natural rate of unemployment

The natural rate of unemployment is the rate of unemployment when the labour market is in equilibrium and is caused by structural, supply-side, factors, such as a mismatch of skills, rather than by demand-side factors.

There are a number of determinants of natural unemployment, including the following:

- Availability of information about jobs: this will be an important factor in determining how quickly the people who are frictionally unemployed find jobs.

- The level of state benefits: relatively generous unemployment benefits may discourage people from taking jobs at the existing wage rate; however, if the level of benefits is low, this will lead to a fall in the natural rate of unemployment.

- Skills and education: the quality of skills and education will influence the level of occupational mobility; that is, a better trained and better educated workforce will be more occupationally mobile.

- The level of geographical mobility of labour: the more willing people are to move to different parts of a country, the more geographically mobile they will be.

- Flexibility of the labour market: trade unions may be able to restrict the supply of labour to certain labour markets, making them less flexible, and this will increase the natural rate of unemployment.

- Hysteresis: a recession may cause a rise in the natural level of unemployment because when people are unemployed for a relatively long period of time, they become deskilled and demotivated, making it more difficult for them to find jobs.

The policy implications

The way to reduce the natural rate of unemployment in an economy is to implement supply-side policies, including:

- better education and training to reduce the occupational immobility of labour

- better information about job vacancies in different parts of a country to reduce the geographical immobility of labour

- greater flexibility of labour markets, such as through the reduction of the powers of trade unions.

Labour productivity

The implementation of supply-side policies could lead to an improvement in **labour productivity**. Labour productivity refers to the efficiency of labour in terms of the output per worker per period of time. Levels of productivity can vary for a number of reasons, including:

- education
- training
- skills
- experience
- technical knowledge
- level of capital available
- working methods and practices
- motivation and engagement.

Key term

Labour productivity: the level of efficiency of a unit of labour in terms of the output that can be produced per person per period of time.

★ **Exam tip**

Be sure not to confuse 'production' and 'productivity'. Production refers to the total output from a given number of resources, whereas productivity refers to the efficiency of an input, such as labour, into the production process.

9.3.5 Patterns and trends in (un)employment

Although economists will be interested in the unemployment rate in an economy at any one moment in time, they will also be interested to discover patterns and trends in employment and unemployment over a longer period of time. They will be particularly interested in finding out whether the trend in the unemployment rate is upward or downward.

★ **Exam tip**

If you are asked to comment in the exam on a pattern or a trend, make sure that you do focus on the overall pattern or trend over time and do not simply describe every figure that is included in the data.

9.3.6 The mobility of labour

The forms of labour mobility

Mobility of labour refers to the ability and willingness of labour to move from one place to another or from one occupation to another. There are thus two types of labour mobility:

- **geographical mobility:** when a worker moves from one place to another within a country or from one country to another

- **occupational mobility:** when a worker moves from one occupation to another, either in the same industry or in a different industry.

Key terms

Geographical mobility of labour: when a worker moves from one place to another within a country or from one country to another.

Occupational mobility of labour: when a worker moves from one occupation to another, either in the same industry or in a different industry.

The factors affecting labour mobility

There are a number of factors affecting labour mobility, including the following:

- Education and training: labour mobility is affected by the extent to which it is educated and trained; the more a person is educated and trained, the greater their occupational and geographical mobility is likely to be.

- Transport and communication: a more developed transport and communication system is likely to encourage labour mobility, especially geographical mobility.

- Job information: the availability of appropriate information about jobs and job vacancies will impact on labour mobility.

- Wage differences: differences in wages in different regions of countries, or in different countries, and in different occupations will have an influence on the extent of geographical and occupational mobility.

- Cost of living: the cost of living can vary a great deal between different regions of a country and between different countries and this could have an impact on the mobility of labour, especially in relation to the affordability of accommodation.

- Immigration policy: the ability of labour to move from one country to another may be restricted by the immigration policies of governments.

9.3.7 Policies to reduce unemployment and their effectiveness

There are a number of different policies that can be used to reduce unemployment and they are of three types: fiscal policy, monetary policy and supply-side policy.

Fiscal policy

Fiscal policy, when used to correct unemployment in an economy, will involve the reduction of taxation, both direct and indirect, to increase the level of consumption. Taxes on the profits of companies can also be reduced to encourage greater investment. Government expenditure can also be increased. A reduction in taxation and/or an increase in government expenditure will increase the level of aggregate demand in an economy and this is likely to correct unemployment.

Monetary policy

Another possible approach to the correction of unemployment is through the use of monetary policy. Interest rates could be lowered and/or the money supply increased to encourage the level of spending in an economy. If the cost of borrowing is reduced, this will encourage people to spend more and save less. Also, if interest rates in an economy are lowered, this is likely to lead to a fall in the exchange rate. If this did happen, it would make a country's exports more price competitive in international markets and this could lead to an increase in the demand for them and therefore an increase in the demand for labour to produce them, correcting unemployment. This assumes that the demand for the exports was price elastic.

Supply-side policy

Whereas fiscal policy and monetary policy operate to influence the level of aggregate demand in an economy, another way to correct unemployment is through the use of supply-side policy measures. Policies could be adopted with the aim of allowing markets to work more efficiently and this would be likely to reduce the level of unemployment. For example, policies to make the labour market more flexible, such as fewer regulations and more restrictions on trade unions, would be likely to bring about a greater level of employment. Government initiatives, such as training and retraining schemes, would also help to make workers more employable.

> **💡 Remember**
>
> Policies to correct unemployment are broadly of three types: fiscal policy, monetary policy and supply-side policy.

> **★ Link**
>
> See Unit 4, section 4.5, on unemployment.

9.4 Money and banking

9.4.1 The definition, functions and characteristics of money

Money performs four functions in a modern economy, which are:

- a medium of exchange
- a measure of value or a unit of account
- a standard for deferred payment
- a store of value or a store of wealth.

Money has a number of distinctive characteristics and these include:

- acceptability
- divisibility
- portability
- durability
- scarcity
- stability of supply
- recognisability
- uniformity
- stability of value.

> **Key term**
>
> **Money:** anything which is universally acceptable as a means of payment for goods and services and a settlement of debt.

> **💡 Remember**
>
> In a modern economy, money in the form of cash is becoming less important and should be seen not just as cash, but in terms of balances held in different financial institutions.

> **💡 Remember**
>
> Money as a medium of exchange essentially depends on its general acceptability in an economy as a way of financing transactions.
>
> Money as a measure of value or as a unit of account makes it relatively easy to compare the value of different goods and services, something that was very difficult to do with barter.
>
> Money as a standard for deferred payment enables people to borrow money and pay it back at a later date; this encourages the provision of credit and so is vital to the development of trade.
>
> Money as a store of value or wealth could be adversely affected if a country experiences a relatively high rate of inflation because inflation will erode the purchasing power of a given sum of money over a period of time, so even though money enables saving to take place, the real value of those savings will fall if an economy experiences inflation.

> **★ Exam tip**
>
> A common error is to confuse the functions of money with the characteristics or attributes of money.

> **Key terms**
>
> **Barter:** the direct exchange of one good or service for another.
>
> **Double coincidence of wants:** the situation in which, in a barter system of exchange, a seller needs to find a buyer who not only wants what the seller is selling, but also has something that the buyer wants.

Barter, cash and bank deposits, cheques, near money and liquidity

Barter refers to the situation that occurs in which, instead of using money, transactions involve the direct exchange of goods and services without the use of any monetary mechanism. The main reason that barter was replaced by money is that it relies on a **double coincidence of wants**, that is, one person offering a good or service needs to be able to find someone who wants the particular good or service and that person also needs to be offering something in exchange that the seller wants.

Money is often regarded as **cash**, but in many economies there is a move towards a cashless society. It is therefore important, in a modern economy, that money is seen as **bank deposits** in a variety of financial institutions, including banks, building societies, friendly societies and credit unions. A **cheque** is simply a means of transferring money; it is not money. **Near money** refers to financial assets that could settle some, but not all, debts. **Liquidity** refers to how easy or quick it is to turn a financial asset into money.

Key terms

Cash: the notes and coins in existence in an economy; this is the most liquid form of asset.

Bank deposits: money that is held in accounts with a financial institution, such as a bank, a building society, a credit union or a friendly society.

Cheques: a written instruction to a financial institution to pay an amount of money from an account; although a method of payment, a cheque is not a form of money.

Near money: an asset that can be transferred into money relatively easily and quickly, but is not actually money; it is therefore sometimes known as 'quasi money'.

Liquidity: a term used to indicate when a financial asset is turned into cash.

Remember

Money should not be viewed in terms of just cash. As economies move towards a cashless society, most money is held in the form of bank deposits, frequently accessed through a variety of cards and electronic transactions.

★ Exam tip

Make sure you recognise that barter refers to the direct exchange of goods and services without the use of money, as well as understanding that the main limitation of barter is that it relies on the existence of a double coincidence of wants, with two people each wanting what the other has to sell.

A number of candidates regard a cheque as a form of money, but this is incorrect; a cheque is simply a means of transferring money from one account to another.

You should also understand that near money refers to financial assets that can settle some, but not all, debts and so it is unable to perform all of the functions of money. In particular, it cannot be used as a medium of exchange because it will not be generally acceptable.

Make sure that you can explain the concept of liquidity. The term simply refers to the ease with which it is possible to turn a financial asset into money. For example, cash is the most liquid type of financial asset.

9.4.2 The definition of money supply

Money supply

The **money supply** refers to the total amount of money in an economy at any one time. It includes both broad and narrow money supply.

Broad and narrow money supply

A **broad money supply** reflects the total purchasing power in an economy at a particular time. It is sometimes called M3 or M4 and includes not only notes and coins but also a wide range of deposits held with different financial services providers.

A **narrow money supply** is mainly the cash in an economy at a particular time. It is sometimes called M0 or M1 and mainly includes the notes and coins held by people and in balances with financial institutions. It is also sometimes known as the **monetary base**.

Key terms

Money supply: the amount of money available to the general public and the banking system in an economy at any one time.

Broad money supply: a measure of the stock of money which reflects the total purchasing power in an economy.

Narrow money supply: a measure of the stock of money in an economy which is mainly cash, that is, notes and coins.

Key term

Monetary base: the cash held by the general public and by the banking system, including the balances of the financial institutions with the central bank of a country.

💡 **Remember**

The monetary base acts as the basis for any expansion of bank lending in an economy.

9.4.3 The quantity theory of money (MV = PT)

The quantity theory of money shows the relationship between the money supply, the general level of prices and the level of output in an economy. It is usually expressed in terms of $MV = PT$, where:

- M is the quantity of money or the money supply

- V is the velocity of circulation, that is, the number of times money changes hands

- P is the general price level

- T is the number of transactions or output.

Key term

Quantity theory of money: the $MV = PT$ equation shows that changes in the general price level (P) are directly proportional to changes in the money supply (M).

💡 **Remember**

It is assumed that V (the velocity of circulation of money) and T (the number of transactions) are constant over a period of time. In this situation, M (the quantity of money or money supply) and P (the general level of prices) are directly linked, although there is likely to be a time lag before this is seen, of perhaps 12, 18 or 24 months.

However, the theory has been challenged, especially as to whether it is correct to assume that V and T will be constant over a period of time. It has also been challenged for being less of a theory and more of an identity that is necessarily true, that is, MV represents total spending in an economy and PT represents the total money received for the goods and services. In essence, it is the same situation looked at from different perspectives.

💡 **Remember**

M and P are directly linked, meaning that if the money supply rises, people will have access to more funds, giving them greater purchasing power, and consequently the general price level in the economy rises, that is, it will lead to inflation.

9.4.4 The functions of commercial banks

Commercial banks perform a number of functions, including the following:

- **Providing deposit accounts:** commercial banks provide a variety of different accounts, including demand deposit or current accounts where money can be deposited and withdrawn at any time, fixed deposit accounts, where money is deposited for a fixed period of time, and various kinds of savings accounts.

- **Lending money:** commercial banks can lend money in different forms, including an overdraft, where a current account is allowed to be overdrawn up to a certain maximum amount, a loan, where a specific amount of money is lent for a particular period of time, and a mortgage, similar to a loan but usually for a longer period of time in order to buy a property.

- **Holding or providing cash, securities and equity:** commercial banks can hold or provide cash, in the form of notes and coins, and various kinds of securities, such as shares in limited companies and government securities.

The reserve ratio and the capital ratio

The **reserve ratio** of a commercial bank refers to central bank regulations that establish the minimum capital reserves that a commercial bank must hold as a percentage of its deposits. The bank reserve ratio is also sometimes known as the cash reserve ratio (CRR) or bank reserve requirement. A higher proportion of reserves indicates financial soundness because a commercial bank would be better able to meet any future losses.

The reserve ratio is a reserves to capital ratio and is calculated by reserves divided by capital. As an example, if the reserve ratio was 11% and a commercial bank had deposits of $1 billion, it would be required to have $110 million on reserve.

The **capital ratio** of a commercial bank measures the funds that it has against the riskier assets that it holds that could be vulnerable in the event of a financial crisis. Commercial banks are sometimes required to carry out stress tests to check that they have enough of a capital buffer to cope with any possible economic or financial circumstances. Commercial banks are usually required to maintain a capital ratio of at least 8%, that is, this is a bank's core equity capital divided by its total risk-weighted assets.

The objectives of commercial banks

Commercial banks have three key objectives, as indicated below:

- **Liquidity:** this refers, as has been indicated in section 9.4.1, to the ease with which assets can be converted into cash. In relation to commercial banks, this refers to their ability to finance all of their obligations when due and these obligations can be in relation to lending, investment, the withdrawal of deposits and the maturity of liabilities.

- **Security:** commercial banks need to clearly demonstrate that they are a safe, secure and trustworthy means of storing money so that customers have confidence in them.

- **Profitability:** commercial banks are usually examples of public limited companies and, like any such company, their main aim is to make a profit for their shareholders.

9.4.5 The causes of changes in the money supply in an open economy

Commercial banks as sources of credit creation and the bank credit multiplier

Financial institutions, such as a **commercial bank**, are able to create 'new' money as a result of additional cash deposits. This is termed **credit creation**. It is understood that only a small proportion of such deposits need to be available to give out to people, allowing the financial institutions to, perhaps, have a **cash ratio** of 10%, enabling them to lend out the remaining 90%. This process is known as **fractional reserve banking** and the ratio of new money created to the initial money deposited is known as the bank **credit multiplier**.

> **Key terms**
>
> **Reserve ratio:** the proportion of the funds that a commercial bank has that it is required to maintain with the central bank and which will not be available for any commercial lending.
>
> **Capital ratio:** the amount of a commercial bank's capital in relation to the amount of risk it is taking.

> **Key terms**
>
> **Commercial bank:** a financial institution in which individuals and firms can save money and obtain loans.
>
> **Credit creation:** the process by which financial institutions are able to use some of the money deposited to expand their lending.
>
> **Cash ratio:** the ratio of the total liabilities of a financial institution that is held in the form of cash reserves.

> **Key terms**
>
> **Fractional reserve banking:** the idea that financial institutions only need to keep a fraction of their reserves in cash, enabling them to lend the remainder.
>
> **Credit multiplier:** the ratio of the new money created to the size of the initial deposit.

The role of a central bank

A **central bank** might want to control the ability of commercial banks to lend money, such as through open market operations. This is the process of buying and selling government securities, that is, bonds or shares that are issued by a government.

> **Key term**
>
> **Central bank:** the main bank in a country that is responsible for the monitoring and oversight of the banking system.

> 💡 **Remember**
>
> If a central bank wants to encourage bank lending, it will buy government securities. If a central bank wants to discourage bank lending, it will sell government securities.

> ⭐ **Exam tip**
>
> Be careful not to confuse a commercial bank and a central bank. A commercial bank has direct dealings with individuals and firms, whereas a central bank has a broad oversight of the entire banking system of a country and can come to the rescue of commercial banks by proving funds in its capacity as a lender of last resort. A central bank is also likely to have responsibility for the issue of notes and coins and for the setting of key interest rates in an economy.

Government deficit financing

A government can plan for a budget surplus, a balanced budget or a budget deficit. If there is a **budget deficit**, this can be financed by the government borrowing money from the central bank and/or the commercial banks. This will lead to an increase in the money supply in the economy. The method is termed **deficit financing**.

Quantitative easing

Quantitative easing refers to a process whereby a government, through the central bank, buys securities, such as bills and bonds, creating more liquidity in the financial system, leading to an increase in bank deposits.

> **Key terms**
>
> **Budget deficit:** a situation in which projected revenue is less than planned expenditure.
>
> **Deficit financing:** the different ways in which a government could finance a budget deficit where there is a gap between public revenue and public expenditure.
>
> **Quantitative easing:** the process whereby the government of a country deliberately buys bonds and bills in order to increase the money supply in an economy.

> ⭐ **Exam tip**
>
> It would be useful if you understood how quantitative easing has been used by a number of countries since the financial crisis of 2007–2008 to stimulate economic activity, increasing the level of aggregate demand in such countries and so helping the countries to get out of a situation of recession.

Changes in the balance of payments

Total currency flow refers to the total inflow and outflow of money as a result of a range of international monetary transactions which are shown in the balance of payments. Such changes in the balance of payments can cause a change in the money supply in an open economy.

> **Key term**
>
> **Total currency flow:** the total inflow and outflow of money as a result of international transactions with other countries which are shown in the balance of payments.

> ⭐ **Exam tip**
>
> Make sure you understand that a net inflow of money in the total currency flow will lead to an increase in the money supply, whereas a net outflow of money will lead to a decrease in the money supply.

9.4.6 Policies to reduce inflation and their effectiveness

There are three possible policies to reduce the rate of inflation in an economy, as indicated below:

Fiscal policy to correct inflation

Inflation can be corrected by fiscal policy. For example, if the inflation is caused by demand-pull factors, a government may decide to reduce the level of aggregate demand in an economy by reducing the level of government expenditure and/or increasing the level of taxation.

The effectiveness of fiscal policy to correct inflation will depend on a number of factors. Higher rates of income tax could reduce aggregate demand, but this could create a disincentive effect, with workers only prepared to work fewer hours. Also, higher rates of income tax may lead trade unions to demand significant wage increases to at least maintain the disposable incomes of their members, and increased wages will lead to increased costs for firms, generating cost-push inflation.

Monetary policy to correct inflation

Inflation can be corrected by monetary policy. For example, if the inflation is caused by demand-pull factors, a government may decide to reduce the level of aggregate demand in an economy by reducing the money supply and/or increasing the interest rate.

The effectiveness of monetary policy to correct inflation will depend on a number of factors. The impact of a rise in the rate of interest will depend on how interest-elastic the demand is for products, but if demand is interest-elastic, borrowing will be discouraged as it is now more expensive. Saving will be encouraged by a higher rate of interest, if demand for savings accounts is interest-elastic.

Supply-side policy to correct inflation

Inflation can be corrected by supply-side policies. For example, if such policies are used to reduce the power of trade unions and make the labour market more competitive, this is likely to increase aggregate supply. If inflation was caused by an excess of aggregate demand over aggregate supply, this will have the effect of reducing the imbalance and so reducing inflationary pressures. Privatisation might also help to increase aggregate supply in an economy if the privatised firms are more efficient.

The effectiveness of supply-side policy to correct inflation will depend on a number of factors. The main factor is that supply-side measures usually take quite a while to have any significant effect, for example, making markets more competitive and flexible is something that can take quite a lot of time and so the impact on inflation may not be immediate.

9.4.7 The demand for money: liquidity preference theory

The demand for money in an economy, and the determination of interest rates, can be analysed through the **liquidity preference** theory.

This Keynesian approach to the demand for money and the determination of interest rates is based on the fact that there are three possible motives for holding money.

Firstly, there is the transactions demand for money. This is where money is used to pay for everyday purchases. This is an **active balance** and is interest inelastic.

Secondly, there is the precautionary demand for money. This is where money is used to pay for unexpected expenses. It is also an active balance that is interest inelastic.

Thirdly, there is the speculative demand for money. This is where money is used to buy government bonds. Unlike the transactions and the precautionary demand for money, it is regarded as an **idle balance** and it is interest elastic. An important influence on the demand for a bond is the **yield**; this is the annual income obtained from the bond as a proportion of its

Key terms

Liquidity preference: the relationship between the quantity of money that people wish to hold and the rate of interest.

Active balance: the demand for money that is not responsive to changes in the rate of interest; it applies to both the transactions and the precautionary demand for money.

Idle balance: the demand for money that is responsive to changes in the rate of interest; it applies to the speculative demand for money.

Yield: the annual income that is obtained from a bond as a proportion of its market price.

current market price. The price of government bonds and the rate of interest will move in opposite directions. Whereas the **transactions demand for money** and the **precautionary demand for money** are price inelastic, shown by a straight vertical line, the **speculative demand for money** is interest elastic, shown by a downward sloping demand curve, that is, as the rate of interest falls there will be a rise in the demand for money. It is even possible, at a relatively low rate of interest, that the liquidity preference (or demand) curve could become horizontal. At this point, the demand for money is perfectly elastic and this is known as the liquidity trap.

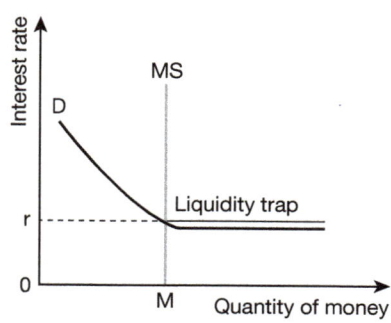

▲ **Figure 9.7** The liquidity preference curve

This can be seen in Figure 9.7. The transactions and precautionary demand for money can be shown by the vertical straight line at M. The speculative demand for money curve is downward sloping. The demand, or liquidity preference, curve D is the combination of the three motives for holding money. Eventually, at a low rate of interest, the demand curve will become perfectly elastic and horizontal and at this point it is known as the **liquidity trap**.

Key terms

Transactions demand for money: money that is demanded to pay for everyday purchases; it is an active balance that is interest inelastic.

Precautionary demand for money: money that is demanded to pay for unexpected expenses; it is an active balance that is interest inelastic.

Speculative demand for money: money that is demanded to pay for bonds; it is an idle balance that is interest elastic.

Liquidity trap: a situation at relatively low rates of interest when changes in the money supply will have no effect on the rate of interest and where the demand for money is perfectly elastic, that is, totally unresponsive to any changes in the rate of interest.

💡 **Remember**

The demand for money is based on three motives for holding money. The transactions demand and the precautionary demand for money are both active balances and, in both cases, will not respond to changes in interest rates. The speculative demand for money, on the other hand, is an idle, rather than an active, balance and is interest elastic, that is, it will respond to changes in interest rates.

It is important you understand that the price of bonds and the rate of interest will move in opposite directions, that is, there is an inverse relationship between them. If the interest rate rises, this will reduce the desire to hold money and the price of the bonds will fall. If the interest rate falls, there will be less of an incentive to switch out of money into other assets and the price of bonds will rise.

Whereas the transactions and the precautionary demand for money are interest inelastic, the speculative demand for money is elastic and so the demand curve for money is downward sloping, until at low rates of interest it becomes perfectly elastic, shown by a horizontal demand curve. This is known as the liquidity trap.

★ **Exam tip**

Make sure you fully understand the speculative demand for money. There are three aspects that need to be stressed:

- Whereas the transactions and the precautionary demand for money are active balances, the speculative demand for money is an idle balance.

- Whereas the transactions and the precautionary demand for money are interest inelastic, the speculative demand for money is interest elastic.

- The price of bonds and the rate of interest are inversely related; that is, when one rises, the other falls.

You need to be able to demonstrate an understanding of how a liquidity preference curve is derived. It comprises three demand curves for money: two of these will be vertical straight lines (representing the transactions demand and the precautionary demand for money) and one will be a downward sloping curve (representing the speculative demand for money).

💡 Remember

Although the liquidity preference, or demand, curve for money is downward sloping, at a relatively low rate of interest it will become a horizontal straight line. This indicates that the demand for money is perfectly elastic. This is known as the liquidity trap.

9.4.8 Interest rate determination: loanable funds theory and Keynesian theory

The Keynesian liquidity preference theory

The Keynesian theory stresses that interest is a reward for parting with liquidity for a specified period of time. According to Keynes, interest is a purely monetary phenomenon and the theory of interest is a monetary theory of interest. The Keynesian theory stresses that the rate of interest is determined by the demand for, and the supply of money. As has already been pointed out in section 9.4.7, the demand for money comes about as a result of three motives: the transactions, precautionary and speculative motives. The supply of money is fixed and controlled by the monetary authority and is perfectly interest-inelastic.

The loanable funds theory

An alternative approach to the liquidity preference theory of explaining the demand for money and the determination of interest rates is the **loanable funds theory**. This states that the rate of interest is determined by the demand for, and the supply of, loanable funds in financial markets; that is, the rate of interest is a price and, just like any other price in an economy, it is determined by the interaction of the demand for, and the supply of, loanable funds, that is, the supply of funds from savings and the demand for funds for investment.

The demand for loanable funds comes from:

- firms wanting to invest

- households wanting to buy consumer products

- a government aiming to fund a budget deficit.

The demand curve for loanable funds slopes down from left to right.

The supply of loanable funds comes from:

- savings.

The loanable funds theory can be seen in Figure 9.8. The supply of loanable funds curve slopes up from left to right and the demand for loanable funds curve slopes down from left to right. Figure 9.8 shows how the rate of interest is determined by the demand for, and the supply of, loanable funds. A rate of interest of r is established for a quantity M of funds.

Key term

Loanable funds theory: the idea that interest rates are determined by the demand for, and the supply of, loanable funds in financial markets.

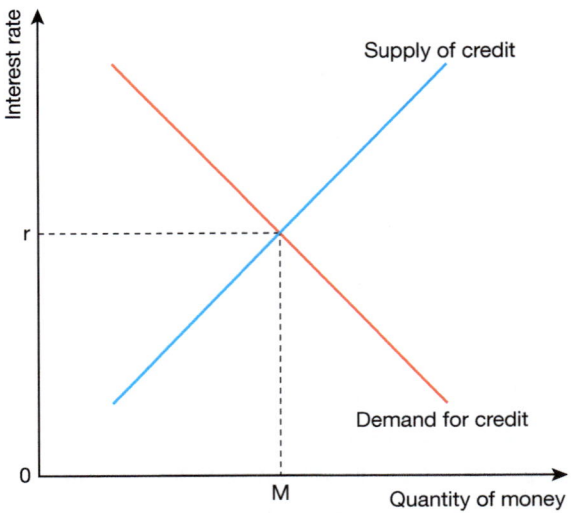

▲ **Figure 9.8** The loanable funds theory

⬆ Raise your grade

Assess how money, in performing its various functions, can facilitate a country's economic progress. [20]

Money is said to have four functions or roles that it performs in a modern economy.

Firstly, it acts as a medium of exchange, enabling individuals, firms and governments to finance transactions. In this role, it is much better than barter which relied on a direct exchange of goods and services without the use of money (1).

Secondly, it acts as a measure of value or unit of account. This allows the value of a product to be directly compared, something that was not easily provided for in a barter system (2).

Thirdly, it has the function of operating as a standard for deferred payment. This is very important in a modern economy as it enables people to borrow money and to pay it back at a later date. Payments can be spread over a period of time and this encourages the provision of credit (3).

Finally, the fourth function of money is as a store of value or wealth. This is where wealth can be stored in the form of money and savings are therefore encouraged (4).

How to improve this answer

1. The candidate has referred to money as a medium of exchange, a very significant role and one that is crucial to a country's economic progress, but it would have been helpful if the candidate had pointed out that this role could only be performed effectively if money was generally accepted as a means of payment for goods and services in an economy. For example, there could have been a reference to the idea of 'legal tender'.

2. The candidate correctly refers to this second function of money, but it would have been helpful if the candidate had also pointed out that this function helps consumers to make economic decisions in terms of buying one product rather than another.

3. The candidate has stressed the importance of money operating as a standard for deferred payment, especially in terms of encouraging the provision of credit, but this point could have been developed more fully, especially in relation to the purchase of products through the use of credit cards, a major factor in the increase in consumption, a key element in a country's economic progress.

4. The candidate has referred to the function of money as a store of value or wealth and has linked this to the encouragement of savings. However, this point could have been developed more fully, such as through pointing out that the savings that are deposited in financial institutions enable these firms to lend to others, facilitating the expansion of borrowing and enabling more people to finance purchases. The candidate could also have pointed out a limitation of this function in countries with relatively high rates of inflation where saving may be discouraged due to the erosion of the real value of those savings.

AO1 and AO2: Level 2   7/14

AO3:   Level 1   3/6

Total: 10/20

Worked Example

Assess how useful is the quantity theory of money in explaining the existence of inflation in an economy. [20]

The quantity theory of money, $MV = PT$, is very useful in explaining the existence of inflation in an economy. It shows that there is a direct link between the money supply in an economy (M refers to the quantity of money and V refers to the velocity of circulation of that money) and the general level of prices in that economy (P refers to the price level and T refers to the number of transactions).

However, although the theory is useful in explaining how inflation can come about in an economy, it has been criticised. Although it emphasises the direct link between the money supply in an economy and the general level of prices in that economy, there is likely to be a time lag of 12, 18 or 24 months before the effect can be noticed. It assumes that V and T are constant over a period of time, but this may not always be the case (3).

The theory has also been challenged for being more of an identity than a theory, in that it could be argued that MV and PT are essentially the same. MV represents total spending in an economy and PT represents the total money received for the goods and services.

Therefore, it can be seen that while the quantity theory of money is quite useful in explaining the existence of inflation in an economy, and is an important element in the Monetarist approach, stressing the link between changes in an economy's money supply and changes in the general level of prices in that economy, it is not without its critics. This is especially the case with regard to the assumptions on which the theory is based and the fact that some economists have argued that it is not really a theory at all, but simply a situation of looking at the same thing from two different angles.

Exam-style questions

1 Sustainability can be defined as a situation in which:

   (a) actual growth is always greater than potential growth

   (b) the economic growth of a country is never more than 2% per annum

   (c) the needs of the present generation are met without affecting the needs of future generations

   (d) the standard of living is guaranteed to be higher in the future than it is today. [1]

2 The four stages of the business (trade) cycle are:

   (a) boom, output, recession, slump

   (b) recovery, boom, recession, depression

   (c) slump, inflation, boom, recession

   (d) slump, recovery, boom, recession. [1]

3 The aggregate demand function is:

   (a) $C + I + G + (X + M)$

   (b) $C + I + G + (X - M)$

   (c) $C + I + T + S$

   (d) $C + I + X + M$. [1]

4 The multiplier is calculated by 1 divided by:

   (a) APS + ART + APM

   (b) MPS + MPC + MPM

   (c) MPS + MRT + MPM

   (d) MPS + MRT + MPX. [1]

5 The quantity theory of money is:

   (a) $MP = VT$

   (b) $MT = VP$

   (c) $MV = PT$

   (d) $TV = PM$. [1]

6 The speculative demand for money is:

   (a) an active balance with interest elastic demand

   (b) an active balance with interest inelastic demand

   (c) an idle balance with interest elastic demand

   (d) an idle balance with interest inelastic demand. [1]

7 A liquidity trap shows the situation when the demand for money is:

   (a) perfectly elastic

   (b) perfectly inelastic

   (c) relatively elastic

   (d) relatively inelastic. [1]

8 The three objectives of commercial banks are:

   (a) liquidity, security, equity

   (b) liquidity, security, profitability

   (c) quantitative easing, security, profitability

   (d) stability, security, profitability. [1]

9 Assess what is meant by structural unemployment. [20]

10 Assess whether frictional unemployment is likely to have a more damaging effect on an economy than cyclical unemployment. [20]

Key topics
- Government macroeconomic policy objectives
- The links between macroeconomic problems and their interrelatedness
- The effectiveness of policy options to meet all macroeconomic objectives

10.1 Government macroeconomic policy objectives

10.1.1 Government macroeconomic policy objectives

Governments usually have a wide range of objectives in relation to macroeconomic policy, but in most cases they tend to concentrate on a combination of these seven aims.

Inflation

One aim is in relation to changes in the general level of prices in an economy over a period of time. Governments generally aim for a relatively low and stable rate of inflation, although what might be considered a relatively low and stable rate of inflation is likely to vary from one country to another.

Balance of payments

A government would aim for the balance of payments to be in equilibrium over a period of time. This means that the inflows of money equal the outflows of money taking into account all aspects of the balance of payments.

Unemployment

Governments aim to achieve full employment, although this may vary from one country to another. Full employment is defined as the situation which exists when all those willing and able to work at the given real wage rate are either in employment or about to take up employment, that is, they are frictionally unemployed.

Economic growth

Governments aim for a high economic growth rate, although there is increasing recognition that the growth rate needs to be sustainable. This means that there should be conservation as well as use of non-renewable resources so that the interests of future generations, and not just those of the present generation, are taken into account.

Economic development

Economic development is a broader aim, focusing not just on growth in terms of real national output, but also on other factors that influence the standard of living and the quality of life of people, such as in relation to the provision of education and health care.

Sustainability

Sustainability refers to the ability to use existing resources to satisfy the needs of the present generation without compromising the ability of future

> **💡 Remember**
>
> You need to understand that governments in all countries have a number of macroeconomic policy objectives and that these relate to inflation, the balance of payments, unemployment, economic growth, economic development, sustainability and the redistribution of income and wealth.

> **★ Link**
>
> See Unit 5, section 5.1, on government macroeconomic policy objectives.

generations to satisfy their needs. Governments aim for sustainable economic growth that takes into account the needs of future generations as well as those of the present generation.

The redistribution of income and wealth

Governments aim for a redistribution of income and wealth by using a variety of different policies to reduce the extent of inequality of income and wealth.

10.2 The links between macroeconomic problems and their interrelatedness

10.2.1 The relationship between the internal value of money and the external value of money

It is important to distinguish between the **internal value of money** and the **external value of money**, but it also needs to be stressed that the two values of money are interrelated. For example, if a country is experiencing a relatively high rate of inflation, this will reduce the internal value of a currency. Exports will become more expensive and if demand for those exports is price elastic, the demand for them will fall, as will the demand for the currency to pay for them. This will lead to a fall, or depreciation, in the external value of the currency.

> **Key terms**
>
> **Internal value of money:** the real value of a given sum of money in terms of its purchasing power.
>
> **External value of money:** the value of a currency in terms of how many units of other currencies it can buy on the foreign exchange markets.

10.2.2 The relationship between the balance of payments and inflation

If there is a relatively high rate of inflation in a country, this will make exports more expensive. This is likely to reduce the demand for them, assuming that the price elasticity of demand for the exports is elastic. The demand for imports, however, may remain unchanged. In such a situation, the money received from exports will fall but the money paid for imports will remain the same. This will lead to a deterioration in the current account of the balance of payments.

10.2.3 The relationship between economic growth and inflation

There can be a conflict between economic growth and inflation. During periods of relatively high economic growth, the rate of inflation in an economy is likely to rise. If an economy grows too quickly, aggregate supply may not be able to respond sufficiently. However, it is possible for an economy to experience both positive economic growth and a low rate of inflation as long as the growth is sustainable and productive capacity increases at a similar rate to the increase in aggregate demand.

10.2.4 The relationship between economic growth and the balance of payments

As an economy grows, it is likely to lead to an increase in expenditure on imported goods. If the increase in import expenditure is greater than the revenue received from the sales of exported products, it could lead to a problem in the current account of the balance of payments.

10.2.5 The relationship between inflation and unemployment

If a country is experiencing a relatively high rate of inflation, its government may decide to deliberately bring down the rate of aggregate demand to reduce the inflation rate, especially if the country is experiencing demand-pull inflation. For example, monetary policy could be used to reduce aggregate demand through an increase in the interest rate or fiscal policy could be used through an increase in taxation. If there is a reduction of aggregate demand in an economy, it is likely to lead to an increase in the level of unemployment.

The traditional Phillips curve

This trade-off between inflation and unemployment can be seen through the traditional **Phillips curve**, as shown in Figure 10.1.

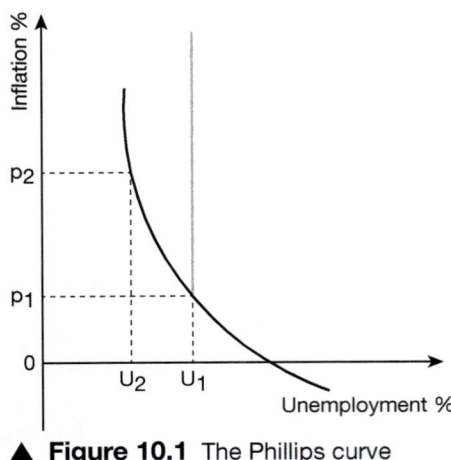

▲ **Figure 10.1** The Phillips curve

The diagram shows that if there is a fall in the level of unemployment from $0U_1$ to $0U_2$; this will have the effect of increasing the general level of prices in the economy from $0P_1$ to $0P_2$. However, some countries experienced **stagflation**, that is, a situation of both relatively high inflation and relatively high unemployment, suggesting that the trade-off did not always apply.

The expectations-augmented Phillips curve (short- and long-run Phillips curve)

This absence of a trade-off between inflation and unemployment is particularly noticeable in the long run. This is because of the expectations of consumers in terms of future prices and the expectations of producers in terms of future costs. This gives rise to the **expectations-augmented Phillips curve** in the long run. This is a vertical line that shows NAIRU: the non-accelerating inflation rate of unemployment. This is shown in Figure 10.2.

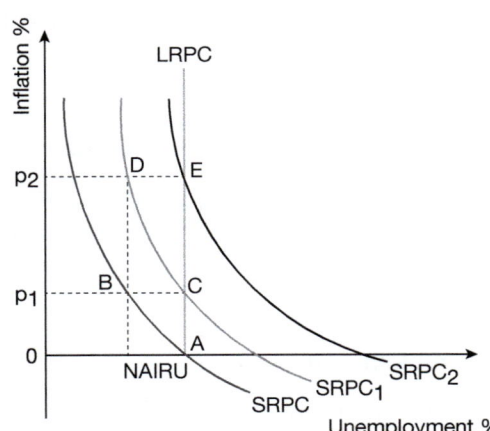

▲ **Figure 10.2** The expectations-augmented Phillips curve

This diagram shows three Phillips curves in the short run: SRPC, $SRPC_1$ and $SRPC_2$. However, although the trade-off relationship can be seen in the short run, in the long-run LRPC is a vertical straight line to indicate NAIRU.

Key terms

Phillips curve: a way of showing the trade-off between the rate of inflation and the level of unemployment in an economy.

Stagflation: a situation characterised by both a high rate of inflation and a high level of unemployment.

Expectations-augmented Phillips curve: the relationship between inflation and unemployment is shown as a curve in the short run, but in the long run it becomes a vertical line.

★ Exam tip

Make sure that you are able to clearly distinguish between the short-run and the long-run Phillips curve.

> 💡 **Remember**
>
> It is important to be able to show the distinction between the short-run Phillips curve and the long-run Phillips curve. In the short run, it is a curve because as the price level in an economy rises, the level of unemployment falls and as the level of unemployment rises, the level of inflation falls. However, in the long run, the Phillips curve is not a curve but a vertical straight line. Any attempt to reduce unemployment by increasing demand will just lead to inflation. This long-run curve is known as the expectations-augmented Phillips curve, that is, it takes into account the expectations that consumers and producers have in relation to prices, wages and costs. This vertical line will show NAIRU, which is the level of unemployment in an economy that does not cause the rate of inflation to increase.

10.3 The effectiveness of policy options to meet all macroeconomic objectives

10.3.1 The effectiveness of different policies in relation to different macroeconomic objectives

Fiscal policy

Fiscal policy is the deliberate adjustment of government spending and/or taxation to achieve particular macroeconomic objectives by changing the level and composition of aggregate demand. There are two types of fiscal policy: discretionary and automatic. Discretionary fiscal policy refers to policies which are implemented by specific one-off policy changes, whereas automatic fiscal policy refers to where existing policy decisions lead to changes brought about by changes in an economy. Discretionary and automatic fiscal policies were covered in Unit 5, section 5.2.5.

The effectiveness of fiscal policy is largely dependent on the balance between taxation and spending and fiscal policy can be either expansionary (when there is a budget deficit) or contractionary (when there is a budget surplus). Expansionary fiscal policy can help to reduce the level of unemployment in an economy and contractionary fiscal policy can help to reduce the level of inflation. Expansionary and contractionary fiscal policies were covered in Unit 5, section 5.2.6. Taxation can fund government projects which could help to stimulate economic growth and progressive taxation can be especially relevant to the redistribution of income and wealth in an economy.

The advantages of fiscal policy include the following:

- Public spending can have a significant impact on the level of aggregate demand in an economy.

- If the spending is on infrastructure, this can help increase economic growth.

- Public spending can help to reduce the level of unemployment in an economy.

- Direct taxes, such as income tax, can help to redistribute income in an economy.

- Indirect taxes can be targeted at altering certain kinds of behaviour, such as taxes on demerit goods such as alcohol and tobacco.

Although fiscal policy can be a very effective way to manage an economy, there are a number of issues involved in its use. The disadvantages of fiscal policy include the following:

- There may be a significant time lag before a particular revenue or expenditure decision begins to take effect, such as between a reduction in income tax and an increase in household spending.

- The potential benefit of a fiscal decision may not be fully seen because of the existence of information failure.

- There may be side-effects of any fiscal policy, for example, unemployment may be reduced, but at the cost of a higher rate of inflation (the possibility of a trade-off between inflation and unemployment has already been covered in section 10.2.5).

- Changing tax rates, allowances and bands is more complex than changing interest rates as part of monetary policy.

- Higher taxes may possibly have a disincentive effect on work and enterprise, for example, higher taxes may encourage people to work less so as to have more leisure time.

- A government needs to be able to estimate reasonably accurately the likely effects of any change in taxation and/or public expenditure, otherwise the desired objectives may not be achieved.

- Some decisions that are justified by economic reasoning may not be taken by a government for political reasons, especially if an election is due in the not-too-distant future.

Laffer curve analysis

The effectiveness of fiscal policy can be considered in terms of **Laffer curve** analysis.

A Laffer curve shows the relationship between the percentage tax rates in an economy and the revenue received by government from the taxation. Figure 10.3 shows the Laffer curve.

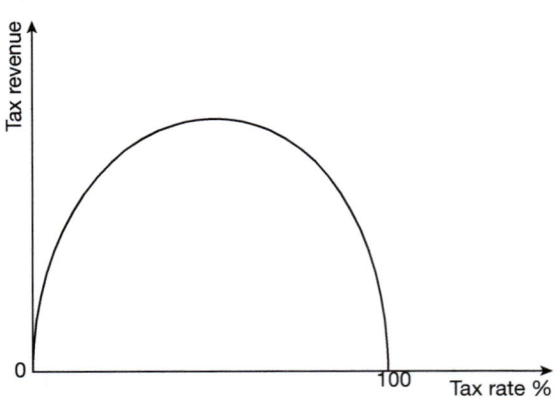

▲ **Figure 10.3** The Laffer curve

The Laffer curve shows that as the tax rate is increased along the horizontal axis, the revenue received from this taxation at first increases and then falls. At relatively high rates of tax, the tax is not worthwhile as it actually brings in less revenue than at lower rates of tax.

Monetary policy

Monetary policy is the deliberate adjustment of the money supply and/or interest rates to achieve particular macroeconomic objectives by changing the level and composition of aggregate demand.

Monetary policy can be either expansionary (when there is an increase in the money supply and/or a decrease in the interest rate) or contractionary (when there is a decrease in the money supply and/or an increase in the interest rate budget). Expansionary monetary policy can help to reduce the level of unemployment in an economy and contractionary monetary policy can help to reduce the level of inflation. Expansionary and contractionary monetary policies were covered in Unit 5, section 5.3.3.

The advantages of monetary policy include the following:

- Changes in interest rates can have a significant effect on spending in an economy, indicating that demand is interest elastic.

- A central bank in many countries where it is independent from government can make decisions about changes in interest rates and/or changes in the money supply without political interference.

- Interest rates can be adjusted on a monthly basis; this contrasts with discretionary fiscal policy which cannot be so easily changed at such regular intervals.

- Interest rate changes can have a relatively immediate effect on levels of confidence in an economy.

Although monetary policy can be a very effective way to manage an economy, there are a number of issues involved in its use. The disadvantages of monetary policy include the following:

- There is a time lag between a change in an interest rate and the impact of that change on an economy; it is difficult to be precise about how long that time lag might be, but a number of economists have suggested that it could be as long as 18 months.

- Various people in an economy may react differently to a change in interest rates, in other words, not everyone will have the same interest elasticity of demand. For example, relatively rich people in an economy are likely to have a relatively inelastic interest elasticity of demand, whereas relatively poor people are likely to have a relatively elastic interest elasticity of demand. This makes it difficult to estimate the likely effects of a change in interest rates in an economy.

- Any increase in the money supply of an economy, such as through the process of quantitative easing at a time of recession, is likely to have an inflationary effect in that economy, resulting from the increase in the level of aggregate demand.

- The accuracy of inflation forecasts may be relatively poor; monetary policy tries to reduce inflationary pressures before they occur, but if

inflation is higher than predicted, the interest rate may be too low to effectively control the rate of inflation in an economy.

- An increase in interest rates to control inflation could have a negative effect on other areas of an economy, for example, it could have a negative impact on investment spending and therefore on economic growth and changes in interest rates could also affect the exchange rate and the balance of payments.

- The money supply may be difficult to control in practice.

Supply-side policy including market-based and interventionist policies

Supply-side policies were covered in Unit 5, section 5.4.3. They can be divided into market-based, such as reducing the size of government, lower taxes and opening up more flexible markets, and interventionist policies, such as regional policies and education and training initiatives.

The advantages of supply-side policy include the following:

- Policies such as better education and training can increase aggregate supply in an economy and improve an economy's productive capacity and potential output, shifting the LRAS curve to the right.

- Supply-side policies are of particular importance in reducing the natural rate of unemployment in an economy, especially in relation to a reduction in structural and frictional unemployment.

- Supply-side policies can improve the level of competition, encouraging greater efficiency in markets.

- Supply-side policies enable sustained economic growth to be achieved in an economy without causing a rise in inflation; they help reduce

inflationary pressure in an economy in the long run because of the achievement of efficiency and productivity gains in the product and labour markets.

- Supply-side policies can not only help to achieve a lower rate of unemployment and a higher rate of sustainable economic growth through their positive effect on labour productivity and competitiveness, but can also help to improve a country's balance of payments.

- Supply-side policy is, on the whole, less likely to create conflicts between the macroeconomic objectives of stable prices, sustainable economic growth, full employment and balance of payments equilibrium compared with the use of fiscal and/ or monetary policy.

Although supply-side policy can be a very effective way to manage an economy, there are a number of issues involved in its use. The disadvantages of supply-side policy include the following:

- There is no guarantee that a firm in the private sector will be more efficient than one in the public sector; privatisation may involve the need to get rid of some workers, leading to an increase in the rate of unemployment in an economy.

- A privatised firm may be in a monopoly position in an economy, so all that has been achieved is a move from a state-owned to a privately-owned monopoly.

- A lowering of unemployment benefits and/or a lowering of taxes might persuade more people to look for work, but this will have no effect if there are no jobs available for them.

- The effects of supply-side policies can take a long time to show, as in the case of improvements to the quality of human capital through initiatives in training and education; the potential benefits of deregulation may also take a long time to have an

effect in markets.

- Supply-side policy can be very costly to implement, such as improvements in the provision of education and training.

- Some supply-side policies may be strongly resisted if they have the effect of reducing the power of certain interest groups, such as trade unions where their influence has been reduced by certain labour market reforms.

- There could be a conflict with the aim of equity, such as when supply-side policies have a negative effect on the distribution of income in an economy, at least in the short run; for example, reductions in the power of trade unions and the movement towards greater privatisation could contribute to a widening of the gap between rich and poor.

Exchange rate policy

The exchange rate of an economy affects the level of aggregate demand through its impact on export and import prices. Deliberate changes in exchange rates to affect macroeconomic objectives can be regarded as a type of monetary policy. Changes in exchange rates have an impact on an economy through their effect on prices, in terms of both exports and imports. Exchange rates were covered in Unit 6, section 6.4.

A lowering of an exchange rate, that is, a depreciation or a devaluation, can have a number of advantages, including the following:

- It can raise the level of aggregate demand in an economy.

- It can increase national output (GDP) and increase jobs.

- It can lead to an improvement in a country's balance of payments, assuming that the PED for exports and imports is greater than one.

An increase in an exchange rate, that is, an appreciation or a revaluation, can have a number of advantages, including the following:

- It can lower the level of aggregate demand in an economy.

- It can reduce the rate of inflation.

Although exchange rate policy can be a very effective way to manage an economy, there are a number of issues involved in its use. The disadvantages of exchange rate policy include the following:

- A depreciation or devaluation, whilst lowering the price of exports, will increase the price of imports, and so it could contribute to an increase in the rate of inflation in an economy.

- An appreciation or revaluation of an exchange rate would increase the price of exports, and so it could contribute to an increase in the rate of unemployment in an economy, depending on the relative size of the export sector in the economy.

- There will be a time-lag between any change in an exchange rate and its impact on an economy.

- The scale of any change in an exchange rate may be extremely small and, in this case, it is unlikely to have much of an effect.

- It is generally assumed that the PED for both exports and imports is likely to be relatively elastic, but this may not necessarily be the case.

- The change in an exchange rate may take place at an unfavourable phase in the business (trade) cycle.

International trade policy

The impact of international trade policy on the macroeconomic objectives of a government will depend on the degree of liberalisation in relation to world trade, especially the extent to which protective trade barriers, such as tariffs and quotas, have been reduced or removed.

The advantages of the liberalisation of international trade policy include the following:

- The promotion of free trade will secure market openings with trade partners.

- This could lead to an increase in the level of exports to such partners.

- This would reduce the level of unemployment in the export sector and encourage economic growth.

However, if a country's international trade policy favours trade protectionism, so as to protect domestic industries, there will be a number of disadvantages, including the following:

- Resources are not allocated efficiently.

- Consumers will have a smaller range of products to choose from.

- Economic growth may be lower than would otherwise be the case if there was no protectionism.

10.3.2 Problems and conflicts arising from the outcome of these policies

It is not always easy for governments to achieve success in all policy objectives and it is often the case that there are conflicts between different policy objectives. For example, a depreciation or a devaluation in the value of an exchange rate could increase the demand for exports and decrease the demand for imports, assuming that the price elasticity of demand for both is elastic (for a devaluation to be successful, the Marshall-Lerner condition states the sum of the two elasticities must be greater than one). However, if the price elasticity of demand for imports is relatively inelastic, the demand for them will not change significantly and the effect of this is that it will contribute to a relatively high rate of inflation in an economy, both in terms of the price of imported raw materials/component parts and imported finished goods.

The Phillips curve shows the possible conflict when a government tries to reduce both the rate of inflation and the level of unemployment in an economy. Policies to reduce the level of unemployment will not usually conflict with a policy of achieving economic growth, but there may be a conflict between the policy objective of high economic growth and the need to protect the environment, especially if the rate of growth is unsustainable, that is, it does not sufficiently take into account the needs of future generations.

A policy objective of redistributing income and wealth, such as through progressive taxation, may have a disincentive to work effect on those workers paying high rates of taxation on their earnings and this could have a dampening effect on the rate of economic growth in an economy.

> ★ **Exam tip**
>
> Make sure that you are able to refer to different examples of problems arising from conflicts between policy objectives on a wide range of macro policy aims.

10.3.3 The existence of government failure in macroeconomic policies

It is possible that a government may fail in its macroeconomic policies. For example, policies to bring about a more equitable distribution of income and wealth in an economy through the use of progressive tax could not only create a disincentive to work effect, but could also lead to people deciding to leave a country in protest at the high rate of tax being paid. Such people are likely to be the most educated and the most skilled in an economy, and this is why such a situation has been referred to as a 'brain drain'.

Information failure could have an impact on the success or otherwise of a government's macroeconomic policies. For example, there may be a time lag between when a policy is introduced and when it begins to have an effect, but during this time lag the economic situation has changed. It has been estimated by economists that a change in interest rates can take up to 18 or 24 months to be fully effective.

A country may be experiencing a relatively high rate of inflation and so the government decides to take appropriate measures to reduce the level of demand in the economy. However, the level of inflation then falls for reasons that have nothing to do with the measures taken, leading to a rise in the level of unemployment as a result of the measures taken, an unintended consequence of the measures taken.

> ★ **Exam tip**
>
> Make sure that you are able to refer to different examples of government failure in relation to macroeconomic policies.

↑ Raise your grade

Assess the extent to which there is likely to be a trade-off between economic growth and inflation. [20]

One of the macroeconomic policy objectives of a government is to achieve economic growth (1). One of the ways to achieve this is to stimulate the level of aggregate demand in an economy in the expectation that the increase in aggregate demand will lead to an increase in aggregate supply.

The difficulty, however, is that any increase in aggregate supply is likely to take a period of time to be achieved (2) and so during this time, when there is excess demand in the economy, there is likely to be an increase in the rate of inflation. It is therefore very likely that there will be a trade-off between economic growth and inflation (3) (4).

How to improve this answer

1. The candidate could have made a distinction between the two types of economic growth, that is, actual growth and potential growth.

2. The period of time required to bring about an increase in aggregate supply will depend on whether an economy is at full capacity. If it is, then an increase in aggregate supply will take a period of time to be achieved, but if there is spare capacity, that is, if some economic resources, such as labour, are being under-utilised, then these resources can be put to productive use in a relatively shorter period of time.

3. The possibility of a trade-off is based on the idea that aggregate demand will rise more quickly than aggregate supply, giving rise to an increase in the rate of inflation. However, if aggregate demand and aggregate supply grow at a similar rate, there will not necessarily be an increase in the rate of inflation.

4. The conclusion is very one-sided, that is, it assumes that there will be a trade-off between economic growth and inflation, but the candidate needs to stress that this trade-off is not inevitable and that it depends on the relative rate of change of aggregate demand and aggregate supply.

AO1 and AO2:	Level 2	6/14
AO3:	Level 1	1/6
Total:		7/20

Worked Example

Assess whether there is a likely to be a trade-off between inflation and the balance of payments.

If a country has a high rate of inflation, it will make its exports more expensive and this could lead to a decrease in the amount demanded. If the value of a country's exports decreases, it could have a negative effect on the trade balance.

However, this will not necessarily be the case. It will depend on the degree to which the demand for a country's exports is price elastic; if demand is price inelastic, it may not have much of an effect on demand. The impact of the inflation will also depend on how the rate of inflation compares with the rate of inflation in other countries. A country may have a high rate of inflation, but the rate of inflation could be higher in other countries. In such a situation, demand for a country's exports could increase if its rate of inflation is lower than in other countries.

Another aspect to consider is that the balance of trade is only one part of the balance of payments. Even if a relatively high rate of inflation has a negative impact on a country's trade balance, this could be offset by movements in the balances of other parts of the balance of payments.

Therefore, although there may be a trade-off between inflation and a country's balance of payments, it is by no means inevitable.

Exam-style questions

1   Governments generally aim for a:

   (a) relatively high and stable rate of inflation

   (b) relatively high and unstable rate of inflation

   (c) relatively low and stable rate of inflation

   (d) relatively low and unstable rate of inflation.   [1]

2   Stagflation refers to a situation in which there is a combination of:

   (a) high inflation and high unemployment

   (b) high inflation and low unemployment

   (c) low inflation and high unemployment

   (d) low inflation and low unemployment.   [1]

3   The long-run Phillips curve is a:

   (a) downward sloping straight line

   (b) horizontal straight line

   (c) upward sloping straight line

   (d) vertical straight line.   [1]

4   The Laffer curve shows that as the tax rate increases:

   (a) the tax revenue at first falls and then rises

   (b) the tax revenue at first rises and then falls

   (c) the tax revenue continually falls

   (d) the tax revenue continually rises.   [1]

5   Assess to what extent the macroeconomic policy objectives of a government are likely to give rise to a conflict between them.   [20]

6   Assess whether the Phillips curve adequately shows the trade-off between the levels of inflation and unemployment in an economy.   [20]

11.1 Policies to correct disequilibrium in the balance of payments

11.1.1 The components of the balance of payments accounts: current account, financial account and capital account

The balance of payments is a record of the transactions that one country has with the rest of the world. It shows all the various payments and receipts arising from a country's involvement in international trade. It consists of the following three components:

- the current account
- the financial account
- the capital account.

The current account was covered in section 6.3 of Unit 6. It is now necessary to cover the other two accounts in the balance of payments.

Financial account

The **financial account** is the part of the balance of payments that records the movement of funds into and out of a country, such as direct investment in the form of building a factory or portfolio investment in the form of the buying or selling of government bonds.

Capital account

The **capital account** is the part of the balance of payments that records capital movements, in terms of various assets and liabilities, into and out of a particular country, such as money brought into and taken out of a country by migrants.

Balancing item

In addition to the three accounts, the balance of payments also includes a **balancing item**. The balance of payments should eventually balance when all of the various accounts are included. However, it is possible that statistical discrepancies may prevent this from happening and so a balancing item is used to ensure that the accounts, when added together, equal zero.

Key terms

Financial account: this account records the inflows and outflows that result from different forms of investment.

Capital account: this account records capital movements, in the form of assets and liabilities, when these are transferred from one country to another.

Balancing item: this is a way of ensuring that the balance of payments, when all of the different component accounts are added together, does actually balance, that is, it equals zero.

11.1.2 The effect of fiscal, monetary, supply-side, protectionist and exchange rate policies on the balance of payments

The effect of fiscal, monetary, supply-side and protectionist policies on the current account have already been discussed in section 6.5.2. It is now necessary to extend this discussion to include exchange rates and to consider the effect of all of them on the balance of payments in full, that is, to cover not only the current account, but the other accounts as well.

Fiscal policy

If a country is experiencing a deficit on the financial account, it is not necessarily a problem as it will bring about an inflow of profits, interest and dividends in the future. The government could reduce taxation and/or increase expenditure. This is likely to improve confidence in a country's economic prospects, encouraging investment and a reduction of the deficit.

If a country is experiencing a surplus on the financial account or the capital account, the government could increase taxation and/or reduce expenditure.

Monetary policy

If a country is experiencing a deficit on the financial account or the capital account, the government could increase interest rates. This is likely to increase the flow of hot money coming into the country in search of higher interest rates.

If a country is experiencing a surplus on the financial account or the capital account, the government could increase the growth of the money supply and/or decrease interest rates.

Supply-side policy

If a country is experiencing a deficit on the financial account or the capital account, the government could use supply-side measures to improve the performance of the economy. For example, privatisation and deregulation will increase competition in markets and make domestic firms more efficient, improving quality and lowering costs. Increased government spending on training and education could also lead to an increase in productivity. This is likely to lead to a movement of firms and funds into the country.

Protectionist policies

If a country is experiencing a deficit on the financial account or the capital account, the government could impose a tariff on imports. This would make the imported goods more expensive and so discourage their consumption, with consumers now more inclined to buy domestically produced substitutes. This would be likely to attract investment and capital into the country.

If a country is experiencing a surplus on the financial account or the capital account, protectionist policies could be used, for example, placing a quota on imported goods.

Exchange rate policies

If a country is experiencing a deficit in the current account, the government could lower the exchange rate to make its exports more competitive in world markets. However, if it was experiencing a deficit in the financial account or capital account, the government could raise the exchange rate to encourage capital movements into the country.

> ★ **Link**
>
> See Unit 6, sections 6.3 and 6.5, for more information on the balance of payments.

11.1.3 The difference between expenditure-switching and expenditure-reducing policies

Expenditure-reducing and expenditure-switching policies

It is important to be able to distinguish between expenditure-reducing and expenditure-switching policies.

Expenditure-reducing policies

Expenditure-reducing policies are those which are designed to reduce the demand for all products in an economy, that is, they are intended to reduce

> **Key term**
>
> **Expenditure-reducing policies:** policies which are intended to bring about a reduction in the level of aggregate demand in an economy.

the demand for imported goods, but the effect is that the demand for all goods, including domestically produced goods, will be reduced.

Deflationary fiscal policy, to reduce expenditure, can include an increase in taxation and/or a reduction in government expenditure. Deflationary monetary policy, to reduce expenditure, can include an increase in interest rates and/or a reduction in the money supply.

Expenditure-switching policies

Whereas expenditure-reducing policies are designed to reduce the demand for all products in an economy, **expenditure-switching policies** are designed to switch demand away from some products and towards others, for example, they could intend to decrease the demand for imports and increase the demand for exports.

There are a number of protectionist methods that can be used to decrease the demand for imports and increase the demand for exports, including tariffs, quotas, subsidies, exchange controls, embargoes and administrative restrictions.

> **Key term**
>
> **Expenditure-switching policies:** policies which are intended to bring about a change in the demand for different products in an economy, especially a reduction in the demand for imports and an increase in the demand for exports.

> **Remember**
>
> A balance of payments disequilibrium can refer to a persistent surplus as well as a persistent deficit.

> **★ Exam tip**
>
> Make sure that you are able to explain the distinction between expenditure-reducing policies, which are designed to bring about a fall in demand for all products in an economy, and expenditure-switching policies, which are designed to bring about a change in the pattern of demand for different products in an economy, for example, reducing the demand for imported products and increasing the demand for exported products.

> **★ Exam tip**
>
> Be careful not to get confused between the idea of deflation, that is, a period of falling prices in an economy, and deflationary policies which are designed to reduce the level of aggregate demand in an economy.

11.2 Exchange rates

11.2.1 The measurement of exchange rates

The definition of an exchange rate was given in section 6.4.1 of Unit 6 where it was stated that an exchange rate refers to the value of one currency in relation to the value of another, that is, it is the price of one currency expressed in terms of another. However, it is now necessary to extend the discussion to include nominal, real and trade-weighted exchange rates.

The distinction between nominal and real exchange rates

Nominal exchange rate

A **nominal exchange rate** is usually the most common way of measuring an exchange rate. It is expressed in money terms, but does not take the effects of inflation into account.

Real exchange rate

A **real exchange rate** is a way of measuring an exchange rate that does take the effects of inflation into account. In this sense, it will give an indication of the purchasing power of one currency compared to another. When real exchange rates are used, they are expressed in terms of **purchasing power parity** by taking into account price levels in different countries.

> **Key terms**
>
> **Nominal exchange rate:** an exchange rate that is expressed in money terms, without taking into account the possible effects of inflation.
>
> **Real exchange rate:** an exchange rate that does take into account the effects of inflation in different countries.
>
> **Purchasing power parity:** the value of a currency in terms of what it is able to buy in other countries.

Trade-weighted exchange rates

A **trade-weighted exchange rate** is where the exchange rates of currencies are considered by weighting the different currencies being compared according to their importance in international trade. This method of measurement is sometimes called the effective exchange rate.

11.2.2 The determination of exchange rates under fixed and managed systems

It is important to distinguish between the different ways in which an exchange rate is determined. Floating exchange rates were covered in section 6.4.2 of Unit 6. It is now necessary to consider fixed and managed systems.

Fixed exchange rate systems

Governments generally aim to avoid large fluctuations in the external value of the currency. This will be easier to achieve with a **fixed exchange rate system**. In this type of exchange rate system, the external value of a currency is determined by the government of the country, that is, the government decides to fix the exchange rate at a particular level, rather than leaving the rate to be decided by market forces as in a floating exchange rate system.

The advantage of a fixed exchange rate system is that a government can intervene in the foreign exchange market on a regular basis in order to maintain a particular rate of exchange with other currencies. If there is a floating exchange rate, this will be more difficult to achieve because the rate of exchange with other currencies will be determined by changes in the demand for, and the supply of, the currency on foreign exchange markets.

However, a disadvantage of a fixed exchange rate system is that a government will need to ensure that it has sufficient reserves in order to be able to intervene in the foreign exchange market to maintain a particular exchange rate.

Managed exchange rate systems

A **managed exchange rate system** is a combination of floating and fixed exchange rates. A government may decide to allow the exchange rate of a currency to be determined by market forces, but only to an extent; it will aim to reduce any large fluctuations in a floating exchange rate system through a degree of intervention and this is why it is known as a managed float.

The government will decide the minimum and maximum rates between which the value will range. If market forces determine the rate above or below those maximum or minimum values, the government will intervene to buy or sell the currency to ensure that its value stays within the predetermined limits.

> **Key term**
>
> **Trade-weighted exchange rate:** an exchange rate that takes into account the importance of a currency in international trade by giving it a weighting to reflect this importance.

> **★ Exam tip**
>
> When writing about exchange rates in an examination, make sure you make it clear what method of measurement of the value of a currency is being used, that is, nominal, real or trade-weighted.

> **Key term**
>
> **Fixed exchange rate system:** an exchange rate system in which the value of a currency is determined by a government, that is, the exchange rate is fixed at a particular value.

> **Key term**
>
> **Managed exchange rate system:** an exchange rate system in which the value of a currency is allowed to float up or down, determined by market forces, but only within certain limits. If the value of the currency moves outside those limits, the government will intervene by buying or selling the currency to bring it back to a rate that is within the predetermined limits allowed for the currency.

> **💡 Remember**
>
> A managed exchange rate system can also be referred to as a dirty float because of the fact that a government will only allow the exchange rate to move between predetermined limits. If the value goes above or below those limits, the government will intervene by buying or selling the currency.

11.2.3 The distinction between the revaluation and the devaluation of a fixed exchange rate

If an exchange rate is lowered in a fixed exchange rate system, it is called a **devaluation**. If the exchange rate is increased in a fixed exchange rate system, it is called a **revaluation**.

11.2.4 Changes in the exchange rate under different exchange rate systems

There are a number of possible factors that can cause changes in exchange rates. These include:

*   the demand for a country's exports from other countries
*   the demand for imports into a country from other countries
*   relative inflation rates in different countries, affecting the international competitiveness of goods and services that are traded between different countries
*   the quality and reliability of products that are traded internationally
*   relative interest rates in different countries, which can be a major factor in the movement of '**hot money**' from one country to another
*   changes in the costs of production in different countries
*   changes in the levels of productivity in different countries
*   differences in the state of technology in different countries.

11.2.5 The effects of changing exchange rates on the external economy using Marshall-Lerner and J curve analysis.

Marshall-Lerner analysis

The **Marshall-Lerner condition** states for a reduction in the external value of a currency to be successful, the sum of the price elasticity of demand for exports and the price elasticity of demand for imports needs to be greater than one. The Marshall-Lerner condition, in relation to the price elasticity of demand for a country's exports and imports, is useful in terms of judging whether a reduction in the value of a country's exchange rate is likely to be successful in improving a country's balance of payment situation.

J curve analysis

A country's exchange rate could be lowered to encourage an increase in exports and a decrease in imports. This aim, however, might not happen immediately and it is possible that there may be a period of time when the situation becomes worse before it gets better. This situation is known as the **J curve effect**. It can be seen in Figure 11.1. Initially the current account situation worsens as a result of the reduction in the external value of the currency, and the situation only improves after a certain period of time has elapsed.

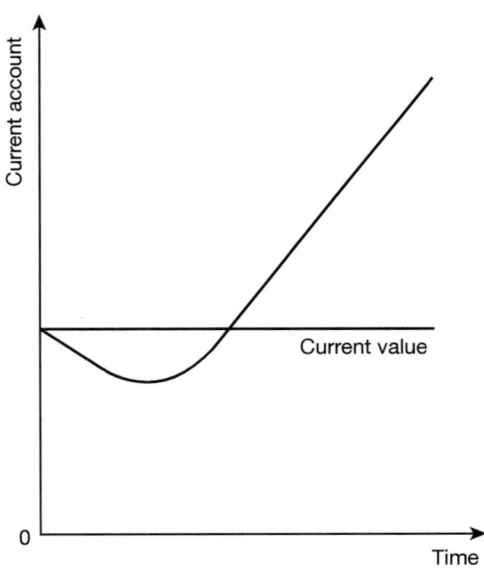

▲ **Figure 11.1** The J curve effect

Key terms

Devaluation: a situation in which an exchange rate decreases in value in a fixed exchange rate system.

Revaluation: a situation in which an exchange rate increases in value in a fixed exchange rate system.

⭐ **Exam tip**

Make sure that you clearly understand the difference between a depreciation and a devaluation and between an appreciation and a revaluation.

Key term

Hot money: inflows and outflows of money between countries, largely as a result of the different interest rates in various countries.

Key terms

Marshall-Lerner condition: this states that the sum of the price elasticities of demand for both exports and imports must be greater than one if a reduction in the value of a currency is to lead to an improvement in the current account of a country.

J curve effect: the short-term response of the current account to a reduction in the value of a country's exchange rate. There will be a certain period of time when the current account gets worse before it eventually gets better.

⭐ **Link**

See Unit 6, section 6.4, for more information on exchange rates.

11.3 Economic development

11.3.1 The classification of economies in terms of their level of development

Economic development is a broader concept than economic growth. It puts the emphasis on the quality of life of people rather than just the material aspects of their standard of living.

Key term

Economic development: an increase in the economic wealth of a country so as to benefit all of its people.

The characteristics of developed, developing and emerging economies

Developed, developing and emerging economies can be distinguished by a number of key characteristics:

Characteristic	Developed economies	Developing and emerging economies
Population growth	Relatively low **birth rates, death rates and infant mortality rates,** leading to slow rate of **population growth**	Relatively high birth rates, death rates and infant mortality rates, leading to high rate of **population growth**
Population structure	Relatively large ageing population	Relatively large young population
Income distribution	Income relatively more evenly distributed	Income relatively less evenly distributed
Economic structure	Relatively high proportion of output from tertiary sector; proportion of output from primary and secondary sectors declining	Developing countries have a relatively high proportion of output from primary sector (although this will vary enormously); in emerging economies, the tertiary sector will be more significant than in developing economies
Employment composition	Relatively high proportion of employment in tertiary sector; proportion of employment in primary and secondary sectors declining	Developing economies have a relatively high proportion of employment in primary sector (although this will vary enormously); in emerging economies, the tertiary sector will be more significant than in developing economies
External trade	In the past, developed economies relied heavily on the exports of manufactured products, but now there is more reliance on the exports of services	Developing economies have relied heavily on the exports of primary products; in emerging economies, there has been an increase in the exports of manufactured products
Urbanisation	A relatively high proportion of the population live and work in urban areas	In developing economies, a relatively high proportion of the population have lived and worked in rural areas, but the extent of urbanisation is now increasing; in emerging economies, the extent of urbanisation is also increasing

Emerging economies are sometimes collectively referred to by an acronym, such as **BRICS**, **MINT**, **CIVETS** or **VISTA**. It will be useful in the exam if you could refer to at least a few of these and the countries that are included within them.

Key terms

Developed economies: economies characterised by a relatively low birth rate, a relatively high life expectancy, a relatively high level of literacy and a relatively high gross domestic product.

Developing economies: economies characterised by a relatively high birth rate, a relatively low life expectancy, a relatively low level of literacy and a relatively low gross domestic product.

Emerging economies: economies that are rapidly growing and going through a relatively fast rate of economic development, mainly located in parts of Asia, Africa and South America.

Birth rate: the number of live births per thousand of population in a year.

Death rate: the number of deaths per thousand of population in a year.

Infant mortality rate: the number of deaths of infants under one year old per thousand live births in a year.

Population growth: the **natural increase of population** in a country, plus the net migration (the difference between the number of immigrants and the number of emigrants), in a year.

Natural increase of population: the difference between the birth rate and the death rate in a country in a year.

Population structure: the population of a country according to the gender and age of the people, shown through a population pyramid.

Urbanisation: the increase in the proportion of people in a country living and working in towns and cities.

BRICS: an acronym referring to the emerging economies of Brazil, Russia, India and China; sometimes South Africa is added as a fifth country.

MINT: an acronym referring to the emerging economies of Mexico, Indonesia, Nigeria and Turkey.

CIVETS: an acronym referring to the emerging economies of Colombia, Indonesia, Vietnam, Egypt, Turkey and South Africa.

VISTA: an acronym referring to the emerging economies of Vietnam, Indonesia, South Africa, Turkey and Argentina.

Although the rate of population growth in a developing economy is likely to be higher than in a developed economy, do not assume that this means that all developing economies have relatively large populations and that all developed economies have relatively small populations. This is clearly not the case.

Also, do not assume that all people in a developed economy are rich and that all people in a developing economy are poor. This is not the case. Some people in developed economies will be very poor and some people in developing or emerging economies will be very rich.

11.3.2 The classification of economies in terms of their level of national income

In addition to classifying different economies in terms of their level of development, they can also be classified in terms of their level of national income.

The World Bank divides the world's economies into four income groups:

- high
- upper-middle
- lower-middle
- low.

This classification on the level of income is based on national income per person using Gross National Income (GNI) per capita.

11.3.3 Indicators of living standards and economic development

There are a number of ways to compare living standards and economic development in different countries, including monetary indicators, non-monetary indicators and composite indicators.

Monetary indicators

Traditionally, real per capita national income statistics, such as GDP, GNP or GNI, have been used to make these comparisons. These national income statistics were covered in section 4.1 of Unit 4. They have to be at purchasing power parity to make the comparisons effective. Purchasing power parity has already been discussed in section 11.2.1 of this unit. However, there are a number of issues of comparison using monetary indicators.

Issues of comparison using monetary indicators

National income statistics can be used as measures of economic growth and living standards. In terms of economic growth, GDP has tended to be used and, in particular, changes in real GDP over a period of time. In terms of living standards, GDP per capita has tended to be used and, in particular, changes in real GDP per capita or per head over time.

However, although real GDP per capita has generally been used to compare living standards in different countries, there are limitations in using such data. These include the following:

- The hidden, informal or underground economy in a country will not be included in GDP data because the income from such economic activity is not declared.

- GDP data will only include goods and services that involve transactions through a market, but in many economies there will be examples of non-marketed products where there is no price attached, for example, DIY (do-it-yourself) activities.

- It may be that in some countries, a great deal of the increase in output involves weapons and military equipment, but this will not directly lead to an increase in living standards.

- There may be an increase in short-run living standards resulting from economic growth, but this will not necessarily lead to a long-term increase in living standards if the economic growth is not sustainable.

- Real GDP can be divided by a country's population to give an average per head or per capita figure, but this average may be very misleading in countries with a very unequal distribution of income and wealth.

- GDP statistics take into account the quantity of a country's output, but not the quality of the goods and services produced.

- Changes in the exchange rates between different currencies will make it difficult to compare the living standards of people in different countries, so to overcome this problem the comparisons of real GDP per capita are usually expressed in terms of purchasing power parities.

- GDP data measures the output produced in a country, but it does not measure how that output is produced, for example, there could be a substantial increase in working hours and a deterioration in working conditions, such as in relation to health and safety.

- GDP will not include information about political freedom and civil and human rights in different countries and yet these can be regarded as important elements of the quality of life.

- The level of literacy may vary between countries, making data collection and interpretation inaccurate.

★ Exam tip

Make sure that when using monetary indicators, such as GDP, GNP or GNI, to compare living standards and economic development between different countries, you take into account the following three aspects. They need to be:

- real
- per capita
- at purchasing power parity.

★ Exam tip

Remember that when living standards are being measured in different countries, it will involve comparisons of real GDP per capita at purchasing power parity.

★ Exam tip

Be careful not to confuse how GDP can be used to measure economic growth and living standards. If economic growth is being measured, changes in real GDP over a period of time should be used. If living standards are being measured, changes in real GDP per capita at purchasing power parity over a period of time should be used.

Non-monetary indicators

Although monetary indicators are often used to compare living standards and economic development in different countries, non-monetary indicators can also be used. However, there are also problems with using these.

Non-monetary indicators can include the following:

- The level of literacy: the literacy rate can vary a great deal between countries and those countries with a relatively low rate of literacy may not produce very accurate data.

- Working hours and working conditions: the GDP data records the quantity of output produced in different countries, but they do not take into account the way in which that output is produced, for example, a country's output may have increased substantially, but this may have been at a cost of a significant increase in working hours and a deterioration in working conditions.

- Political freedom: although not directly an economic example, it could be argued that political freedoms and civil/human rights also need to be taken into account when assessing the quality of life in different parts of the world.

Composite indicators

The issues of comparison using monetary indicators and non-monetary indicators have been considered and so composite indicators are now increasingly being used which combine both monetary and non-monetary elements.

The three most commonly used composite indicators are:

- the Human Development Index (HDI)
- the Measure of Economic Welfare (MEW)
- the Multidimensional Poverty Index (MPI).

The Human Development Index (HDI)

The **Human Development Index (HDI)** is a composite measure that takes into account three elements of living standards:

- average income in terms of real gross national income (GNI) per capita or per head at purchasing power parities in US dollars

- life expectancy

- years of schooling.

There is also an **Inequality-adjusted Human Development Index (IHDI)**. This was introduced in 2010 to take into account the extent of inequality in different countries.

> **Key terms**
>
> **Human Development Index (HDI):** a measure of economic development that uses average income in the form of real GNI per capita at PPP, years of schooling and life expectancy.
>
> **Inequality-adjusted Human Development Index (IHDI):** the HDI after taking into account the extent of inequality in a country.

> ★ **Exam tip**
>
> Be sure not to be confused by what is included in the HDI. For example, many candidates seem to think that the quality of drinking water is included in the HDI. The quality of drinking water is NOT included in the HDI, although it is included in the MPI.

Measure of Economic Welfare (MEW)

The **Measure of Economic Welfare (MEW)** is a broader measure of living standards and economic development than real GDP per capita and takes into account such elements of living standards as:

- leisure hours
- crime rates
- the value of childcare and looking after the sick and the elderly
- depletion of natural resources and changes in the natural environment
- levels of pollution.

> ★ **Exam tip**
>
> You will need to remember that although the Human Development Index used to use real GDP per capita as a way of measuring the average level of income in economies, since 2010 it has used real GNI per capita.

The Multidimensional Poverty Index (MPI)

The **Human Poverty Index (HPI)** was used as an indicator of living standards and economic development for many years, but in 2010 it was replaced by the **Multidimensional Poverty Index (MPI)**. This uses ten indicators in three categories or dimensions (health, education and living standards):

- child mortality
- nutrition
- years of schooling
- child school attendance
- provision of electricity

- sanitation
- quality of drinking water
- type of floor
- type of cooking fuel
- ownership of assets.

The Kuznets curve

The **Kuznets curve** shows that as an economy develops over time, economic inequality first increases and then decreases. This is shown in Figure 11.2. The vertical axis shows the level of income and wealth inequality, or Gini coefficient, in a country and the horizontal axis shows the economic development, or income per capita, in the country. The curve is an inverted U-shape and shows that as an economy develops initially, the level of inequality increases, but after a certain level of economic development, and per capita income, has been reached, the level of inequality decreases as the benefits of economic growth and economic development extend to a greater number of people in the country.

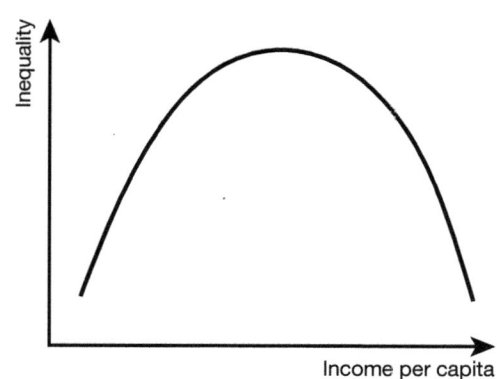

▲ **Figure 11.2** The Kuznets curve

11.3.4 The comparison of economic growth rates and living standards

Economic growth rates can be used to make comparisons of economic development and living standards in two ways:

- over time
- between countries.

Over time

Real GDP data can be analysed over time to recognise trends in economic growth in a country. These may relate to significant upturns or downturns at particular times which will have important effects on standards of living. For example, many countries experienced a downturn after the financial crisis of 2007–2009. Economic growth rates can be averaged out so that comparisons over time can be made.

There are a number of factors to take into account when comparing living standards over time:

- Changes in productivity rates can help to explain economic growth rates over time.
- It is necessary to consider whether a country is experiencing a persistent trade deficit and, if it is, by how much; if a country is experiencing a persistent trade deficit, it means that it is living beyond its means.
- It is also necessary to consider changes in the level of public debt and especially whether the level of debt is rising or falling as a percentage of GDP.

Between countries

The comparison of economic growth rates and living standards between countries has already been discussed in the previous section of this unit under 'issues of comparison using monetary indicators'.

There may be similarities in economic growth rates between countries, especially in the long run, for a number of reasons. These could include the following:

- Technological developments: a key factor in determining similarities in economic growth rates and living standards is the development and implementation of new technologies; all countries have been able to benefit to some extent from similar technological developments.

- The role of multinational companies: multinational companies (see section 11.5.3 of this unit) operate in many economies all over the world and this can contribute to improvements in productivity in those countries where they are located.

- Global shocks: all countries, to varying degrees, are subject to the same global shocks, such as when there is a significant rise in oil prices or an international financial crisis.

However, there may be differences in economic growth rates between countries, especially in the short run, for a number of reasons. These could include the following:

- Government demand management policies: governments in various countries may pursue different macroeconomic policies, for example, one country may pursue deflationary policies of higher taxes and lower spending while another country may pursue reflationary policies of lower taxes and higher spending.

- Industrial relations: some countries may experience better industrial relations than other countries, contributing to higher levels of productivity growth.

- Entrepreneurial culture: some countries may experience a greater level of dynamism and innovation than other countries, perhaps because of differences in the level of government support for the encouragement of the development of an entrepreneurial culture.

★ **Link**

See Unit 4, section 4.4, for more on economic growth.

11.4 The characteristics of countries at different levels of development

11.4.1 Population growth and structure

The measurement and causes of changes in birth rate, death rate, infant mortality rate and net migration

The birth rate

The **birth rate** is the number of individuals born into a population in a given amount of time. It is measured as the annual number of live births per 1,000 inhabitants.

Changes in the birth rate are caused by:

- the need for large families, so that children can work at an early age, can contribute to an increase in the birth rate

- improvements in education and health care can contribute to a decrease in the birth rate.

The death rate

The **death rate** (also known as the mortality rate) is the number of deaths in a particular population during a particular period of time. It is measured as the annual number of deaths per 1,000 inhabitants.

Changes in the death rate are caused by:

- an epidemic or pandemic can contribute to an increase in the death rate

- better food and nutrition and improved health services can contribute to a decrease in the death rate.

The infant mortality rate

The **infant mortality rate** (also known as the infant death rate) is the number of deaths in a group younger than one year of age. It is measured as the annual number of deaths of those under one year old per 1,000 live births.

Changes in the infant mortality rate are caused by:

- an increase in infectious diseases can contribute to an increase in the infant mortality rate

- better health care can contribute to a decrease in the infant mortality rate.

Net migration

Net migration is the difference between the immigrants coming into, and the emigrants leaving from, a country. It is measured by the number of immigrants minus the number of emigrants over a given period of time.

Changes in net migration are caused by:

- an increase in the number of immigrants coming into a country, with the number of emigrants constant, will increase net migration

- a decrease in the number of immigrants coming into a country, with the number of emigrants constant, will decrease net migration.

The optimum population

The **optimum population** refers to the ideal population that a country should have, after taking into account its available resources. It is not a fixed or rigid population size, but is variable depending on possible changes in the quantity and quality of resources and in the level of technology. It is therefore defined as that size of population enabling maximum per capita output to be achieved, accompanied by the highest possible standard of living within a given set of economic and technological conditions.

The level of urbanisation

Another aspect of population structure that needs to be considered is the level of urbanisation in a country. It needs to be pointed out that the definition of what constitutes an urban area can vary between countries. Urbanisation describes the movement of people from rural areas, that is, hamlets and villages, to urban areas, that is, towns and cities. As countries become more developed, the level of urbanisation increases. Today, 55% of the world's population live in urban areas, a proportion that is expected to increase to 70% by 2050.

11.4.2 Income distribution

The Gini coefficient and the Lorenz curve

The **Lorenz curve** is a graphical representation which shows the extent of inequality in the distribution of income in an economy. The more unequal the distribution of income, the more divergent the Lorenz curve will be from the diagonal line of total equality. This can be seen in Figure 11.3.

In country Y, the Lorenz curve is quite close to the 45-degree line of absolute equality and so income is distributed relatively evenly. In country X, however, the Lorenz curve is further away from the 45-degree diagonal line and this shows that income is more unevenly distributed in country X than in country Y.

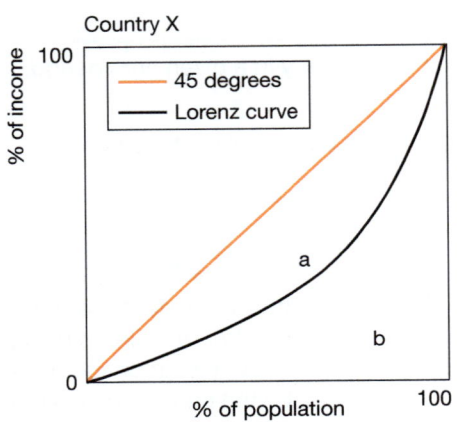
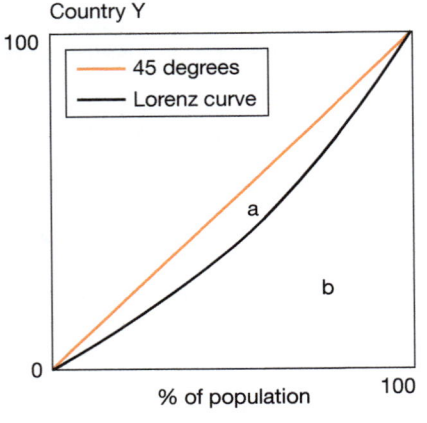

◀ **Figure 11.3:**
A comparison of income equality in two countries

The **Gini coefficient** was discussed in section 3.3.2 of Unit 3. It is a way of measuring the extent of inequality in the distribution of income in an economy. It is measured as the ratio of the area between the 45-degree diagonal line of total equality and the Lorenz curve to the total area under the diagonal. In Figure 11.3, it is area 'a' divided by area 'a' and 'b'. The lower the value of the Gini coefficient, the more even is the distribution of income; for example, in many developed countries, the coefficient is about 0.3. The higher the value of the Gini coefficient, the less even is the distribution of income; for example, in many developing countries, the coefficient is about 0.5.

> **Key term**
>
> **Gini coefficient:** a statistical measure of the degree of inequality of income in an economy.

> 💡 **Remember**
>
> The lower the figure of the Gini coefficient, the more equal is the distribution of income in a particular economy. The higher the figure of the Gini coefficient, the less equal is the distribution of income.

> 💡 **Remember**
>
> A Gini coefficient figure of 0.5 or above is considered relatively high, for example, Brazil. A Gini coefficient of between 0.3 and 0.5 is considered medium, for example, Vietnam. A Gini coefficient of less than 0.3 is considered relatively low, for example, Austria.

> ★ **Exam tip**
>
> Make sure that you do not mix up these two terms, referring to a Lorenz coefficient and a Gini curve. The correct terms are Gini coefficient and Lorenz curve.

> ★ **Exam tip**
>
> Make sure you realise that a high Gini coefficient is an indication of a low level of equality in the distribution of income, not the other way round.

> ★ **Link**
>
> See Unit 3, section 3.3.2, for more on the Gini coefficient.

11.4.3 Economic structure

This involves two aspects:

*   employment composition: primary, secondary and tertiary sectors of employment
*   the pattern of trade at different levels of economic development.

Employment composition

Production in an economy can take place in three sectors: the primary sector, the secondary sector and the tertiary sector.

As a country becomes more developed, its employment structure and composition changes, as indicated below:

- **Primary sector:** as a country becomes more developed, mechanisation of farms reduces the need for farm workers and so the percentage of workers employed in the primary sector decreases.

- **Secondary sector:** as a country becomes more developed and goes through the **industrialisation** process, many workers will leave jobs in agriculture, forestry and fishing, that is, the primary sector, and take up jobs in the secondary sector, for example, manufacturing. However, as a country develops further, there will to some extent be an element of **deindustrialisation** and the percentage of people employed in the secondary sector, having first increased, will then decrease.

- **Tertiary sector:** as a country becomes more developed, the decline in the proportion of people working in the primary and secondary sectors will continue and the proportion of people working in the tertiary sector will increase, for example, service occupations such as education and finance.

The UK is an example of this change in employment composition as it has become more developed. The following table shows the change in the employment composition of the UK between 1920 and 2020.

Sector	1920	2020
Primary sector	15%	1%
Secondary sector	35%	18%
Tertiary sector	50%	81%

Key terms

Primary sector: production that takes place in agriculture, fishing, forestry or mining.

Secondary sector: production that takes place in manufacturing or construction.

Industrialisation: the process by which an economy is transformed from primarily agricultural to one based on the manufacture of goods.

Deindustrialisation: a reduction in the size or share of the manufacturing sector in an economy.

Tertiary sector: production that takes place through the provision of services.

The pattern of trade at different levels of development

As a country becomes more developed, its pattern of trade also changes. Developing countries tend to have economies that are largely based on agriculture and so most of their exports are agricultural products and most of their imports are manufactured products.

However, developed countries tend to have economies that are largely based on manufacturing and services, so most of their exports are from the secondary and tertiary sectors.

This pattern of trade at different levels of development tends to favour developed, rather than developing, countries in that the price of agricultural products tends to be lower than the price of manufactured products.

11.5 The relationship between countries at different levels of development

11.5.1 International aid

It is necessary to have an understanding of:

- the forms of international aid
- the reasons for giving international aid
- the effects of international aid
- the importance of international aid.

Key term

International aid: the process of developed economies and/or international agencies providing different types of financial support to developing economies.

The forms of international aid

One policy approach towards developing economies is the provision of **international aid**. There are various types of aid from developed to developing economies, including different types of financial grants and loans. Sometimes the aid is **bilateral aid**, involving just two countries, and sometimes the aid is **multilateral aid**, involving a number of different countries and/or agencies. Sometimes the aid is conditional or tied aid, that is, conditions are attached to the aid, and sometimes the aid is unconditional or untied aid, that is, there are no conditions attached to the aid.

It is possible to distinguish between the following forms of aid:

- humanitarian assistance, for example, aid for medical reasons
- emergency short-term aid, for example, after a disaster
- food
- investment projects.

The reasons for giving international aid

There are a number of reasons for giving aid, including the following: It helps:

- countries fight diseases
- countries to respond to disasters and humanitarian emergencies
- those countries affected by a hunger crisis
- countries to improve their health and education systems
- to save the lives of people living in poverty around the world
- countries around the world to improve their infrastructure, for example, in relation to water supply.

The effects of international aid

As has been indicated, international aid can help to assist the social and economic development of a country and/or help it to more effectively respond to a disaster.

There have, however, been a number of problems in relation to international aid and it has been criticised as contributing towards a situation of **dependency** where developing countries have become, to some extent, dependent on the help of the governments of other countries and/or international agencies.

> **Remember**
>
> There are a number of potential problems with the international aid that has been given to developing economies, including the following:
>
> - Some aid has been in the form of financial support for investment projects that have been relatively unsuccessful once they have started operation.
> - There is some evidence of an element of corruption in a few countries where the aid has been concentrated in the hands of a few.
> - Some aid has been counterproductive and has made a situation worse, for example, the provision of food has reduced prices, making it more difficult for the farmers to survive.
> - Some of the financial aid has involved the payment of interest, putting many countries in a state of debt.

Key terms

Bilateral aid: aid that involves just two countries.

Multilateral aid: aid that involves a number of countries and/or international agencies.

Key term

Dependency: a situation in which one country depends on the help of another country and/or an international agency, or a number of countries and/or international agencies.

★ Exam tip

Make sure that you are aware of the different types and forms of aid that can exist and that you are able to consider both the potential advantages and the potential disadvantages of aid.

Remember

Although there are a number of potential advantages of aid to developing economies, there is a chance that it will create a situation of dependency.

The importance of international aid

International aid has been of importance for a number of reasons, including the following:

- It helps the economy of the receiving country to grow.

- It helps to improve the level of employment in a country.

- It helps a country to improve its balance of payments position.

- It allows for experts to come into a country to provide technical advice and assistance.

- It can save the lives of millions of people living in poverty around the world.

- It helps to address health, education, infrastructure issues.

- It helps to address humanitarian emergencies.

- It helps to promote international trade.

- It helps to redistribute global wealth.

11.5.2 Trade and investment

The theory of comparative advantage shows that all countries can benefit from free trade as long as there are differences in the opportunity cost ratios of production in the different countries. International trade will therefore lead to an increase in world output and this will lead to an improvement in the standard of living and quality of life, including developing economies. The **World Trade Organization** (WTO), consisting of 164 member countries, exists to promote trade between countries. It deals with the global rules of trade between countries and its main function is to ensure that trade flows as smoothly, predictably and freely as possible.

It will also be useful if investment is encouraged in developing economies. Investment is often relatively low in developing economies because of the lack of savings (the savings ratio tends to be lower in developing economies compared with developed economies) and/or the lack of financial institutions with the funds to substantially support investment. However, if investment can be encouraged, with the help of developed economies and/or international agencies, it may be possible to create a **virtuous circle**.

> **Key terms**
>
> **World Trade Organization (WTO):** an international organisation, established in 1995, replacing the General Agreement on Tariffs and Trade (GATT) which had been set up in 1948, to promote free trade in the world through the reduction of trade barriers; it establishes, monitors, reinforces and regulates the rules of trade between countries.
>
> **Virtuous circle:** the links between an increase in investment, an increase in productivity, an increase in income and an increase in savings.

> **💡 Remember**
>
> Although the encouragement of trade between developing economies and developed economies should be encouraged, there are potential problems with such trade, including the following:
>
> - Many developing economies rely on the production of primary products and the prices of these tend to be generally lower than those of manufactured products.
>
> - The prices of primary products also tend to be less stable than those of manufactured products.
>
> - The demand for primary products tends to be more income inelastic than the demand for manufactured products.

11.5.3 The role of multinational companies (MNCs)

The definition of a multinational company (MNC)

A **multinational company (MNC)** is one that has facilities and other assets in at least one country other than its home country. It generally has factories and/or offices in different countries. It is not enough for a company to just sell products in other countries to be described as a multinational; it needs to actually have operations in those countries, such as factories.

> **Key term**
>
> **Multinational company (MNC):** a firm that has facilities and other assets in at least one country other than its home country.

The activities of multinational companies (MNCs)

Investment in economies can come about through the decisions of multinational companies to locate in such countries, such as by building a factory, and this is known as foreign direct investment (FDI) (see section 11.5.4).

Multinational companies are involved in a range of various activities in different countries, including:

- producing and selling goods and services
- exporting goods and services
- making significant investments in those countries
- buying and selling licenses.

★ **Exam tip**

Make sure that you are able to compare and contrast both the potential advantages and the potential disadvantages of a multinational setting up in another country.

The consequences of multinational companies (MNCs)

The potential advantages of a multinational company locating in an economy include the following:	However, there are also potential disadvantages of a multinational company locating in an economy, including the following:
• There can be an increase in employment, creating more income and through the multiplier effect, this can lead to an increase in the standard of living and quality of life. • They can provide more choice for consumers. • They can lead to an increase in the revenue received from taxation, such as from taxes on the profits of the multinationals. • The multinationals can bring technical knowledge which could lead to an increase in levels of productivity in the developing economy. • They can contribute to an increase in economic growth. • If some of the output produced is exported to other countries, this could lead to an improvement in the current account of the balance of payments.	• They may use capital-intensive, rather than labour-intensive, methods of production, with the result that any increase in employment will be relatively small. • The jobs that are created may be relatively unskilled (such jobs are sometimes called 'screwdriver' jobs). • Although some of the profit made may be taxed by the developing economy, much of it will be repatriated to the home country and not re-invested in the local economy. • The operation of the multinationals may lead to damage to the environment, in the form of additional pollution, and they may contribute to the further depletion of natural resources. • The multinationals may attempt to influence the government of the country, giving rise to the possibility of corruption.

★ **Exam tip**

Make sure you do not think that a multinational is simply a firm that sells its products in another country. A multinational is one that does more than simply sell its products in another country; it actually operates in another country, such as by building a factory to produce products.

11.5.4 Foreign Direct Investment (FDI)

The definition of FDI

Foreign direct investment (FDI) has already been referred to in section 11.5.3 in relation to the activities of multinational companies. It can be defined as the establishment of production units in another country.

Key term

Foreign direct investment (FDI): investment by a firm in another country.

The consequences of FDI

Foreign direct investment in an economy is important for a number of reasons, including the following:

- Foreign expertise can be an important factor in the improvement of the existing technical processes in a country.
- It can help to improve the quality of products and processes in particular sectors of an economy.
- It can help in the creation of jobs and so reduce the level of unemployment in an economy.
- It provides a source of external capital for a country that can improve its level of economic development.
- It provides a source of tax revenue to a government.

11.5.5 External debt

The causes of external debt

External debt refers to the portion of a country's debt that has been borrowed from foreign lenders, including commercial banks, governments and international financial institutions.

External debt (also known as foreign debt) represents the amount that a particular country owes to other countries. It includes both public sector debt and private sector debt. It also includes both short-term liabilities, for example, loans which need to be repaid in the near future, such as within one year, and long-term liabilities, for example, loans which need to be repaid over a longer period of time.

The causes of the existence of external debt include:

- outstanding loans to foreign private sector financial institutions, including the outstanding interest
- payments due to international organisations, such as the International Monetary Fund (IMF)
- outstanding payments for a balance of payments deficit.

The consequences of external debt

The existence of external debt can be a major obstacle to the economic growth and economic development of a country. The repayment of the debt, including any interest payments, can become a major burden for a country, despite the efforts of such organisations as Jubilee 2000 and Make Poverty History to cancel or reschedule the debt.

There is also an opportunity cost involved with external debt, as there is with any form of expenditure. The funds that are being used to pay the debt could have been used in other ways that would have been more productive in terms of the economic development of a country, such as spending on health care and education.

11.5.6 The role of the International Monetary Fund (IMF)

A number of international organisations have been established since 1944 to encourage free trade and to reduce the extent of trade protectionism in the world market. One of these is the **International Monetary Fund (IMF)**.

The IMF was established in 1944 to promote international trade through such measures as providing financial support in the form of a loan to help a country overcome, or at least reduce, a deficit in the current account of the balance of payments.

The IMF aims to:

- reduce the extent of global poverty
- encourage international trade
- secure financial stability
- promote sustainable economic growth
- promote high employment
- foster global monetary cooperation.

> **Key term**
>
> **The International Monetary Fund (IMF):** an international organisation that offers advice to governments and central banks and provides loans to countries in severe economic difficulties.

It achieves these aims by overseeing economic development, lending and capacity development. It has played a significant role in stabilising exchange rates and thereby facilitating international payments. It has also helped to enforce monetary discipline among its 189 member countries.

11.5.7 The role of the World Bank

The **World Bank** was established in 1944 to provide finance to countries, particularly developing economies, to help with various kinds of capital investment projects. It actually consists of five agencies, of which the most important and most well-known is the International Bank for Reconstruction and Development (IBRD). It has 180 member countries.

> **Key term**
>
> **World Bank:** an international organisation that provides loans to developing economies to facilitate capital investment.

The World Bank aims to:

- provide low-interest loans, interest-free credit and grants to middle-income and low-income countries to reduce the extent of poverty

- improve the health, education and infrastructure facilities of countries

- modernise the financial sector, agriculture and natural resources and environmental management of different countries.

The World Bank has set two goals for the world to achieve by 2030:

- to end extreme poverty by decreasing the percentage of people living on less than $1.90 a day to no more than 3%

- to promote shared prosperity by fostering the income growth of the bottom 40% for every country.

11.6 Globalisation

11.6.1 The meaning of globalisation and its causes and consequences

The meaning of globalisation

Globalisation refers to the increase of trade around the world, especially by large companies producing and trading products in many different countries. It involves an increase in international competition through the development of a global free market, with companies able to gain a competitive advantage. It refers to the free movement of goods, services and people across the world and involves a process that enables financial and investment markets to operate internationally.

> **Key term**
>
> **Globalisation:** the process whereby there is an increasing world market in goods and services, making an increase in multilateral trade more likely. It has been made possible by a number of factors, including progress in trade liberalisation.

The causes of globalisation

Globalisation describes an economic interdependence of countries around the world fostered through the development of trade liberalisation and free trade. The reduction of protectionism, involving the removal or reduction of tariffs and other import controls, has been a significant cause of globalisation. It is also the result of deregulation and improvements in communications technology.

> ★ **Exam tip**
>
> In any question on the consequences of globalisation, make sure that you consider both the advantages and disadvantages of globalisation.

The consequences of globalisation

Globalisation has led to the increased spread of products, technology, information and employment across national borders. It has created new jobs and enhanced economic growth through the international flow of goods, capital and labour. Companies have been able to reduce costs by manufacturing abroad and have been able to gain access to millions of new customers. Significant improvements in standards of living have been achieved in many countries, with free markets and free trade a means of reducing the extent of poverty in the world.

However, this job creation and economic growth has not been distributed evenly across industries or countries. Specific industries in certain countries have suffered disruption or collapse as a result of increased competition. Globalisation has benefited large multinational companies, but its impact remains mixed for particular workers and firms around the world, in both developed and developing countries. It can also have a significant effect on the environment. It can create a domino effect where a crisis or economic downturn in one country can have a severe impact on many other countries in the world.

11.6.2 The distinction between a free trade area, a customs union, a monetary union and full economic union

It is important to be able to distinguish between different forms of economic integration.

Free trade area

A **free trade area** is where countries come together to trade freely with each other, but each of these member countries will retain their own trade barriers with other countries outside the free trade area, that is, there is no common external tariff in existence.

Examples include:

- the European Free Trade Area (Iceland, Liechtenstein, Norway and Switzerland)
- the North American Free Trade Area (USA, Canada and Mexico).

Customs union

A **customs union** is where countries come together to trade freely with each other and they also have a **common external tariff** with other countries outside the customs union.

Examples include:

- the Caribbean Community (CARICOM) (15 full member countries including Jamaica, Barbados and Trinidad and Tobago).

Monetary union

A **monetary union** is where countries come together and adopt a single currency. Certain policies may also be adopted to support the operation of the currency and there is usually one single central bank.

Examples include:

- the eurozone (19 member countries of the European Union have adopted the euro as their currency, including France, Italy and Germany).

Full economic union

A **full economic union** is where countries come together and adopt a number of common economic policies that apply to all member countries. Full economic union usually involves the countries adopting a single currency, but this is not absolutely essential.

Examples include:

- the European Union (19 of the 27 member countries have adopted the single currency)
- the Eurasian Economic Union (Russia, Belarus, Armenia and Kazakhstan, but each of the four countries have retained their own currency).

> ★ **Exam tip**
>
> Make sure you do not assume that all countries in an economic union will adopt a single currency. This is not always the case. For example, in the European Union, only 19 of the 27 member countries have adopted the euro as their currency.

11.6.3 Trade creation and trade diversion

It is important to distinguish between trade creation and trade diversion.

Trade creation

If there is some form of economic integration between a group of countries, there will be fewer trade barriers between them. This is likely to lead to

> **Key terms**
>
> **Free trade area:** a situation in which a group of countries come together to promote free trade between themselves, while retaining their own separate trade barriers with other countries.
>
> **Customs union:** a situation in which a group of countries come together to promote free trade between themselves and to impose a common external tariff on imports from countries outside the customs union.
>
> **Common external tariff:** a situation in which a group of countries impose the same common tariff on trade with all non-member countries.

> **Key terms**
>
> **Monetary union:** a situation in which a group of countries come together and adopt a single currency. The member countries are likely to have a number of common monetary policies to support the operation of the single currency.
>
> **Full economic union:** a situation in which a group of countries come together and agree to integrate their economies as much as possible through a variety of laws, regulations and policies. They may or may not have a single currency.

> ★ **Exam tip**
>
> It is important that you can distinguish between the different forms of economic integration that can exist between countries in different parts of the world.

> 💡 **Remember**
>
> There are varying degrees of economic union between countries. In a full economic union, it is likely that all of the member countries will have adopted a single currency, but not necessarily.

trade creation as new markets are opened up within the member countries and firms take advantage of new opportunities. There is therefore likely to be increased specialisation and more trade between the countries.

Trade diversion

However, it is also possible that economic integration may lead to a degree of **trade diversion**. For example, the member countries are likely to focus more on trade between themselves and less on trade with non-member countries.

Key terms

Trade creation: the creation of new trade resulting from the reduction or elimination of trade barriers between member countries of a trading bloc.

Trade diversion: the loss of some existing trade between a trading bloc and non-member countries as a result of the imposition of trade barriers.

★ Exam tip

Remember that in a 'discuss' question on economic integration, there are potential benefits in the form of trade creation as well as potential drawbacks in the form of trade diversion.

 Raise your grade

Assess how economic integration can lead to both trade creation and trade diversion. [20]

Economic integration, whether in the form of a free trade area or a customs union (1), can lead to both trade creation and trade diversion.

Trade creation can take place when countries form a trading bloc which has the effect of reducing (2) the trade barriers between the member countries. Free trade will be encouraged and there will be more opportunities to conduct business between the countries (3).

However, at the same time, although increased trade between the member countries is encouraged, trade with non-member countries may be discouraged (4). The member countries will tend to look inwards towards the trading bloc, possibly reducing or cutting off trade with countries that they previously traded with.

How to improve this answer

1. The candidate has referred to two types of economic integration, but could also have referred to the two other types of economic integration, a monetary union and a full economic union.

2. It is not simply that the trade barriers have been reduced; it is also possible that such barriers have been eliminated entirely, increasing the scope for trade creation.

3. The candidate could perhaps have included an example to support the point being made. This could have included an example of a free trade area, such as the North American Free Trade Area, or of an economic union, such as the European Union.

4. The candidate has referred to the discouragement of trade with non-member countries, but this point needed to be developed more fully, such as in relation to the existence of a Common External Tariff which the European Union has with all non-member countries.

AO1 and AO2:	Level 2	8/14
AO3:	Level 1	1/6
Total:		9/20

Worked Example

Assess the main characteristics of a developing economy. [20]

A developing economy will have a number of key characteristics.

It is likely to have a relatively high rate of population growth, resulting from the natural increase in the country's population arising from the difference between the birth rate and the death rate. The increase in the country's population will also be affected by net migration. There is also likely to be a relatively high proportion of young people.

Income levels will tend to be lower than in a developed economy and there is also likely to be a relatively high level of inequality in the distribution of that income. It is also likely that a majority of the population will be employed in the primary and secondary sectors, with a lower proportion employed in the tertiary sector compared with a developed economy. A relatively smaller proportion of women are likely to be employed in a developing economy compared with a developed economy. There are a number of possible social, cultural and religious reasons for this.

In terms of external trade, many developing economies will rely on the export of primary products, such as agricultural produce, and there is often a high level of price instability associated with such products. There is likely to be a high degree of urbanisation taking place in developing economies and this rural–urban migration can put a great deal of pressure on resources in the urban areas, such as in terms of overcrowding. Many developing economies have accumulated a great deal of external debt; in some developing economies, the level of debt can be over 100% of Gross National Product.

A developing economy is also likely to have a lower Human Development Index value than a developed economy; whereas a developed economy is likely to have an HDI value of 0.8 or 0.9, a developing economy is likely to have an HDI value of 0.3, 0.4 or 0.5.

Exam-style questions

1 An exchange rate that takes into account changes in prices is called a:

(a) J curve exchange rate

(b) nominal exchange rate

(c) real exchange rate

(d) trade-weighted exchange rate. [1]

2 The Human Development Index uses:

(a) GDP

(b) GNI

(c) GNP

(d) NNP. [1]

3 The MPI is the:

(a) measure of poverty index

(b) monetary poverty index

(c) multidimensional poverty index

(d) multinational production index. [1]

4 When a government intervenes in a floating exchange rate system, it is known as:

(a) a managed float

(b) a special float

(c) a stable float

(d) an interventionist float. [1]

5 For a devaluation to be successful, the Marshall-Lerner condition states that the price elasticities of demand for exports and imports should be:

(a) equal to one

(b) equal to zero

(c) greater than one

(d) less than one but more than zero. [1]

6 A relatively high Gini coefficient indicates that:

(a) prices are relatively stable in an economy

(b) taxes in an economy are extremely progressive

(c) the distribution of income in a country is relatively less even

(d) the distribution of income in a country is relatively more even. [1]

7 Assess whether a decision by a multinational company to produce in a country will always be of benefit to that country. [20]

8 Assess whether economic integration is likely to lead to more trade creation or more trade diversion. [20]